T0307279

LIONS IN
AFRICA

LIONS IN AFRICA

The British & Irish Lions and
the Hunt for the Springboks

CHRIS SCHOEMAN
AND DAVID MCLENNAN

AMBERLEY

First published 2021

Amberley Publishing
The Hill, Stroud
Gloucestershire, GL5 4EP

www.amberley-books.com

Copyright © Chris Schoeman and David
McLennan, 2021

The right of Chris Schoeman and David
McLennan to be identified as the Authors of this
work has been asserted in accordance with the
Copyright, Designs and Patents Act 1988.

ISBN 978 1 3981 0828 8 (hardback)
ISBN 978 1 3981 0829 5 (ebook)

British Library Cataloguing in Publication Data.
A catalogue record for this book is available
from the British Library.

1 2 3 4 5 6 7 8 9 10

Typesetting by SJmagic DESIGN SERVICES,
India.
Printed in the UK.

CONTENTS

FOREWORD BY WILLIE JOHN MCBRIDE

The British Lions tours happen only every four years, and even in today's professional world, to be a Lion is still as special as it always was. To me, having been considered as one the thirty players of the four countries to go on tour, that's special, very special, and that bond that you've created, in my case for the last time over forty years ago, it's still there; that's why it's a remarkable game. It still makes me sort of glow inside.

I toured South Africa three times with the Lions, in 1962, 1968 and finally in 1974. When we toured there in 1974, there was a lot of opposition in Britain because of South Africa's policy of apartheid. As far as I am concerned, I don't associate the political and the sport, I never have done. And let's be honest, my own beloved province of Ulster in 1974 when I left was in turmoil with the strikes, so I was not going to have any influence on the political scene at home, so I don't see how I was going to have much political influence on what was happening in South Africa.

I remember I was asked to accept a petition from a guy called Peter Hain of the Anti-Apartheid Movement and I read it to the team, and I said, 'I'm going to South Africa, it will be my last tour as a player. I have one objective, and that is to win the series, to beat them in the four Test games.' And I also said, 'It has nothing to do with politics, absolutely nothing, and if anybody has any doubt in this room, about going on this tour, the door is open, please leave now. Don't come to me in a week, don't come to me tomorrow, don't come to me in three weeks, because you're no use to this team and if you have the slightest doubt, you are certainly of no use to me.' And I can remember for what seemed like minutes I sat there, and nobody moved. And I said, 'Okay, we are now on the road.'

When we arrived in South Africa, we were welcomed like long-lost brothers. But we didn't have the numbers of fans in the stands as they have nowadays; they were virtually all South Africans in the stands. We were fifteen against all that, and I always felt it was important to go out and say we're here and we're here to beat you, we're here to win, and we did that in '74. Each time was just great.

For obvious reasons the tour of 1974 is the one that stands out. The one good thing that the management achieved was to make sure there were no cliques. Welsh guys for instance didn't stick together – and there were quite a few Welsh guys in that squad – so we mixed immediately. Whether you were a steelworker, a labourer or a barrister, once we were on the field we were just a bunch of rugby players.

The tour also became well known for its '99' call. While our previous Lions teams had flair, most floundered in the face of South African rugby aggression. But this time we decided it was going to be different. We had to show the opposition that they couldn't punch us and kick us any time they wanted, so we had to have this unity. I was ready to fight fire with fire – we didn't want to be messed around – and that suited some of our players. I remember when I told Bobby Windsor that there will be a bit of fisticuffs, he said 'Oh, this is for me!' With the game against Eastern Province, when the fists were really flying, it was suggested that the Eastern Province players would have liked to see what we were made of. Well, they soon found out.

It's history now that the first Test at a wet Newlands set the tone for the series. It's amazing as you put on that shirt, that shirt you covet most, I think you really get bigger, and I remember walking down that tunnel and you get bigger and bigger and you feel stronger and stronger; this is the biggest moment of your rugby life.

The Boks were playing with the wind and they actually took the lead with a drop goal. I said to the team, 'This is not what we've come for,' and it just lifted the players. Gareth Edwards later sealed the match for us with a marvellous drop goal, and I'll never forget when the ball went over the crossbar, how everyone who wasn't white jumped into the air! They supported us, because it was the height of apartheid and they dearly wanted to see us beat the Springboks. It was a great team effort ... and to have had rain like that in South Africa, what more can you ask for! Victory gave everybody that tremendous feeling, that we were dominant, and we were believing in ourselves.

Before the second Test, we were singing on the bus on the way to the stadium, and that's really where the *Flower of Scotland* came to prominence. We handed the Springboks their biggest ever Test defeat. To illustrate how seriously people in South Africa take their rugby, the government had to answer questions in Parliament about the state of South African rugby!

With the third Test – the so-called 'Battle of Boet Erasmus', we had to wait for the Springboks to come out of the tunnel, and it was not the captain's team talk that caused the delay, but the Minister of Sport's motivational speech in the dressing room, can you believe it. The Springboks came steaming out of that tunnel like men possessed and it was probably the hardest first twenty minutes of my rugby life. There were free-for-alls, but we stuck it out and we again beat the Boks convincingly to take the series.

Even on Robben Island, where Nelson Mandela was still in captivity, the prisoners were celebrating and one of the warders warned them not to talk about the British Lions while they were working in the stone quarry!

We controversially drew the final Test but still returned home undefeated. And the funny thing was, all those politicians who didn't want to know us before the tour, for all kinds of reasons, were now clamouring to be part of the party on our return! Yes, that was a wonderful time and as I've said, that bond that we created all those years ago, it's still alive, and to have been a British Lion is still as special today as it was then – something the Lions of 2021 will also cherish when they've worn the red.

WILLIE JOHN MCBRIDE
BRITISH LIONS 1962–74

FOREWORD BY
HANNES MARAIS

Throughout my rugby career, I have always been very much aware of the great tradition of British Lions rugby, and I first played against a British Lions touring side in 1962 for the Southern Universities against Arthur Smith's team at Newlands. Six years later, when Tom Kiernan's Lions toured here, I had a taste of the real thing when I played in all four Tests of the series. Except for the final Test, which we won 19-6, scores had been close, with the second Test drawn. When the Lions of 1974 were due to tour, everyone in South Africa expected the same series results as with previous tours – the Springboks to win again.

Originally, I would not have been part of it. We would have toured New Zealand in 1973, but it was called off for political reasons and I decided to retire; I then felt I had had my share of rugby. But then Prof Johan Claassen, the convenor of the South African selectors, contacted me to say that they needed me for the British Lions tour, and I agreed to lead the team. I have to admit, the prospect of the tour did not bother me much; I thought the team would be just another bunch of British players who in the beginning would be giving their best, but be too soft and succumb under the physical pressures of a long tour.

But how we underestimated them. Their coach, Syd Millar, knew well that to beat the Springboks, they had to beat us in the scrums.

Their captain, Willie John McBride, was on his third Lions tour to South Africa, and his approach was direct and uncompromising. I thought the Lions had a 'decent' pack, but what an understatement that was! At the end of the tour, these guys were all legends. The Lions arrived in South Africa as just another group of British players, but they actually never left again – till this day they are being remembered with awe and respect.

It was when they played Eastern Province in Port Elizabeth – I was the captain on the day – that we realised that the Lions were not going to turn the other cheek. Gareth Edwards was twice hit hard without the ball, and at the next line-out the Lions just forgot about the ball and executed their notorious '99' call. They hit out in all directions and afterwards it was clear that no team was going to 'soften them up'. For the first time in this country we had come up against organised retaliation and we were caught completely unawares, and it did have an effect in the series.

Our defeat in the first Test was not the end of the world, but the rugby public at the time just couldn't accept that we could lose against a British Lions side. Their general attitude was one of total disbelief; they were looking everywhere to put the blame – it must be the captain, it must be the selectors, it must be the coach. Unfortunately, the many changes to the national side were detrimental to building team spirit and cohesion, with the result that we were no match for the opposition, we were in serious trouble.

The third Test of course was do or die for us, and in the first half we still held out well. But in the second half we ran out of steam and the Lions calmly took control, and their class and tactical nous were too much for mere passion.

I was terribly disappointed and after the match function I couldn't wait to get back to my farm, some two hours away from Port Elizabeth. I just had to escape from the pressure and humiliation of the series defeat, and I sat there alone in the dark for hours. But the sun rose the next morning and I was ready to look the world in the face again – to have lost against a side like the 1974 Lions was no disgrace. Three years earlier, after all, they had handed the mighty All Blacks a series defeat in New Zealand.

We were desperate for them not to achieve a complete whitewash, and for the fourth Test in Johannesburg I somehow felt more positive going into the match. By finally managing to put a lot of pressure on Gareth Edwards we slowed their momentum and salvaged a draw. But the bottom line was that they beat us 3-0 in the series and by ten tries to one, and with that no one could argue about who the better side was. To me, as a Springbok who had been used to much more winning than losing, the defeats were bitter and hard to swallow. But I always made sure that I was the first to go into the Lions changing room with my beer in my hand. They were a team worthy of admiration and respect and I wanted to show them that.

In the years after the tour, I was invited to two 1974 British Lions reunions, and every time I had to sit there and listen to the '74 heroes' stories of their triumphant tour in South Africa. But during one of these functions, Stuart McKinney walked over to me, took off his Lions blazer and gave it to me. That just shows you the true spirit of brotherhood that exists between players from all over the world, irrespective of nationality or results.

Looking back, what struck me most about the 1974 British Lions was what a close unit they were. For that I must praise the team's leadership in Willie John McBride, the captain, and Syd Millar, the coach, both from Ballymena. They knew what was required to beat the Springboks in their own backyard, and how well did they plan and execute that, setting a standard that was going to be very hard to follow for future British Lions tours to South Africa.

HANNES MARAIS
SPRINGBOK CAPTAIN 1971–74

I

THE 1891 BRITISH ISLES TOUR TO SOUTHERN AFRICA: THE PIONEERS

In the course of the nineteenth century, as transport links across England, Scotland, Wales and Ireland expanded, so did the playing of team sport, with the improved methods of transport allowing players to move rapidly between towns and counties. By the middle of the century, the various forms of what would become known as rugby were starting to be codified and clubs established. In late 1870, Edwin Ash and Benjamin Burns initiated a meeting of all those who played a 'rugby-type' game. As a result of this gathering in Regent Street, London, the Rugby Football Union was formed in early 1871. A few months later, the first international rugby game, between England and Scotland, was played in Edinburgh.

The type of rugby played in that game would not be easily recognisable to the modern rugby supporter. There were twenty players a side, with thirteen in the forwards and three full backs. In the years that followed laws were drawn up, teams reduced to fifteen players a side, referees introduced, and a scoring system agreed upon.

The last quarter of the nineteenth century can be viewed as the apogee of the British Empire. Queen Victoria's portrait hung in the place of honour in locations across a quarter of the globe and as her emissaries established military and trading outposts that became colonies, they also took English traditions, sporting and cultural, with them. Cricket, soccer and rugby all began to take root in outposts from Calcutta to Cape Town, Auckland to Adelaide and further afield.

Canon George Ogilvie is attributed with bringing 'the handling game', as rugby was sometimes known, to southern Africa. Educated at Winchester and Oxford, he was advised to seek warmer climes for his health. Initially, he taught at a school in Buenos Aires, but in 1861 he took up a position as the teacher in charge of St George's Grammar School in Cape Town. He later moved to the school founded by the Bishop of Cape Town, Robert Gray, in 1849. This school was located on a farm in the Cape Town suburb of Rondebosch. It was here that Ogilvie, known to the boys of 'the Bishop's school' as 'Gog', taught them to play rugby, or 'Gog's game'.

Gog's game became popular in Cape Town and it was here that the first two clubs formed in southern Africa, Hamilton and Villager, came into being in 1875 and 1876 respectively. Games were played on the Green Point Common and on fields laid out at the Wynberg military camp on the road midway between Cape Town and Simon's Town.

By the end of the 1870s, rugby had spread to the towns and villages of the Cape hinterland such as Malmesbury, Paarl and Stellenbosch. At the same time the political situation in southern Africa had required increasing numbers of military personnel to be sent out to the eastern Cape and Natal, which in turn had led to the spread of the game into those areas. In 1885, a rugby club was formed in Potchefstroom and by 1888 matches were being played as far afield as Pretoria, Barberton and Johannesburg, where the Pirates Club was formed that year. The proliferation of rugby clubs across southern Africa led to the establishment of rugby unions to organise competitions, codify laws and provide direction. The first such union was the Western Province Rugby Football Union (WPRU) founded in Cape Town in 1883 followed by Griqualand West RU in 1886 and others thereafter.[1]

The spread of rugby throughout southern Africa had not gone unnoticed in Britain. In other parts of the Empire, most notably Australia, Canada and New Zealand, the game had also taken root and begun to expand. In 1888 an unofficial team from Britain under R. L. Seddon undertook a tour of New Zealand. The team toured for nine months and played fifty-four matches, but none against a representative national side.

Over the southern summer season of 1888–89, a team of cricketers also went on tour. Led by Major R. G. Warton and captained by C. A. Smith, they toured around southern Africa playing nineteen matches in the two British colonies of the Cape and Natal, as well as two matches in Johannesburg. Johannesburg, established because of the discovery of gold on the Witwatersrand, was part of President Paul Kruger's Zuid-Afrikaansche Republiek (ZAR), a country that had fought a full-scale war against Britain just seven years previously.

In London and Edinburgh, the success of the tour organised by Major Warton had been noted. The Seddon tour to New Zealand had also made the news in the Cape. Correspondence between the RFU and its equivalent in Cape Town, the South African Rugby Football Board (formed in Kimberley in 1889), took place in mid-1890. Joe Richards was going to visit London and was tasked by the WPRU to contact the RFU and suggest the tour in person. The RFU was interested, but the Honorary Secretary, G. Rowland Hill, made it plain that the tour could only go ahead if the South Africans agreed that there would be 'nothing of a professional character about it'. Hill was wary, since it later appeared that the Seddon tour had been 'essentially a commercial enterprise'.[2]

He also sought cast-iron financial guarantees before any players would be contacted. Cecil Rhodes 'took the whole financial responsibility upon himself' to bring the team out to the Cape and President Paul Kruger of the ZAR 'gave the tour his blessing and promised any support he could give'. The two rugby unions consequently agreed upon a tour to take place during the southern hemisphere winter of 1891.

The RFU called for 'applications' to join the tour by May 1891. *The Athletic News* could report that a 'very large number of applications' had been received, which would lead the team to be 'fairly representative'.[3] They concluded that those who could spare the time to travel so far and be away for such a long period would enjoy a 'most pleasant trip'. There were suggestions that some clubs in the Cape played a 'good strong game', but the team selected was considered certain to win most of their matches. They cautioned that those selected should be 'men who can put up with a bit of rough work'.[4]

The squad, chosen in late May, comprised nine backs and twelve forwards and would be led by W. E. 'Bill' Maclagan of London Scottish and Scotland, with an Englishman, John Hammond of Cambridge University, as his deputy. The manager was to be Edwin 'Daddy' Ash, who twenty years previously had been instrumental in forming the RFU. On Saturday 20 June 1891, the team set sail from Southampton on the *Dunnottar Castle* and sixteen days later (a new record for the travel time between the two ports) reached Cape Town.

When Maclagan and his men stepped off the vessel onto African soil for the first time, they were initiating a tradition which, unbeknownst to them, would be built upon and grow over the next 130 years into one of the great rugby events of the world. The first British Lions had arrived!

The Team and the First Matches in Cape Town

The team that arrived on 6 July in Cape Town had been carefully chosen. It contained four Scots in Maclagan, P. L. Clauss, W. Wotherspoon and R. G. MacMillan. There were two players each from Manchester, B. G. Roscoe and T. Whittaker, and from Yorkshire, W. E. and E. Bromet. The remaining thirteen hailed from southern England. It was very much a team of gentlemen: twelve were from the University of Cambridge and two from Oxford.

On the eve of their departure, Sir Donald Currie held a gathering for RFU members, well-wishers and journalists in the magnificently appointed first-class dining room of the *Dunnottar Castle*. Venison stew, Malay curry, sherry and champagne were served before Sir Donald rose to propose a toast to the team. Wishing them well, he announced that, as with the cricketers who had headed to southern Africa in 1888, he was sending a cup to be played for by future rugby teams in 'all the states up to the Zambesi'. Maclagan gave a short response to the toast, whereupon Rowland Hill, representing the RFU, gave, according to the journalist, an earnest, solemn and lengthy address.[5]

Hill's address was focused on a matter that was to irreparably divide the rugby-playing fraternity in England four years hence. By the time Maclagan's team were cleaning their boots and packing their bags to leave for Cape Town, the split between north and south England was already becoming painfully apparent. The wealthier south played rugby for enjoyment and recreation. The poorer northern counties began to suggest that players should be compensated for loss of wages that occurred due to practice, or when teams travelled further afield to compete. In 1895, the north would break away and form what became the Rugby Football League, where compensation was allowed.

The arranging of this tour thus takes on a different light. The preponderance of southerners and university players could be seen as an attempt by the amateur establishment to make playing their form of the game more attractive. In 1890 the International Rugby Football Board (IRFB) had been formed and Hill would have been very aware of the spread of the game across the whole of the Empire. By holding out the chance of tours both to and from overseas British colonies and other nations, he was strengthening the hand of the RFU in the ongoing bitter battle against their northern League brethren.

Hill alluded to the fact that he knew all South African players were even more against the 'pros' than he was and played the game in a 'proper and noble' spirit. *The Athletic News* journalist covering the gathering, tongue in cheek, indicated that Rowland Hill 'did not regard professionals as God's creatures ... merely earthly encrustations'! Finally, 'Daddy' Ash concluded the speeches and all present adjourned to the deck to enjoy cigars and coffee.[6]

In later years, Paul Clauss would recall the team's arrival and first days in Cape Town with fondness. Unlimited hospitality prevailed. Smoking concerts, dances and a ball at Government House, lunch on board HMS *Penelope* lying off Simon's Town (the headquarters of the Royal Navy in southern Africa) and a picnic in Hout Bay were but some of the attractions. Clauss concludes that the team were 'royally entertained'. In between the social whirl they tried to get in some practice and three days after their arrival, on 9 July, the first match of the tour, against Cape Town Clubs, was held in the lee of Table Mountain at the new rugby ground owned by the Western Province Rugby Union in the leafy suburb of Newlands.[7]

It was the Scot, William Wotherspoon, of Fife and Cambridge University, who was the man who took the 'leather', and facing Table Mountain in his red-and-white striped rugby jersey on that balmy afternoon, hoisted the ball into the air 'shortly after the advertised time' to begin the contest.[8] Five minutes into the match Wotherspoon kicked a penalty to open the scoring. Little did he know what a tradition he had initiated.

The visitors won the match easily in front of a good crowd of 6,000 by scoring four tries against the one try scored by the local team. That try, by Charles 'Hasie' Versfeld, one of a trio of brothers who were playing for Cape Town Clubs, was significant. It turned out to be the only points scored against Maclagan's men during the whole tour comprising nineteen matches![9]

The visitors defeated Western Province on 11 July and the Cape Colony on 13 July in a convincing manner, both matches being played at Newlands. In the evening after the third match, they were seen off by a large crowd at the Cape Town train station when they set off for Kimberley.

The Karoo and Kimberley

Maclagan's tour party had already experienced one aspect of touring southern Africa that was destined to have an impact, sometimes severely, on rugby tourists in years to come. The non-stop hospitality extended to the tourists had its delights, but also created problems. Now the team was about to experience a second aspect of touring this huge land that would create difficulties for those intent on playing competitive rugby. A 36-hour rail journey awaited them. The first part of the journey was through the beautiful Hex River Valley, but in the darkness they saw none of it.

When they awoke, they found themselves in the 'Karoo or desert with a few bushes' and at 8.30 a.m. they halted for breakfast at the siding of Matjiesfontein where the owner of the hotel, James Logan, entertained them. Logan was a forty-four-year-old Scot who had survived a shipwreck off the Cape coast and had then remained at the Cape. Starting work as a porter on the Cape Town station, Logan, an enterprising individual, had quickly worked his way up through the Cape Government Railway ranks. He purchased a farm in the Karoo and established the village of Matjiesfontein. Matjiesfontein became both a water refuelling stop for trains and a destination for those who wanted to imbibe the 'clear airs' of the Karoo for health reasons or to have a relaxing break. A keen sportsman, Logan had already entertained cricket teams who had visited the Colony and Maclagan's men would meet him again towards the end of the tour.

In the late Tuesday afternoon, the train reached Beaufort West. It had thus taken them nearly twenty-four hours to travel just 500 kilometres. At midnight they reached the village of De Aar, deep in the Karoo. They were woken, given a meal in freezing conditions, and then hastened back to their beds to 'roost'. They arrived at Beaconsfield station outside Kimberley the next morning at 8.45. Little did the team know that this railway journey would be one of the most comfortable and relaxing of the journeys they would undertake during the tour.

At Beaconsfield station they were met by the mayor of Kimberley and a crowd of over 2,000. Almost immediately a series of social engagements began. That afternoon the team were shown the splendour of the De Beers diamond sorting rooms and the evening was a 'giddy whirl', with many local belles in attendance. On Friday morning, they were transported 800 feet down into the De Beers mine, attended the theatre in the evening and on Saturday morning got their first look at the Eclectic field on which they would play the game against Kimberley Clubs that afternoon.[10]

Here Maclagan's men confronted a third aspect of touring in Africa that would affect their ability, and that of future tourists, to play the type of rugby they knew at home. One correspondent sarcastically indicated that the Eclectic field had at least 'three blades of grass' present and was primarily 'sandy gravel'.[11] The *Sporting Life* correspondent recorded the ground consisted of 'hard red sand, and the dust puzzled our men'.[12] The tourists could not believe that they were expected to play on such a 'field'.

It is hard to imagine a place further from home for the tourists. Kimberley's dry, cold winters leave the veld in the area dusty, barren and brown. In 1891, every tree or bush in the countryside for a circumference of over 50 kilometres around the city had been cut down to supply either firewood, or more importantly, mining headgear. The lack of wood meant construction using bricks was impossible. The whole town was constructed of corrugated iron or variants thereof. Even wooden floors were hard to find. Ceilings were often stretched canvas that sagged as they collected dust and debris. The novelist Anthony Trollope had visited Kimberley some years earlier. His verdict: 'I doubt whether there was a blade of grass within twenty miles... Everything was brown as though the dusty dry uncovered earth never knew the blessing of verdure ... an uglier place I do not know how to imagine.'[13]

The Kimberley team, however, was used to the conditions and the tourists found they played rugby at a furious pace, aided by the rock-hard field. Quick on the break and with men snapping up every dropped pass or mis-kick, Maclagan's men battled against a team comprising players hardened by years of tough physical labour.

It is pertinent to record that the touring team were much bigger men than the locals. This would not be the case in future years, but the tourists were large men, led by Froude 'Baby' Hancock at 250 lbs and 6'5" and with three men in the backs over 6 foot, Maclagan's men withstood the initial attacks and began to wear the Kimberley team down. Whittaker scored a good try, which proved to be the only score of the half. In the second half MacMillan scored a try far out that was not converted and finally Clauss rounded off some good passing by the tourists to score a further converted try.

The victory came at a price, however. Thompson was tackled so hard that he suffered numerous cuts to his face and some of the players did not acquit themselves well under the pressure exerted by the local team. Marshall, for example, was forced to hurry his passes from the base of the scrum and provided his fellow half-back, Rotherham, with poor service. The real problem for the visitors was that 'the dust from the ground nearly blinded the players ... and it was extremely difficult to see the ball'. The strong sun created shadows that also confused Maclagan's men and made their passing of the ball difficult. Future rugby tourists would all testify to southern African conditions making the playing of their natural games more difficult, if not impossible.

There was a further aspect of the match commented upon by *The Athletic News* correspondent. In Cape Town, the games had been played in a good spirit and the spectators had been even-handed in their applause for the teams. In Kimberley, they found the local players uncompromising and the 4,000-strong crowd vociferous in their support for the home team. The damning verdict from the visiting gentlemen was that the match had not been played 'in such a nice spirit'.[14]

Notwithstanding this criticism, the concerts and dinners continued throughout the rest of the weekend. On the Monday afternoon, the visitors faced a Griqualand West side at the same ground. This time around, there were 3,000 spectators. Griqualand West was essentially the same side as the Kimberley team they had beaten on the Saturday with only two new players, Trenery and Shackleton, coming into the side. In Maclagan's team, Marshall was replaced by the tough Roscoe of Manchester.

Once again, the local men took it to the visitors. This was to prove the closest game of the whole tour and the Griqualand West half-back pairing of De Melker and Powell played an 'off-side' game so hard did they press, according to the few in the crowd supporting the side from overseas. The crowd once again played their part and 'hooted' at the tourists and generally showed their displeasure at Maclagan's tactics of kicking the ball into touch to relieve pressure. It was alleged by the tourists that some in the crowd were 'ignorant of the game'!

De Kock intercepted a pass and was on the verge of scoring when pulled down by the full back Mitchell in a superb tackle. Roscoe was also having a 'capital' game and provided good service to his backs, who gradually began to dominate their opponents.

After a period of hard dribbling, Paul Clauss picked up the ball and finally crossed the Griqualand West line, but once over, 'sacrificed the good of his side to a little gallery play by trying to go behind the posts, the ball being mauled away for him' by the uncompromising locals. It was not to be Clauss's day. He later went to ground so hard that he was effectively *hors de combat* for the entire second half. In the end it was left to the captain himself to rescue his team and Maclagan scored a crucial try. Before the final whistle, the visitors scored once more. This 'close struggle' was marked by scrummage after scrummage. Here again, tourists in years to come would echo a similar refrain regarding the tactics used by South African teams.

On to Port Elizabeth and the First Test

The team entrained for the coastal city of Port Elizabeth late on Thursday. This time, the journey took thirty-six hours, and the novelty of the Cape was beginning to wear thin for *The Athletic News* correspondent. Travel in this country was 'monotonous', he concluded. However, he reported that the African sunrise witnessed at the breakfast stop in the village of Cradock the next morning was 'impressive'.[15]

When the team arrived in Port Elizabeth, exhausted by their long journey, they were not formally welcomed. However, the local inhabitants broke barriers at the station to get to them and simply 'smothered us' according to one player. The team found they were going to lodge with leading members of the local community. Once again, concerts took place as well as deep-sea fishing and some players were also invited to the 'married men's club on the Zwartkops River'.

On Saturday 25 July, the team played against Port Elizabeth Clubs. To their 'great relief', they found they would be playing on grass and the result was a walkover for the visitors: six goals and four tries to nil. Once again, Mitchell played well and showed impressive kicking abilities, whilst both Wotherspoon and Whittaker scored two tries. Three days later they beat Eastern Province by an impressive seven goals to nil with Arthur Rotherham converting all seven tries. Now Maclagan's men would face South Africa in what would be the first 'Test' match in the history of this incipient rugby nation.

The first match between 'South Africa and the British Isles' was played on the Port Elizabeth Cricket Club ground on Thursday 30 July 1891. The referee was Dr John Griffin. On a bright, fine winter's day, over 6,000 spectators lined the four edges of the field.

The team of 'South Africa' was led by Herbert Hayton Castens. Castens was a local man, his father the President of the Eastern Province Rugby Union. He had acted as referee in the two previous matches Maclagan's men had played in Port Elizabeth. During this tour, in all three Tests, the local union was responsible for the selection of the national team. It put the local men at a huge disadvantage, as the team they were facing had grown into a battle-hardened unit, while the South Africa team tended to have a local flavour and had never played together before.

For this, the first team to represent South Africa, Castens selected six players from his union, Western Province, three from Griqualand West and two from Eastern Province. These men had already played against the tourists. The last four he selected played for Transvaal, the rugby union located in Johannesburg in the Zuid Afrikaansche Republiek. The local team played in the white jerseys of the Crusader Club.

In years to come, Paul Clauss would recall the match as being a 'hard-fought', forward-dominated duel. *The Sportsmen* reporter described it as a 'capital' game but did not provide any further information. *The Edinburgh Evening News*[16] was more specific and indicated that although the 'Africans' were the losers, they had enjoyed the best of the play and had 'pressed' throughout.

The local team might have pressed the visitors, but early in the match it was the tall midfielder Randolph Aston of Cambridge University who crashed over for a try. Shortly thereafter, T. Whittaker of Lancashire dotted down, and Arthur Rotherham, another Cambridge man, converted. At half-time both teams remained on the field and received instructions from their backers while enjoying 'lemons and sundry'.

The second half saw more sustained pressure from the local men, but to no avail. The score remained unchanged and thus Bill Maclagan's team won the day 4-0. The consensus was that whilst Maclagan's men deserved the win, the local team had acquitted themselves well.

Into the Eastern Cape Interior
The day after their Test victory the team travelled to Grahamstown, where they faced the local team, easily, beating them 9-0. This match was followed by a splendid dinner and, on the Sunday, a concert was held at the home of the local bank manager, Mr Simpson. Several of the team went hunting buck on the nearby farm belonging

to the Lovemore family. They found that it was hard work tracking and finding the elusive animals and only W. E. Bromet, Jackson and John Hammond managed to bring one to ground.[17]

A trip of twelve hours in an uncomfortable Cape-cart on a rutted and very bumpy road saw the team reach King William's Town on the Monday night. Here, on the 4th, they played the town team and on the 6th a combined team of King William's Town and East London. They won both matches easily, but Paul Clauss felt the team was getting 'stale'.

Another bumpy journey back down to the coast followed and late on 8 August the tourists boarded a small tug in East London harbour. The tug conveyed the team 'over the bar' to meet the large steamer *Melrose* heading towards Durban. Once over the bar and away from the protection of the harbour, the full force of the strong wind became evident. In the windswept darkness the tug pilot misjudged the approach to the waiting *Melrose* and, to the horror of all on board the smaller vessel, the *Melrose,* towering over them, caught her a glancing blow. Clauss was convinced that had the collision been amidships the tug would have sunk and many on board would have lost their lives. As it was, the tug's bow was hit, but the vessel remained upright. The team was able to clamber on board the *Melrose* with their kit. It had been a narrow escape and would have undoubtedly ended the tour abruptly with the whole concept of tours being called into question.[18]

Natal and the Transvaal
Arriving in Durban harbour on 10 August, the team entrained immediately for Pietermaritzburg. The railway climbed into the Drakensberg foothills until it reached the Natal capital. During the South African War in 1899, Winston Churchill would travel this same route describing the trip thus: 'As the railway zigzags up and down hill and contorts itself into curves that would horrify the domestic engineer, the journey occupies four hours.'[19] Here they recorded the largest win of the tour on the 11th, before heading further northwards. The railway to the Witwatersrand ended at the Charlestown siding and here the squad split up, with most heading on to Standerton and

then Johannesburg in coaches pulled by ten horses. The remainder of the squad hired horses and rode up to Majuba Hill.

In 1877, Britain had unilaterally annexed the ZAR. After initial acceptance of the situation, in 1880 Boer commandos, marshalled by Paul Kruger, took up arms and began to fight for their freedom. Boer forces laid siege to several towns and cities in the ZAR, trapping British forces.

On 27 February 1881, Major General Sir George Pomeroy Colley's force was heavily defeated, and he was killed by Boer forces on the summit of Majuba mountain. Colley and his force had been en route to the ZAR to try and lift the sieges imposed by Kruger's commandos. Colley had occupied the heights of Majuba the previous day but gave no order to dig trenches or defences. Boer commando members scaled the steep sides of the mountain under fire. Once they reached the summit, they outflanked the defenders and Colley's poor planning was exposed, with many in his column being killed or wounded. Gladstone's government in Westminster, already hesitant about going to war, signed a peace treaty after the battle that reinstated the ZAR's independence. Eighteen years later, the slogan 'Remember Majuba' would be a rallying cry to British troops in the second South African War, 1899–1902.

On Saturday 15 August, despite the visitors' exhaustion after the long journey, Maclagan's men soundly defeated a Transvaal Country team. The following Wednesday, they defeated a Johannesburg team and finally on the Saturday thereafter, a full Transvaal team. All three of these matches were played at the Wanderers ground in Johannesburg. The hardest match was against the Transvaal team. The visitors' line was crossed in this match, the first time since Versfeld had achieved that feat in the first match. Jimmy Anderson was the Transvaal player who crossed the white line, but before he could dot the ball down Maclagan picked him up bodily and carried him back into the field of play and averted the crisis!

Johannesburg was a city full of hard living and adventurous individuals. It was a 'city of unbridled squander and unfathomable squalor'.[20] It is no wonder that it was reported that the team had a 'hectic' time whilst staying on the Witwatersrand.

Second Test and Back to Cape Town for the Third

Early on the Sunday after the third match, the team left in two coaches for Klerksdorp, where they would spend the night. The one coach made good time, the second lost a wheel and the unlucky passengers spent a cold night on the veld. The entire next day was again spent in the coaches and they reached Bloemhof stiff, tired, and cold at 2 am. On the third day, after a mere nine hours in the coaches, they reached the railhead at Fourteen Streams and gratefully boarded a train for Kimberley, which they finally reached on Tuesday night at 11 pm. The next day they played a match against the Cape Colony. And won it!

On Saturday 29 August, they played the second Test against South Africa, again on the barren Eclectic ground. This was to prove the toughest and best contested match of the entire tour. Bob Snedden, who had played so well for the Cape Colony in the match the previous Wednesday, captained South Africa. The team wore the jerseys of Griqualand West RU, their hosts. His team showed nine changes from the one defeated in Port Elizabeth and included nine players from Griqualand West. Maclagan changed just three of his players.

The Reuters correspondent in attendance reported that the entire game evoked 'the greatest excitement' in the 3,000 spectators. It was once again a game confined to the forwards with few highlights. The 'Colonials' pressed the visitors hard throughout. The entire match produced just one scoring moment, which, as in the first Test, was early in the first half. The back Bill Mitchell dropped a 'beautiful' goal, according to Clauss, from a mark 'at the touch-line close to the centre flag' that bounced twice on the crossbar before going over. That is how the game ended and Maclagan's men thus won by a slender 3-0.[21]

The return trip to Cape Town was, in comparison to what they had experienced during the tour, an easy journey. Once again, they stopped off in Matjiesfontien and here lost the only match of the tour! James Logan had arranged for a Western Province cricket team to be on hand to face them, and the hosts won by 18 runs. The railway journey through the Hex River Valley was accomplished in daylight hours, thus allowing them to admire the views.

On 3 September, they beat a Cape Colony team at Newlands 7-0 with Herbert Castens the referee. Two days later, again at

Newlands, they faced South Africa for the third time, on this occasion under the captaincy of Alf Richards of Western Province. Maclagan's team showed just one change from the second Test, whilst South Africa made eight changes.

The day of the match, 5 September, was a pleasant one in Cape Town. *The Cape Argus* reported that conditions were 'delightful to the spectators' with not a breath of wind, but that the sun was 'a little too bright for the players'. Possibly this was because, with the field running east to west, the afternoon sun must have shone straight into the eyes of the team playing towards Table Mountain. The field would be swung to run parallel with the railway in years to come, thus avoiding this problem.

The Cape Government Railways arranged several special trains to run to Newlands station. Mr Price, the Newlands stationmaster, and his staff erected a ticket box on the station platform to sell tickets to the ground to alleviate the press at the gates. An hour before kick-off, the ground was 'thickly lined by a huge crowd'.

The visitors won the toss and chose to play with the sun behind their backs. It was Ben Duff who kicked off towards Table Mountain for South Africa. The ball was immediately carried into the home team's half where 'a long series of scrums followed'. At this stage of the game, the Colonial forwards, ably led by Alf Richards, 'were seen to great advantage'. The description of the game that appeared immediately after its conclusion provides few clues as to the actual course of play. Maclagan appeared to be cool under pressure and cleared the ball well into touch. Clauss put in several good runs that were hard to stop. The large centre, Randolph Aston, also proved his value.

On the local side, Chubb Vigne played well whilst William Bisset showed his fine dribbling skills. Only good work by the British full back Bill Mitchell kept the Colonials out. Towards the end of the first half, both Alf Richards and Duff had to 'touch in defence'. BH (Fairy) Heatlie, the largest man on the South African side, proved a tower of strength and made some good touch kicks. When the half-time whistle went it was 'received with loud cheers by the spectators'. There had been no score by either team.

If the 3,000 Capetonians present that day had hoped that, for the first time on the tour, Maclagan's men had met their match, they were in for a disappointment. The second half saw the tourists step up the tempo. The 'bladder travelled from one to another and back like lightning as has never been seen in South Africa'. Only desperate defence by Jim McKendrick and Van Renen saved the day. Then an event occurred which swung the game the tourists' way. Marthinus 'Oupa' Versfeld was 'knocked down' and had to receive attention to a 'nasty wound to the head, which necessitated the stopping of the game for some five minutes'. The tourists now attacked the South African line with great 'vigour' and an 'ugly rush by the English forward division was stopped by Vigne' while the passing of the tourists 'baffled' the home team. It does not sound good from a South African perspective and so it is no surprise to read that shortly thereafter, Maclagan made a 'grand rush' for the line and although caught and 'grassed', was awarded a try. There is confusion as to who took the conversion, with the *Argus* reporter suggesting it was Wotherspoon, but official records indicating Arthur Rotherham. At the death, Aston also scored a second try that was unconverted and Maclagan's tourists had won 4-0, ending their tour undefeated.[22]

Maclagan's Men Return Home

That evening a smoking concert was held in the Drill Hall. The Hall was packed and the band of HMS *Raleigh*, then anchored at Simon's Town, played as the English team entered, this event 'being marked by a considerable display of enthusiasm' by those present. Comic songs by Mr Williams (RN) and several on the banjo by Mr L. Estrange went down well, but it was a song by Maclagan that was 'cheered to the echo'!

After several more musical items, the British team made a presentation to David Pargiter, who had acted as their local manager. It was during this speech that Maclagan hinted, to much acclaim, that another tour might be undertaken in the same manner. The concert then proceeded 'amid great hilarity' until it concluded at a 'late hour with all singing Auld Lang Syne together'.

On Sunday morning at 9 o'clock, a party of thirty persons met outside the Royal Hotel in the city and after several hours the whole party again gathered together, this time on the summit of Table Mountain. Significantly, only a dozen members of the touring party were able to make the climb – the remainder obviously sleeping off the effects of the match and the smoking concert! Those that made the climb walked along the plateau after a cold lunch and were 'greatly impressed by the magnificent scenery, of which the atmospheric conditions enabled them to get a fine view, and after undergoing the inevitable photographic process, and signing their names in the visitor's book at the ranger's cottage, the descent was commenced'. They returned to their hotel by 6 p.m. 'greatly pleased with the day's excursion'.

On the Monday, the team travelled to Stellenbosch where they were entertained on a local wine farm and played a 'picnic game' against a local team that was not considered an official game. They then returned to Cape Town where they were the guests of honour at a ball.

On 9 September, a farewell lunch was held on the *Garth Castle* where the Currie Cup, donated by Sir Donald Currie, was handed over to the team that the tourists felt had played the best game against them. Griqualand West was adjudged that team and their officials promptly offered it as a challenge cup to be played for by the South African rugby unions. Then the 'all ashore' was sounded and the homeward voyage for Maclagan and his men began.

In early October, *The Athletic News* ran a short story on the tour. Some in the English rugby fraternity had been concerned that the 'exertions' of the tour would 'impair the playing' of the party for the forthcoming season. Instead, they found the players in 'grand trim' although missing a 'few yards of skin from their knees, shins and elbows'.[23] Wherever the team travelled they received a 'reception such as might fitly be accorded to heroes'. [24]

A short advertisement was also carried, notifying those interested that a 'Memoir' of the tour could be purchased for 1 shilling from Fenchurch Street. It carried full particulars of all the matches and details of the tourists and some of their opponents.

In Retrospect

The tour undertaken by Bill Maclagan and his team, with no support staff or coaches, might be long forgotten and the type of rugby they played unrecognisable from the modern game, but the role they played in popularising and encouraging rugby in southern Africa was vital. They helped lay the foundations, together with the local teams they faced, of what became a mighty edifice. Traditions that would be followed by other tours across the world in years to come were begun by Maclagan's tourists.

South African rugby historian Paul Dobson points out that whereas the British team fielded but eighteen players in the three Tests, South Africa used twenty-eight.[25] For the British Isles, twelve men played in all three Tests: for the South Africans only five. The tourists carried much too much firepower in terms of experience and number of Test caps. This would be a common refrain in future years. Other refrains from this tour – or rather complaints – which would echo down the years were about the interminable journeys in poor transport faced by the tourists between venues, and the high altitude that sucked the breath out of one's tired body in the dying moments of tough matches played on hard and dusty fields.

Paul Clauss, writing in Ivor Difford's *History of South African Rugby Football* more than four decades later, recalled the factors mentioned above, but he also noted with pleasure the 'boundless hospitality' the team experienced during the tour with many festivities which 'lasted far into the night'. He admitted that no modern team would be able to act in the way they had, but he also pointed out that they had a 'margin of superiority' which no other team in South Africa would enjoy, at least not for another eight decades.[26]

Rowland Hill's vision had been fulfilled. Southern Africa had indeed warmly embraced the team he sent out and thereby the amateur rugby game he so valued. Other southern hemisphere colonies witnessed the success of this tour and the seed of home and away tours across the equator was successfully planted. It would, however, be another fifteen years before a team from South Africa landed in Britain. That event was postponed by a savage war that took three long years to conclude and cost many lives, both South African and British. But when that team did arrive under Paul Roos and Paddy Carolin in 1906, it showed the RFU, and all those who enjoyed rugby in Britain, that the lessons taught in 1891 on the rocky, dusty Eclectic field, on the damp and verdant Newlands and even in far-away Grahamstown and Pietermaritzburg, had been well learnt.

1891 TOURING PARTY
Manager – Edwin Ash

Backs
W. E. 'Bill' Maclagan (Capt.) (Scotland)*
Randolph Aston (England)*
William Bromet (England)*
Paul Clauss (Scotland)*
Howard Marshall (England)*
William Mitchell (England)*
B.G. Roscoe (England)
Arthur Rotherham (England)*
Williams Wotherspoon (Scotland)*

Forwards
Edward Bromet (England)*
John Gould (England)*
John Hammond (England)*
Froude Hancock (England)*
Walter Jackson (England)
Robert MacMillan (Scotland)*
Edwin Mayfield (England)*
Clement Simpson (England)*
Aubone Surtees (England)*
Robert Thompson (England)*
William Thorman (England)
Thomas Whittaker (England)*

* Played in at least one Test match

Bill Maclagan (1858–1926)

William Edward Maclagan was born in Edinburgh and educated at Edinburgh Academy. After school he joined Edinburgh Academical RC and was chosen to represent Scotland at the age of twenty whilst playing for that club. He played for London Scottish, a club he helped start, from 1880 until he toured southern Africa in 1891.

Maclagan became a vital part of a strong Scottish team and in 1884 he was named as captain, a role he would fulfil nine times. In all he played twenty-six times for Scotland between 1878 and 1890. He was the most capped player and winger of his day and was a natural choice to lead the inaugural tour of southern Africa.

An imposing figure both on and off the field, it was suggested he was one of a few men who not only controlled his own team, but also, by force of his nature, influenced those who played against him. He was known as a man almost impossible to stop when close to the line: 'Maclagan within reach of the line was something to see to be believed ... he was the most powerful man behind the scrummage ever to have played for Scotland,' one obituary stated. In his later years he worked as a stockbroker and became President of the Scottish Rugby Union, 1894–1896, but even when no longer holding office, his word on rugby matters was considered *suprema lex*!

In later years he played a good game of golf, travelling every summer to join his brother D. D. Maclagan to play the courses of Perthshire.

At the time of his death his role in rugby was assessed as his life had encompassed the whole early history of international rugby. His role in southern Africa rugby was recalled as being especially important. The 1891 British Isles team he led to Africa 'fired the enthusiasm of the whole Dominion' and inspired a generation who laid the foundations of Springbok rugby. South Africa owes Bill Maclagan a debt of gratitude. (*Dundee Evening Telegraph*, 13 October 1926)

2

THE 1896 TOUR: HAMMOND'S TEAM WIN NEARLY EVERY MATCH

The steamship *Tartar*, carrying the second squad of rugby tourists, sailed from Southampton, reaching Table Bay on the evening of 8 July 1896. This tour party was composed of players from England and Ireland. The captain was an Englishman, John Hammond, and the vice-captain an Irishman, Dr Tommy Crean.

The *Tartar* sailed via Funchal in Madeira where the vessel re-coaled. This allowed the team to disembark briefly and climb the peak behind the town where a convent was situated. The climb in the extreme heat took the team an hour and a quarter. The trip down on wooden sledges (steered by locals) took just ten minutes.

The voyage between Funchal and the Cape was taken up with deck games, concerts, resting on deck and meals. The members of Hammond's team, understandably, dominated all aspects of the sporting activities on board. Crean won the ½ mile event in 2 minutes and 4 seconds; Magee took the 40 yards and the ¼ mile. Other members of the team swept to victory in quoits and other deck games.

Tug-of-war was keenly contested. It pitted first-, second- and third-class passengers against each other, the winners facing off against the crew's teams. Once these preliminary contests had been resolved, the firemen were summoned from 'down below' to confront the winners. The firemen always won. Eight of

Hammond's men, representing first class, got through to the final. The firemen defeated them, as was expected.

The team challenged the firemen to a second round and, one suspects, keen on revenge, some planning was undertaken. This time around, to much surprise and acclaim, the team twice pulled the firemen's team of eight right off their feet. Beware teams in South Africa![1]

Arrival and First Matches
On the morning of 9 July, John Hammond's team began, like Maclagan's men five years before them, to experience what it was like to be on tour. Tugs and other vessels came out to meet the team, circling the *Tartar* lying in Table Bay. The President of the Western Province Rugby Union (WPRU), William Simpkins, scrambled aboard to be the first to greet them. On the dockside, the mayor of Cape Town, J. W. Attwell, and a huge throng of local inhabitants waited to welcome them and convey them to the Royal Hotel.

Two days later, the first match was played against Cape Town Clubs at the Newlands ground. The tourists found the good food and cramped conditions on board ship had left them sadly out of condition. They also found, to their dismay, that the local men had a much better grasp of rugby than had been the case five years previously. Hammond's men struggled and at one stage the Reuters correspondent watching the match thought they were 'going to pieces'. Hammond, however, rallied his men and by half-time they led 6-3. Tries by Alexander Todd and Osbert Mackie and three successful kicks by John Byrne saw them run out winners 14-9. In the process, however, Hammond was severely 'damaged'.

John Hammond was by this time thirty-six years old. He had been playing rugby at the highest level for fifteen years and during the 1891 tour had played every match. The damage done must have been severe, as he would sit out the following thirteen games and only play in seven of the twenty-one during the tour. Tommy Crean became the de facto captain.

On the Sunday following the first match, the team were conveyed around the Peninsula by car. In Hout Bay, they met the mining magnate Barney Barnato (who was on holiday in the Cape) and then returned to the Royal Hotel by way of Oudekraal. On Monday afternoon they faced, and beat, a Cape Town Suburbs team 8-0. Two days later, they faced the Currie Cup champions, Western Province, again at Newlands. Before the Western Province match, the WPRU had arranged for the tourists to be entertained to lunch by the new Premier of the Cape Colony, Sir Gordon Sprigg. Tommy Crean, captain for the day, had decreed that his players 'were to limit themselves to four tumblers of champagne'. The game ended in a 0-0 draw.[2]

After the Western Province match, a banquet was held at the Royal Hotel where more toasts were drunk, the last of which was 'bon voyage'. At nine o'clock that same evening, the team departed by train for Kimberley, the cheers of the local populace and the counter cheers from the team filling the station.

Kimberley

The pace of the tour now slowed considerably. In fact, it became 'painfully slow'. The train took until Friday morning at 9 o'clock to arrive in Kimberley. There they were met by the President of the Griqualand West RU, Percy Ross Frames, and conveyed to the recently constructed Central Hotel. On Friday afternoon, the team were taken to see the De Beers diamond mine. It was not what they had expected. The mine resembled nothing more than a 'rubbish tip' and they saw no evidence of wealth, only dusty, hard-bitten miners. De Beers executives then took them to the diamond sorting rooms where the riches that were driving the growth of Kimberley were on full display, including one diamond of 503 carats.

On Saturday 18 and Wednesday 22 July, the visitors faced the Griqualand West team. Both matches were won by the tourists, both games being hard-fought contests. The first match was especially tough. Watched by nearly 5,000 spectators and played at a furious pace, the victory margin was just two points (11-9).

The second contest saw a wider margin of victory (16-0) and it had become obvious that the team was beginning to combine well.

On the Sunday, the team was again taken over De Beers properties, including the workers' compounds. The team was dismayed by what they were shown. Home to 2,500 workers from tribes across southern Africa, the correspondent reported they were 'practically prisons'. Being a Sunday, the miners were not working, but rather participating in 'war dances' accompanied by thunderous singing and noise. It was, he concluded, an experience the team would 'ever remember'.

In stark contrast, the De Beers executives took them to the suburb of Kenilworth on the Monday morning, where they were shown the houses provided for white workers. They were also treated to a slap-up lunch during this part of the visit. The differences could not have been starker.[3]

Down to the Coast and First Test

The performance of the team was indeed on the up. After a lengthy railway trip down to the coast, they defeated a team from Port Elizabeth 26-3 on Saturday 25 July and three days later, an Eastern Province team 18-0.

The first Test match of the 1896 tour was played at the Crusader ground in Port Elizabeth on Saturday 30 July. Whilst the English & Irish team chose a settled combination, the South Africans chose a squad dominated by players from the Eastern Province, which the tourists had already disposed of easily. The result was a victory for Hammond's team by 8 to 0, which does not sound like a big win. However, most of the match was played in the local men's half and almost all the attacks mounted were by the tourists. Paul Dobson concludes that the South Africans put up a 'poor display' and the forwards especially 'fell apart'.[4]

Four more matches were played in the Eastern Cape. In each case they travelled laboriously and slowly over bad roads between the venues on Cape carts. Accommodation was in humble hostelries, but the team enjoyed the hospitality and the fact that in all four cases the towns came to a halt to allow the populace to view the contests. First, Grahamstown was defeated 20-0 in a heavy downpour that broke the local drought. Then King William's Town (25-0), East London (17-0) and finally Queenstown (25-0) were all easily conquered. In East London, they attended a political debate involving Sir Gordon Sprigg, the Premier, who was a leading local supporter of Rhodes. In the Queenstown game, Syd Bell of Cambridge, who was not selected to play by Crean, acted as referee.

The Transvaal

After the match against Queenstown on the afternoon of 8 August, the team travelled further inland by rail via Springfontein to Bloemfontein, the capital city of the Orange Free State (OFS). There they enjoyed a short break before entraining for Johannesburg.

They were met early on Tuesday morning at Vereeniging by four members of the Transvaal Rugby Union (TRU), including the vice-president, R. H. Blakeley, and J. B. Stone, the secretary. Vereeniging lay on the border of the Orange Free State and the Zuid-Afrikaansche Republiek (ZAR) and the four TRU officials helped the team complete the required customs formalities to allow them to enter the ZAR. Blakeley and his Entertainment Committee had been working feverishly to prepare for the team's arrival and had many interesting events planned for their stay. The TRU had also been expanding the Wanderers ground, where all five of the matches on the Rand would be played. Additional entrances, enclosures, and seating for 2,000 had been constructed.

The train bearing the team to Johannesburg reached Park Station at 10.30 a.m. on Tuesday, where hundreds of flag-waving fans awaited them. They were escorted to the Hotel Victoria, which would serve as their base for the next two weeks. In the afternoon, a team run was held on the Wanderers ground to stretch their travel-weary legs. Despite the ground being regularly and expensively watered, John Hammond was dismayed by what he found. He informed the correspondent of *The Johannesburg Times* that, while the city had changed out of all recognition since his visit five years previously, Wanderers was 'harder than any field they had played on' during the tour and was still 'rocky'.[5] That evening a smoking concert was held in the Hotel Victoria during which three members of the touring team also gave solo performances. On Wednesday afternoon, the first match was played on the Rand against a Johannesburg Country team.

The TRU had not only been preparing the Wanderers field and entertainment for Hammond's men, but also the teams to face them. There was a feeling that if any local team was to beat the tourists, it would be that of Transvaal. Johannesburg, just a decade old, now boasted a population of over 100,000 so there were plenty of potential players. The altitude and, as we have seen, the hard field, worked in their favour, as did the fact that most of the local players were hardened by mine work or physical labour. Three trial matches, confusingly called 'test' matches, had been played on the Rand in the run-up to Hammond's team's arrival, to allow the selectors to assess all the local players. Teams led by Ferdie Aston of Diggers RFC and Jim Crosby of Pirates Club had battled it out. On the eve of the first game at Wanderers against the visitors, a meeting of the TRU executive under the chairmanship of R. L. Cousens was held. Team selection was the most important matter on the agenda.

The first part of the meeting consisted of the usual administrative matters. Minutes were read and approved, and a short discussion followed about final arrangements for the matches. Then Alexander Tait (who died in a train accident near Laingsburg in the Karoo in 1898, while on his way to play for Transvaal in Cape Town) stood up and a made an unexpected proposition. He suggested that, while acknowledging the role of foreign-born players in the various local teams, he would like to see one of the teams to be made up of only 'Colonial-born' players. This team, he suggested 'would be likely to draw a good gate' and an 'interesting game would result'.

This unexpected intervention was met with some surprise and a lively discussion ensued. Alex Tait's historic suggestion had two powerful backers. G. E. 'Tiger' Devenish, who had played for

South Africa in 1891, seconded his proposal, and N. Platnauer also spoke in support of what Tait, defensively, called an 'opinion'. Platnauer rejected the idea that Colonial-born men played an 'inferior' game and he made a point that would resonate in years to come. Platnauer suggested that in many teams he had seen play, the 'Africander' was often the strongest player. This proposal was now put to a vote and approved. The Transvaal Country team thus became known in the local press as the 'Colonials'. It was a seminal moment in South African rugby.[6]

It is no surprise that the team had an 'Africander' look to it. Japie Louw and the two Pretoria men, Andreas Kriegler and C. Maartens, were picked as forwards. Other locals included William Rowlands, who lived in Roodepoort; Hume, who was educated at SACS near Newlands; C. W. 'Toski' Smith of Kimberley; Frank Maxwell, who farmed on the Natal border; and David Cope, who was educated at Bishops in Cape Town (he would also die with Alex Tait in the Laingsburg train crash two years hence). George Devenish of Kimberley was elected captain by the team on the eve of the game. The selectors however did call on some players from further afield: Ben Andrew of Lancashire and the stylish Alf Larard of Yorkshire. Both went on to represent South Africa.

The reports of this match make interesting reading. The game was played under threatening skies and there had been rain earlier in the day. As a result, most ladies stayed away. The ground was, however, still packed with spectators. Alex Tait had been correct. The visitors outweighed the local team by a full stone per player and while six of the English & Irish combination were over 6 feet tall, just one of the locals matched this height. The 'Colonials', however, had something to prove and played with great energy. It took twenty minutes of grinding forward rushes and tenacious tackling for Osbert Mackie finally to cross the line and, despite the close attentions of both Cope and Devenish, he 'held the treasure' and scored for Tommy Crean's visitors. Byrne missed the conversion.

The second half saw several near misses by the local team. A rush by Kriegler and 'Toski' Smith saw the ball bounce into touch just feet from the try line. Alf Larard played a blinder for the Colonials and twice saved certain tries by brave play. Late in the match the visitors finally sunk their plucky Colonial opponents when Byrne put the ball over the crossbars for a 'beautiful goal'. The final whistle saw the visitors run out winners 7-0. It had, concluded *The Johannesburg Times* correspondent, been a 'hard and fast ... rattling' game. The Colonials had stood their ground. Of the five matches to be played on the Rand by Hammond's men, this would be the most fiercely contested.[7] Even the Test match to be played ten days later would see the visitors win by a wider margin. In years to come this too would become a familiar refrain: touring teams beware the provincial teams on the Highveld.

The following day saw the visitors enjoy a conducted tour around the City and Suburban mine and then spend their evening, for once, without entertainment. They were preparing for their second game against the technically stronger Transvaal team, on the Saturday afternoon. Rowland Hill would have been appalled, but this was a frontier town and the Johannesburg gamblers were placing large wagers on the outcome of the Saturday match. Significantly, the word on the street was that the Transvaal team could win, and 'no odds could be obtained on either side'. Bets were also placed on a draw.

Recriminations Mar the Transvaal Clash

Saturday the 15th saw the weather return to a traditional Highveld winter's day. A light breeze and bright sunshine meant that many ladies were present amongst the 6,000-plus who attended. *The Johannesburg Times* concluded 'a larger concourse to assemble than ever before met on the Rand to witness an exposition of the manliest of manly games'. The Wanderers band entertained this great concourse until the teams appeared to sustained applause.[8]

The match was dominated by the consequences of one event: a severe ankle injury. Playing for Transvaal was Jack Orr, whose reputation preceded him. Bishop Walter Carey recalled decades later that Hammond's team (of which he was a member) heard from the minute they arrived in Cape Town that Orr, 'a regular man-killer, was waiting to put us all in hospital. He did seem very formidable.'[9] Early in the first half, Orr seriously injured his ankle. In 1896, replacements were not allowed. Orr bravely remained on the field, but his presence actually weakened his team, as he was but a passenger and inevitably missed tackles and was easily dealt with when he did receive the ball.

Byrne opened the scoring for the visitors with a long-range penalty. And then, in the midst of great excitement, Kriegler crashed over for a try for Transvaal. Aston missed the conversion, but the scores were even. Then Orr was injured. The Transvaal team fought on and only late in the first half did Crean speed over for a try in the corner. Ben Duff, one of the smallest men on the field, did his utmost to steer Tommy Crean into touch and the Transvaal team (and their supporters) queried the try with the referee, the English international Wardlaw B. Thomson. He went across to the touch judge, W. M. Bisset, himself a South African international, and asked his opinion. Crean, Bisset felt, had indeed grounded the ball before being 'slung into touch'. Thomson awarded the try, to huge dismay.

The Transvaal team tried to 'hide' Orr in the forwards in the second half, but to no avail. Further tries by Bulger and Mackie, one converted by Byrne, saw Crean's team win 16-3. A further disruption to the Transvaal team occurred at half-time when some wealthy local patrons of the game insisted on awarding Alf Larard an engraved solid gold medal (this was the Rand after all!) in recognition of his outstanding and 'unselfish' play for the 'Colonials' in the Wednesday clash. Larard indicated, in his short acceptance speech, that he would 'cherish the medal as one of his dearest possessions'. But it must have interrupted the team talk.

That the Crean try was controversial, coming in the manner it did at a crucial stage of the match, can be judged by the fact that the referee was interviewed by *The Johannesburg Times* after the contest. *The Times* correspondent was at pains to point out that

Mr Thompson was a 'thorough sportsman', but he was asked to explain why the try had been awarded. In years to come, this theme would emerge repeatedly during tours to South Africa in relation to interpretations by referees, but this was the first time it attracted such specific attention. The English & Irish team also made their complaint. They suggested that the pass that put Kriegler away for his try had been forward. Mr Thomson also hit back. He suggested that Alf Larard's play had been 'tricky' and that the local team should not 'grumble'.[10]

W. B. Thomson was indeed an English rugby international, but had been born in 1871 in the wilds of Matabeleland where his father served as a missionary. He had however, been schooled in England and under the rules applying in 1896, could play for both teams. Such was the feeling against him in Johannesburg that he declined to play for South Africa in the Test match at the Wanderers on the following Saturday, even though selected. He never did receive another invitation to play for the country of his birth. He also did not officiate at another match during this tour.

That evening, the team attended a performance at the Empire theatre in high spirits. On Sunday the 16th the team spent the day visiting Doornkop.

The trip began at their hotel and the team and supporters, '60 jolly spirits', travelled in four large 'picnic wagons'. A commissariat wagon set off separately. Along the route they stopped to stretch their legs and take refreshment from local tap houses. As there was no sign of the commissariat wagon when they reached Doornkop at 1.30, the men walked all over the battlefield and had a tour of the sites. Whilst waiting for the picnic wagon to arrive, some of the men had a swim in the river at the bottom of the gorge where Boer forces had been located some months previously. *The Johannesburg Times* correspondent noted that there was a 'snapshot fiend' present who captured some of the team swimming 'as Nature first introduced them to this world'. Finally, at 3 o'clock the wagon arrived with food and beverages and the party could eat and drink.

A VISIT TO DOORNKOP

Southern Africa was to prove a political minefield for the British Empire. In the twentieth century, sport, especially rugby, would be placed centre stage in political battles. As rugby tours expanded and traditions became enshrined, differing trends appeared. Tours to Australia and New Zealand and elsewhere were, on occasion, controversial or fraught, but in relation to the playing of rugby and incidents on and off the field. However, tours to South Africa saw rugby increasingly become part of a much wider political battlefield. This undoubtedly affected the games themselves and placed extra pressure on both local and visiting sides.

Political controversy surrounding rugby in southern Africa was not just a twentieth-century phenomenon. By visiting Doornkop, Hammond's men, either wittingly or unwittingly, made a specific political statement. It was an overtly political act that showed implicit support for a certain viewpoint. To understand the situation, one must examine the background.

In 1795, Britain took control of the Cape from the Dutch East India Company (VOC) that had governed the Cape for the previous century and a half after defeating local forces at the Battle of Muizenberg. The Dutch, or Batavian government, as it had become known, had briefly been put back in control by the Treaty of Amiens in 1803. In 1806 however, Britain, keenly aware of the strategic nature of the Cape ports on an African coastline that offered very few harbours, regained control of the Cape, this time after the Battle of Blaauwberg. Vessels heading to and from India, the 'jewel' in the British Empire, especially needed easy access to these ports. They in turn would exercise control over this region for a further century and a half. Disgruntled Cape farmers, used to lax rule by the weak VOC, were dismayed by the idea of British control, which promised higher taxes, equality for persons of colour, an end to slavery and increasing interference in their way of life. They moved, or 'trekked', further into the interior to escape this control.

This 'Great Trek' began in 1838 and saw the eventual creation of two independent Boer states: the Orange Free State (OFS) and the South African Republic (ZAR), governed by conservative men and women who considered themselves 'Africanders', part of Africa. The two Boer republics had a sometimes fraught relationship with the British colonies (Britain had annexed the area known as Natal in 1846 to prevent Boer expansion, thereby acquiring the port of D'Urban) and also with the Zulu, Pedi, Sotho, Swazi, Venda, Griqua and Basotho kingdoms. Alliances were loose and changed often.

As we have seen in 1877, Britain had unilaterally annexed the ZAR, but after their victory at the Battle of Majuba, the Boers had their full independence restored in 1881. In 1879, Britain, concerned about growing Zulu power, had initiated a war which, after initial setbacks, had seen the comprehensive defeat and subjection of the Zulu nation.

The economic value of this part of Africa, previously an almost exclusively agrarian economy that cost the Crown considerably more than it earned, changed dramatically in 1866. Diamonds were discovered on the land of De Beer, a Boer farmer near Kimberley. A dispute over which nation, (Griqua, Tlaping or Boer), owned the diamondiferous land, was resolved by the simple exercise of power. A commission headed by the Lieutenant-Governor of Natal, Robert Keate, was called to adjudicate. Keate found in favour of the Griquas. The Griquas turned in due course to Britain to help them exercise control over the swarming diggers who rapidly came to exploit the richness of the finds – only for Britain to imprison and subjugate their leader, Nicolaas Waterboer, and his people. De facto control of Kimberley and the northern Cape was now vested in Westminster.

One of the early diggers was Cecil John Rhodes. As his wealth grew, so did his acquisition of political power. This power was enormously enhanced when gold was discovered on the Rand, where he made substantial profitable investments. Gold finds had been a feature of life in the ZAR from the 1870s, but the find on the farm Langlaagte, in what is today the middle of Johannesburg, surpassed all previous gold finds. Tens of thousands flocked to the Rand, as this area became known. Gradually, the realisation grew that the gold-bearing reef under the Rand was almost limitless. Johannesburg was poised to become the centre of southern Africa, and if you believed some, the richest city in the world. It was controlled by an elderly Boer statesman who bore no love for the British Empire, believed the earth was flat and wanted nothing more than to be left alone with his 'volk' to farm and hunt: Stephanus Paul Kruger.

Cecil Rhodes was a product of his time. He believed implicitly in the expansion of the British Empire in Africa. His plan to join Cape Town and Cairo by railway was but one of his endeavours. To this end, he unliterally annexed the lands north of the Limpopo River. In later years, this area would be named Northern and Southern Rhodesia. Control was vested in the British South Africa Company (BSAC), with Rhodes its principal shareholder.

Rhodes, by now Premier of the Cape, decided that by taking advantage of the substantial number of non-Boer diggers, or Uitlanders, located in Johannesburg, he could initiate a takeover of the ZAR. Only very few Uitlanders had become ZAR citizens and could thus vote. Calls for an expanded franchise went unheeded by Kruger's government, who feared that Uitlanders would soon outnumber local inhabitants.

Rhodes' trusted lieutenant to lead this incursion was Leander Starr Jameson. Using BSAC troops based in the Rhodesias, and with the connivance of certain Johannesburg digger leaders, the 'Reform Committee', Jameson and his force entered the ZAR early on the morning of 30 December 1895.

From the start, things went wrong for the men who would come to be known as the Jameson Raiders. Meant to cut telegraph lines to limit news of the incursion to Pretoria, they instead cut fences. Kruger allowed them to travel slowly towards Johannesburg, sending out skirmishers to delay them. General Piet Cronje led them into a trap and thirty Raiders were killed on a farm called Doornkop to the west of Johannesburg. The Raiders were all captured and imprisoned. The British government, aghast at the amateurishness of the coup attempt, quickly distanced themselves from the fiasco. Rhodes had to resign his premiership and subject himself to humiliation at the hands of the press and MPs at Westminster. The Westminster enquiry was a sham and crucial evidence was withheld, thus leaving matters inconclusive.

Boer leaders in Pretoria were also dismayed by events. They realised that once again, they were firmly in the cross hairs of the British Empire. Their unexpected and unwanted wealth had made them a target. A young, brilliant Cambridge-educated Boer lawyer, Jan Christiaan Smuts, authored a cutting analysis of the Raid, or as he labelled it, a 'conspiracy' to attack the 'South African Republic with an armed band in order to assist the Capitalist revolution of Johannesburg in overthrowing the Boer Government'. He concluded the Boers should have shot Jameson's 'robber gang' instead of pardoning them.[11] The historian Cornelius de Kiewiet points to the Raid as a turning point in local history: 'Not now nor for many bitter years to come would Great Britain be at rest in South Africa... the grief caused by the Jameson Raid, and a bitterly tragic war would have to be fought.'[12] The battle lines were being drawn and Hammond's team became part of that narrative on the day they elected to visit the battlefield of Doornkop.

The party returned to the hotel for a late dinner. A concert at the Wanderers Club completed the day's events. The highlight of the evening was the rendition by Madame Emma Miller of 'When twilight comes', which was well received and Matthew Mullineux duly presented her with a huge bouquet of flowers arranged in the shape of a rugby ball as a sign of the TRU's appreciation.[13]

The pace of the tour did not let up. The next day, the 1896 tourists faced and defeated a Johannesburg Town team 18-0. This was the easiest of the five matches they played on the Rand. Most of the local team came from the Pirates Club and they were never able to mount much of a challenge. John Hammond returned to play for the first time since he was seriously injured in the first match of the tour. The return of their captain was welcome news for the squad, as midway through the second half Matthew Mullineaux seriously injured his knee and was carried off the field. It was to be the end of his tour but not his rugby career. He would lead the British Isles team to Australia in 1899.

Indicative of the depth of talent available to Hammond was the fact that apart from four tries by Mullineaux (before his departure on a stretcher), Mackie, Bulger and Bell, the standout moment of the match was a superb piece of rugby by C. O. Robinson of Northumberland. He only participated in eight of the games on the whole tour, yet late in the second half he collected the ball when isolated in his position on the wing and avoiding 'half-a-dozen' of the local team, he made some yards before pivoting and putting over a 'beautiful' drop goal from far out.

A mere two days later the tourists again trooped out onto the, by now, familiar, rock-strewn surface of the Wanderers. This time they faced a Transvaal team for the second time. It was impossible, *The Johannesburg Times* reported, to get anyone to back the local lads with the bookies!

The dispute surrounding the refereeing by Thompson led to an extraordinary decision. James Magee of Dublin, a member of Hammond's squad, was invited by the TRU to referee the game. He accepted and the first person he penalised was his younger brother, Louis, playing half-back for the tourists! Hammond's men had by now got their Highveld boots on and they won easily, the match never rising to any great heights. Tries by Bulger and Meares and three successful kicks by Byrne saw the tourists score 16 points. Thirteen of those points were on the board by half-time.

Late in the second half the Transvaal team finally combined well, quickly moved the ball wide, and 'amidst great enthusiasm' Alex Tait dotted down, with David Cope converting the try. The final score was 16-5.[14]

That night 1,600 people filled the Wanderers Club to attend the splendid annual ball of the TRU. Present was a veritable who's who of the Rand, including many 'randlords' such as the Ecksteen, FitzPatrick, Phillips and Farrar families. Women outnumbered men considerably and so many were present that dancing was almost impossible. A report in *The Johannesburg Times* waxed lyrical about the splendid dresses on show and confirmed that the 'smart set' were in full attendance.

The team assembled early the next morning outside their hotel and travelled to Pretoria. Here they were entertained by Eddie, Tom and George Bourke, keen sportsmen and successful local businessmen with Irish roots. Their first stop was to visit 'Karri' Davis and Aubrey Wools Sampson, languishing in the Pretoria goal. These two Uitlander 'hardliners' had declined to accept President Kruger's generous treatment after their capture at Doornkop and refused to accede to his demands. Kruger finally released them on Queen Victoria's Diamond Jubilee in 1897. Their stand was viewed as the 'highest manifestation of Uitlander solidarity'[15] and they were heroes in Johannesburg.

Extraordinarily, they then met President Kruger in the Volksraad. Here was the leader of a country that had been invaded and annexed by the rugby players' fellow countrymen agreeing to the meeting. Louis Cohen, who lived in the ZAR for many years, wrote several books on his experiences. To understand Kruger's attitude to foreigners, Cohen records attending a meeting in Krugersdorp where the President addressed those present thus: 'Kruger commenced his oration by harshly bellowing: "Burghers, friends, thieves, murderers, newcomers and others".' Significantly, the newcomers, or Uitlanders, were mentioned far down the list. [16] Rugby had indeed succeeded in breaking down barriers!

Second Test

The TRU was criticised in the press for their selection of the South African team for the Test on 22 August 1896 at the Wanderers Ground, Johannesburg. No fewer than five selected players could not travel the long distance to the Rand to play and had to be replaced. At the last moment Frank Maxwell also had to withdraw and was replaced by Theo Samuels of Griqualand West. The team that ran out in front of 5,000 on a cold, overcast and windy day was thus heavy with Transvaal players and a sprinkling of four Griqualand West representatives. Just two players were from elsewhere: J. J. Wessels of WP, and A. M. Beswick from Queenstown. The team had never played together and only gathered to practise late on the day before the Test.

On the other hand, Hammond's team showed just three changes from the first Test, Hammond himself returning to the fray at the expense of Mullins. Mullineaux, forced out by injury, was replaced by a Cambridge man, Sydney Bell, at half-back, and James Magee took over the full back position from Cecil Boyd.

Most of the first half was played in the centre of the field with neither side gaining much advantage. Then late in the first half, Hammond's men got the luck of the bounce. George Devenish kicked for touch from the base of the scrum. Osbert Mackie, the tall centre, charged the kick down and the ball bounced awkwardly for all the players, except for the forward Alexander Todd of Blackheath, who collected it well and crashed over for a try that was converted by Byrne. The half-time score was 5-0 to Hammond's men.

The second half produced many more points and saw the ball moving back and forwards across the field. Shortly after the restart, the visitors' solid forward pressure saw them 'invading the African line' and as a result Tommy Crean was able to dot down for a try. Byrne converted with a splendid kick. The gap between the teams widened further when a few minutes later 'Baby' Hancock secured line-out possession and was bundled over the nearby African try line by his forwards; 13-0 to the visitors.

It was then that the South African team began to run the ball at the tourists. Bill Taberer of Griquas made a fine break and was only bundled out on the English 25 by Mackie. In the resulting line-out Paul Scott of Diggers stole the throw-in and Devenish flipped the ball to Ashton, who, drawing his man, put Theo Samuels over for the first ever try by a South African in a Test. This historic event was marked with 'great enthusiasm' by the crowd.

More was to follow. A few minutes later, after a sweeping South African movement upfield, Ashton again neatly drew his man, and again Theo Samuels, the speedy Griqua wing, crossed the whitewash and his fellow Bishops friend Davey Cope converted. The score was now 13-8. The 'excitement of the spectators was great'. Could the Africans indeed win a game on the Highveld?

The game was now being played at breakneck pace. The speedy Bulger got away and was only forced out on the African line. In return Alf Larard, playing a blinder, broke free only to be run down short of the English & Irish line. How many times in years and decades to come would spectators of matches between the descendants of these two teams watch the last ten minutes of a game on their feet, breathlessly following every aspect of the play? And as often happens, one man stepped up and coolly concluded matters. In this case, it was Osbert Mackie of Cambridge. After Hammond's forwards held on to possession, they passed the ball down the line and Mackie neatly side-stepped Hilton Forbes and Ferdie Aston, to put over a beautiful drop. When time was called, the visitors had won a pulsating match 17-8.

That evening, the final dinner on the Rand was held at the team's hotel. Toasts were drunk and Hammond made a short speech indicating the team's deep appreciation for the nearly two weeks they had spent on the Rand. The team was then escorted to the station where a huge crowd had assembled. As the team boarded, a spontaneous 'God Save the Queen' was rendered by the entire crowd. As the train pulled out of the station at 11.15 p.m. bound for Kimberley, cheers were given by those remaining behind. The team, leaning out of the carriages, responded with cheers for Johannesburg.[17]

Back to Kimberley and the Gravel Field

Contrasting the furious pace of the social and rugby aspects of the tour, the train steamed slowly southwards. It took until Monday midday to reach Bloemfontein, the capital of the Orange Free State. There, members of the local Irish community met the train and hosted a lunch for the team. Kimberley was reached late on Monday.

On Wednesday afternoon the tourists faced and defeated a Cape Colony team. Observers noted that even though one of the Colonial backs had to leave the field in the first half, Hammond's men were 'scarcely up to their best form' and struggled. It was only late in the second half that Byrne put over a 'wonderful' kick from a mark. And then, in the final minutes, the correspondent noted a move that any rugby team of whatever age would welcome and strive to achieve. It was reported that the 'leather travelled with clock-like precision' down the line, allowing Mackie to dive over in the corner. The final score was thus 7-0 to the tourists. Two of the Cape backs played outstandingly under the circumstances. Theo Samuels showed his class, as did his fellow wing, Percy Twentyman-Jones. Both would be selected for the South African team to face Hammond's men that Saturday in the third Test. That night a ball was held for the visiting team in the Drill Hall.

For the third Test in a row, Ferdie Aston was asked to captain the local team, which this time carried seven Griqualand West players and ten new faces in all. Hammond's team showed just two changes. Hammond himself did not play this Test and was replaced by R. C. Mullins, while Arthur Meares replaced the injured Magee at full back.

Third Test

Such was the English & Irish dominance of local teams that barely 2,000 individuals were present to watch this match on 29 August 1896 at the Ecelectic Ground, Kimberley. On a bright sunny day, with a light breeze behind him, Tommy Crean kicked off, the ball bouncing all the way to the try line! The early part of the contest saw both sides putting in long kicks to try and gain advantage and most of the play took place in the middle of the field. Robert

Johnston of Ireland was stopped just short of the African line after one good break and Theo Samuels was called upon to field many long, raking kicks from Magee and Bell, the visitors' half-backs. The only score of the half came when Cotty, the Griqualand West scrum half, caught a relieving kick on the English 25, broke though the visitors' backline and put Twentyman-Jones away for him to score behind the posts. Inexplicably, Twentyman-Jones missed the conversion. At half-time the South Africans led 3-0.

Tommy Crean, captaining the team in Hammond's absence, spoke sternly to his men during the break and the second half saw the visitors run the ball 'at every opportunity'. This expansive game had its perils and Bertie Powell, a local man playing his first Test, intercepted a wayward pass and put in a 'capital' run, only being apprehended just short of the try line. The 'excitement of the spectators was intense' since the local team seemed to be getting the better of the mighty visitors. Larry Bulger had other ideas however, and gaining possession he skipped the other backline players in a clever move that put Osbert Mackie clear and allowing him to dot the ball down. Byrne converted. The visitors now led 5-3.

In the dying moments Byrne put the game to bed for the visitors by putting over a 'beautiful' kick. The final score was 9-3, but it had been a close-run thing. The Africans had, for long periods, more than held their own. Being largely forced to select their teams from the local unions rather than the whole country put them at a disadvantage, especially when playing what was by now a well-drilled unit.

That night a banquet was held and then the team entrained for the Cape. The last two matches were to be played on the soft and green turf of Newlands.[18]

Back to Cape Town and the Fourth Test

Hammond's team took the slow train back to Cape Town. There they faced and destroyed Western Province on Thursday 3 September. They had already faced this team in the third game of the tour and on that occasion, after a champagne-fuelled lunch, the teams had played out a 0-0 draw. Not this time. Possibly the joy of once again seeing a lush green field or whether in retribution for the previous contest, the English & Irish combination swept aside their hosts, scoring eight tries in the process. The victory margin was the largest of the whole tour: 32-0.

Now just the last Test remained to be played. The record achieved by Maclagan's men five years previously, of not losing a game for the duration of the tour, was in sight.

The Test was played on 5 September. It was a clear day with a stiff south-easter blowing, which, according to *The Cape Argus*, was 'strong enough to militate against accurate place kicking'. September in the Cape does not tend to be warm, which, together with the wind, accounts for why only 3,000 spectators were present – a much smaller crowd than the 7,500 who had been present in Port Elizabeth, the best attended of the four Tests.

Barry 'Fairy' Heatlie of Western Province was appointed the South African team captain for the last Test. He was a product of a local school, Bishops. After leaving school he had founded the Old Diocesan Union RFC. He and his wife, Jessie, had designed the rugby jersey for the club. Since the dominant colour in the ODURFC tie was bottle green, that was chosen as the jersey's colour. Heatlie, as captain, decreed that would be the jersey the South African team would wear at Newlands.

The referee was Alf Richards, who had played for South Africa in the 1891 series, and he was to have a major influence on the game. As scrums developed, it became apparent that Richards was not going to allow the tourists to swing or 'screw' the scrum and then pounce on the ball – he blew them up for being off-side. *The Cape Argus* noted that Richards used 'plenty of whistle during the game – a little too much considering the teams playing'.

The teams were evenly matched and hard rugby was played. 'Every man played up grandly,' it was felt, but several players were picked out for excellent play including Biddy Anderson and Heatlie who, together with Van Broekhuizen and Beswick, helped the local pack of forwards more than stand up to the tourists. The British 'flyers', Magee of Ireland and Mackie of Cambridge University, the latter having scored ten tries on the tour, were kept well in check with Magee especially 'being regularly run to a stand-still' whenever he got the ball. Twentyman-Jones and Hepburn did exceptional defensive work for the Colonials.[19]

The crucial break came late in the first half. Crean, playing at number eight, took the ball at the back of the line-out. The ball was passed to Magee, Bell and Byrne in the centre, but Byrne was thunderously tackled by Ferdie Aston of Transvaal. Whilst still on his back, the ball was grabbed from his arms by Biddy Anderson who darted downfield and flipped a pass to his fly-half Alf Larard, up in close support, who went over under the posts. Tom Hepburn converted the try. There were some on Crean's team who felt Byrne should have been given time to place the ball after the tackle, but Richards allowed the try to stand.

The significance of this score became more apparent as the second half progressed. The South African scrum did not concede any ground as had happened in the earlier Tests and *The Cape Argus* concluded that the local lads packed finely and 'almost invariably got the ball'. The clock wound down and eventually Richards used his whistle for the last time and sounded 'no side'. South Africa was victorious.

When the teams left the field there was 'a scene of the wildest enthusiasm, South Africa winning by 5 points to nil'. The celebrations did not end there. When the players emerged from the humble wood and iron changing rooms to catch the train home, ecstatic supporters 'carried Heatlie, Twentyman-Jones, Larard and Theo Samuels ... around Newlands in triumph'.[20] It was the first Test match South Africa had won.

Twentyman-Jones, writing nearly forty years later, recalled the result as being 'hailed with delight throughout the country', and that it 'indicated that the pupil had learnt his lesson so well that he was able to compete on terms of equality with his one-time teacher'.[21]

That the defeat rankled with the visitors was undoubtedly true. Osbert Mackie gave two interviews upon his return to England. In the *Sheffield Daily Telegraph*, he indicated that the team had been 'swindled out of it' and it was 'disgraceful'.[22] The *Yorkshire Evening Post* reported him using more diplomatic language. The team, he said, 'had a distinct grievance against the referee' in the last match for 'calling them off-side every time they spun the scrum'. In this interview he conceded that South African teams were 'not to be despised' and their hosts had been 'most hospitable and very sportsmanlike'.[23] Even forty years later, Walter Carey bitterly echoed those sentiments! The referee's actions in stopping them turning the scrum was, he recalled, 'very unsatisfactory' as it was a 'keynote' of our attack and 'we thought he was wrong'.[24]

But South Africa had won, and it was the forwards who had laid the foundation for the victory. 'Heatlie inspired the South African pack to come back at them with the sort of fire and determination which was a foretaste of the type of Springbok forward play which opponents were to become all too aware of in future years.'[25]

Heatlie's role was to grow and he played more important games for South Africa in years to come. It was his belief that the wearing of the green ODRFU jerseys had been a good omen for the team in 1896. When the South African team won the 1903 Test at Newlands, again under Heatlie and again wearing the same green jerseys, his forceful personality saw to it that henceforward that jersey would be worn by the South African side. Paul Roos' side added the collar and more importantly, the Springbok to the breast.

It was on that bright winter's day in 1896, in the lee of Table Mountain, that South African rugby came of age.

After the Game

That evening an 'Irish Banquet' was held for the visiting team in the Masonic Hall in Cape Town. All the leading figures of Cape society were there. Sir James Sivewright proposed a toast to 'our welcome guests'. He indicated that the visit would be 'enshrined' in local memories and the result had indicated that the local team had 'learnt their lesson well'.

John Hammond thanked the assembled guests for their hospitality and also thanked the Irish members of his team for their participation. Tommy Crean rose thereafter and while admitting that on occasion Irishmen could be 'agin' the government of the day, he personally would in future go 'hand in hand with England as long as he lived (cheers)'. This final function of the tour went on very late into the night.[26]

The next rugby tour to southern Africa would not happen for seven years. In the intervening years, the South African War (1899–1902) was fought. Two members of the 1896 team who played that day at Newlands were awarded Victoria Crosses during the conflict. Both were Irishmen: Major Robert Johnston and Captain (Dr) Tommy Crean, who, true to his word, did not fight with the Boer forces as so many of his countrymen did, but fought for Britain. Crean had stayed on in the Transvaal after the tour and when war broke out, he joined a Cape regiment, the Imperial Light Horse. During an engagement with Boer forces at Tygerkloof on 18 December 1901, he was shot as he tended the wounded but continued with his task. When he was wounded a second time, he was reputed to have called out 'By Christ, I'm kilt entoirely.'[27] He survived.

Newlands on 5 September was a battlefield of a different kind, and for the first time, a colonial team had done the impossible and defeated Goliath. The visitors from England and Ireland had won the series. No visiting team would win a series in South Africa for more than six decades after this tour.

1896 TOURING PARTY
Manager – Roger Walker

Backs
Sydney Bell (England)*
Cecil Boyd (Ireland)*
Larry Bulger (Ireland)*
Fred Byrne (England)*
Osbert Mackie (England)*
James Magee (Ireland)*
Louis Magee (Ireland)*
Matthew Mullineaux (England)*
C. O. Robinson (England)

Forwards
John Hammond (Capt.) (England)*
Thomas Crean (Vice-Capt.) (Ireland)*
Walter Carey (England)*

Andrew Clinch (Ireland)*
Froude Hancock (England)*
Robert Johnston (Ireland)*
G. W. Lee (England)#
Arthur Meares (Ireland)*
William Mortimer (England)*
R. C. Mullins (England)*
Jim Sealy (Ireland)*
Alexander Todd (England)*

Replacement
* Played in at least one Test

Johnny Hammond (1860–1907)

John Hammond gained a Cambridge rugby 'blue' in 1881. He was described as an 'honest, hard-working forward' who also did his part defending and assisting backline players as he was quick around the field. He played for the South in four games against the North but was never selected for England. Possibly he was viewed as being too light for international play on the heavy fields of the day. The harder fields in Africa suited him well.

After Cambridge he became a barrister and had rooms at Old Square, Lincoln's Inn. He played rugby at Blackheath for many years before moving to Richmond. At the time of his death, following complications after an operation, he was serving on the committee of the RU.

Shy and retiring by nature, he was a popular player and leader. In the 1891 tour of southern Africa he played in every match, including the unofficial game tacked on to the end of the tour. During the 1896 tour, which he captained, he was injured early on and thus only played in seven matches, including two Tests. In the 1903 tour he acted as manager and when the 1906 Springboks arrived in Great Britain, it was Hammond who was on hand to meet them and guide them through their tour.

Hammond's knowledge of southern African conditions was unrivalled and when he died it was reported that he would be missed by rugby followers in Africa as much as in London.

3

THE 1903 TOUR:
MORRISON'S MEN STRUGGLE

Barely more than a year after the cessation of the brutal South African War of 1899–1902, it was decided to send a rugby team from the British Isles to tour all four territories that had been involved. The scars from this conflict were still very raw and the tour must be seen in the light of the British post-war policy, masterminded by Sir Alfred Milner, High Commissioner for South Africa.

To redress the enormous damage that had been done to all four territories, Milner implemented reconstruction at a furious pace. It was in the Orange Free State (now called the Orange River Colony) and Zuid-Afrikaansche Republiek (now called the Transvaal Colony), which had been forced to capitulate to the huge forces the British Empire had been able to bring to bear upon them, that most damage had been inflicted. Fundamental to Milner's policy was his intention to anglicise these two, previously Boer, states. The tour would include matches in both capital cities of these two new colonies.

The 1903 British team, managed by John Hammond and captained by Mark Morrison, was more representative of the British Isles than had been the case in 1891 and 1896. The 1903 touring party contained eight players from England, seven Scots (including Morrison), five Irishmen and one Welshman. The lone

Welshman made up for the lack of Welsh numbers by being one of only two players to play in every game.

The team might have been representative of the Home Unions, but the selection did not reflect recent results between the four teams. Between 1897 and 1902, England had only been able to win five out of their twenty-one matches, with three drawn. Wales on the other hand, had been victorious in thirteen of the eighteen they had played.

When the SS *Briton* steamed into Table Bay early on the morning of Tuesday 7 July, the team were all on deck to witness their arrival at the foot of the 'magnificent' Table Mountain. In a similar fashion to the previous two tours, the hectic whirl started immediately. They were met on the docks by a great congregation, who ferried them to their hotel. They then lunched with the deputy mayor and many members of the Cape Legislative Assembly. In the afternoon they practised on Newlands field and in the evening attended a performance of *My Lady Molly* at the opera house. On the following day, they again practised on Newlands and Alfred Tedford, the Irish forward, felt they were ready for the fray.

A Poor Start

On Thursday 9 July, just two days after landing, the team took the 3.35 p.m. train from Cape Town station to Newlands for the first game against Western Province Country. Prior to the kick-off at 4.15 p.m., Hammond and Morrison were introduced to the Governor-General, Sir Walter Hely-Hutchinson. The team was warmly welcomed onto the field by the spectators.

Despite it being mid-winter in Cape Town, the weather for this and the subsequent two matches at Newlands was bright and fair. This resulted in full houses, including leading politicians Louis Botha, Sir Pieter Faure and Jan Hofmeyr. Tedford, recalling these matches at Newlands thirty years later, commented: 'Every tree around the ground bore its human fruit.'[1] He was also impressed at overhearing two Malay spectators provide complete statistics of his and another visiting player's careers. He was impressed at 'how closely they kept in touch with the game' from such a distance.

Team members also noted the large number of Malay spectators occupying the southern side of Newlands.

Despite the warnings from the experienced John Hammond, the tourists found the Newlands field much harder than anticipated, the ball blown up too 'tightly' for their liking, the pace of the game very fast and the crowds overwhelmingly on the side of the locals. To their dismay, they also found the players in this corner of South Africa showed 'unexpected form in their running and fine stopping power'. They were not to know that the rugby gods had seen fit to provide Western Province with four outstanding backs. Joe Barry, Paddy Carolin, J. D. 'Japie' Krige and Bob Loubser would grace the backline of this province and South Africa for years to come.

The first points scored on this tour were by Japie Krige for the hosts. It was the result of good combining by the two fastest men on the field:

> Krige, picking up in the loose, made a splendid opening, and at the right moment passed to Loubser, who tore down the right wing, being grassed a yard from the line, but, the ball rolling loose, Krige, who had followed up well, picked it up and ran around behind the posts scoring the first try for the Country men amidst wild enthusiasm.[2]

The first three matches, played over the space of just five days at Newlands, were disastrous for the tourists; all were lost. First against W. P. Country (7-13), then W. P. Town (3-12) and, finally, W. P. (4-8). Seventeen days on the SS *Briton,* with limited chance of exercise and generous meals, had left the team in poor shape. Their hosts, the WPRU, also made sure that the good catering continued! After the Thursday match a dinner dance was held at Rondebosch that saw the team get back to Cape Town station via a train specially laid on by the Union, at 3 am. After the Saturday match a banquet was held at the Mount Nelson Hotel. On Sunday, the team travelled to Groote Schuur and were entertained to a 'sumptuous lunch' by Leander Starr Jameson's secretary, Gordon le Sueur. Dr Jameson had moved into the house upon the passing of C. J. Rhodes, but was unable to be present on the Sunday. After the lunch, a tour of the park-like grounds, including the zoo, was led by Le Sueur.

Newspaper reports of the three matches are interesting. Having got used to Maclagan and Hammond's teams, the reports keep stressing that the team was bound to improve or 'find their feet', but there was increasingly a realisation that maybe that would not occur. Tedford records that during discussions with members of the touring squad after the initial matches, 'We came to the conclusion that we were rather a poor side.'[3]

On the side of the tourists, Reg Skrimshire, the lone Welsh representative, was the outstanding back on display, playing at centre. His name appears regularly in the accounts of matches and he put in good runs, defended well, and kicked a penalty and drop goal. *The Sportsman's* reporter indicated that he showed 'great form' and that the forwards played with considerable fire. The remaining backline players, the reporter decided, did not play 'brilliantly', and needed to improve.

After this sobering introduction to South Africa, the team enjoyed a gala dinner at their hotel, accompanied by many toasts, before entraining for Port Elizabeth.

The Eastern Cape Allows Some Momentum
This first train journey was a lengthy one, as the route was via the junction of De Aar in the freezing Karoo. On the first night the team were 'disconcerted', according to Tedford, to find there were not enough blankets to go around. Lots were drawn to see who would sleep in their greatcoats! The five matches in the Eastern Cape played between 18 and 27 July were all won by the tourists. Four were easy victories, one a narrow escape.

Upon reaching Port Elizabeth the team stayed, 'snugly', at the Grand Hotel. First Port Elizabeth and then the Eastern Cape team were easily beaten. The field was pronounced a good one, bar the fact that a concrete cricket pitch was present in the middle! Skrimshire scored in both games and five tries in total were run in. Local pundits still felt, however, that there was no 'dash' in the visitors' backline.

Festivities continued apace. A ball, a sea fishing trip and, after the Sunday picnic was called off due to the weather and the food donated to a local charity, the team rowed instead on the river at Redhouse. A shorter train journey followed to Grahamstown, where Skrimshire scored two tries and the team eight in total. Then it was on to King William's Town by cart, where Skrimshire scored four tries and the team nine in total. The latter game was described by the local newspaper as a 'splendid display' by the tourists.

The last game in the area, on a field close to the sea in East London, was played in strong wind and occasional driving rain. Skrimshire again came to the rescue, putting over a drop in the last minute to see his side home 7-5, after an earlier try by Ian Davidson of Ireland. After the game, Mark Morrison called the East London players 'tough beggars'.

Once again, the team boarded the train, leaving behind the cool coastal region and heading for dry, dusty Kimberley. John Hammond would have explained to his team what awaited them at this stop. Since his last visit, the town had, famously, been besieged by Boer forces for 124 days, and there was still much evidence of bombardment damage to be seen. Additionally, the summer of 1902–03 had proved to be a very dry one across southern Africa and so the Kimberley Athletic Club field was drier and harder than even he had expected. It was not to prove a happy stop for the 1903 tourists.

Griqualand West Leaves the Team Very 'Dilapidated'

Morrison's team faced Griqualand West, Currie Cup holders, on Saturday afternoon, 1 August, and again two days later. Both games kicked off at 4 p.m. to avoid the extremely hot conditions that prevailed. A crowd of over 5,000 was present for the first game to be played on a field that made no pretence to be grassed. It was simply rolled gravel and thus required an 'entirely different game to that which we are accustomed in the old country' according to the reporter from *The Sportsman*.[4]

The score at half-time was 0-0, despite the match being played at a quick tempo, mainly between the forwards. Shortly after half-time, G. F. Scott for Griqualand West stole the line-out ball and handed it to his half-back, Fred 'Uncle' Dobbin, who passed to W. Cotty in the centre. Cotty broke through the visitors' backline and passed to Syd de Melker, who scored in the corner 'amidst tremendous cheering'. Dobbin failed to convert.

A few moments later, Gilbert Collett of Ireland spilled the ball and Jackie Powell snapped it up and sped down the touchline before passing to 'Klondyke' Raaff, who went over for Griquas' second try. This time P. Rowe, the local full back, made a 'poor' attempt at the conversion, which failed. Griqualand West led 6-0.

That score became 11-0 when, on the stroke of full-time, J. Gartrell and M. Fitzpatrick attacked together, with the former scoring. Arthur Williams converted. Once again Morrison, David Bedell-Sivright and other forwards had been 'magnificent' but had been let down by their backs.

That evening a 'smoker' was held under the auspices of the mayor of Kimberley and on the Sunday, Morrison's men attended mine dancing in the De Beers compound and inspected 'Long Cecil' and other artillery pieces that had defended the city during the war. On Monday, the squad attended a hunt with the Seddon Coursing Club. Numerous springbok were sighted, but few were brought down. Those playing in the match on the Tuesday afternoon could ride horses, those not playing had to walk in pursuit of their prey in extremely hot conditions.

Mark Morrison had contracted a 'chill' and so he sat out the second match in Kimberley and Reg Skrimshire took over the captaincy. The early part of the match was dominated by the tourists until Skrimshire mis-kicked a ball and Cotty collected it 'smartly', passing to Jackie Powell who 'romped' over under the poles. Dobbin converted. A sure sign of the pressure being exerted by Skrimshire's men was the fact that several kicks at goal were tried by the local team to no effect. The half-time score remained 5-0.

The second half saw continued pressure from the visitors. Finally, Jimmy Gillespie of Scotland executed a neat cross kick that was well collected by Collett, who scored in the corner. Frank Stout of England could not convert. A few minutes later the backs finally came good and after the ball was passed across the width of the field at speed, Collett again scored in the corner. Stout again missed the conversion. Skrimshire's men now led 6-5.

The visitors continued exerting pressure and 'rush' after 'rush' was thwarted on the locals' line. William Cave and Tom Gibson, both of Cambridge University, were prominent in the forwards. Against the run of play, the Griqualand West side broke out and got into their opponent's half, where a penalty for 'feet up' was given and Arthur Williams succeeded with a penalty from a 'rather difficult angle'. Despite 'desperate attempts' from Skrimshire's men, that is how the match ended, with a second victory to the local team, 8-6. The 1903 tourists were unlucky not to win this encounter. Play by their backline was much improved, but the bounce and referee's whistle did not assist them.

That night a ball for 400 was held, which carried on into the early hours of the morning. On Wednesday afternoon, the tourists boarded the train for Johannesburg, arriving there on Friday morning with the team feeling, according to *The Sportsman* reporter accompanying them, 'very dilapidated'.⁵ There was no let-up: they went straight to a garden party in Barnato Park.

On the Reef and Down to the Coast – Briefly

Just twenty-four hours after their arrival in Johannesburg, Morrison's men trooped out onto the Wanderers pitch to face the Transvaal team, one full of talent. About half of the South African side the tourists would face in due course were in its ranks. So, it is no surprise that despite holding the local team in the first half, the tourists lost the match 12-3. They only let the ball go down the backline twice during the whole match. *The Sportsman's* correspondent noted that, instead of playing this 'Scotch game', they should have played like England did! That evening they watched the South African heavyweight championship fight between Mike Williams and Harry Duggan at Plunkett's Pavilion. Williams won in the eighth round, but both pugilists showed evidence of 'severe punishment'. Morrison's men could relate to that.[6] On the Sunday, the team were taken by motor car to Bedford, the farm of the randlord Sir George Farrar. They spent the day relaxing and enjoying a picnic lunch in quiet surrounds outside Johannesburg.

Three days later, on Tuesday 11 August, the team travelled northwards and beat a team representing Pretoria 15-3. This match was refereed by Ben Duff, himself a former international player for South Africa. In this match, Frank Stout excelled, scoring a try, a penalty, and conversion. Watching the match was Viscount Milner's new appointee as the Lieutenant-Governor of the Transvaal, Sir Arthur Lawley, later 6th Baron Wenlock.

Early the next morning the team entrained at Pretoria station for Natal. On Thursday afternoon, their train arrived in Pietermaritzburg. They were conveyed straight to the Imperial Hotel and then on again to the rugby ground where, in the late afternoon, they met and defeated the local town team 15-0, scoring five tries. In the process Frank Stout missed all five conversions, including one for his own try from right in front of the posts. Once again, the contest took place in great heat and on a 'dreadfully hard' surface. There had been no rain in the city for over six months.

As Pietermaritzburg was the capital of the colony, the match was preceded by Morrison and his team being introduced to the Governor, Sir Henry McCullam by the president of the Natal Rugby Union, Sir T. K. Murray. Also present were the Chief Justice of Natal, the mayor and mayoress of Pietermaritzburg and Sir A. Hime. The crowd included ladies in 'full finery', many waving Union flags.

The following day, the team drove a short distance from the city to Swartkop where they witnessed 200 Zulu warriors perform a 'war dance' that left them extremely impressed. After its conclusion, the team met the warriors, drank beer with them and swapped tour memorabilia for beadwork. On the return journey one of the cars conveying the team was involved in a bad crash, but luckily no one was injured.

That afternoon, a short train trip saw them arrive in Durban, to be greeted by the local mayor and many 'notable' sportsmen. The match against a Durban team, played on Saturday 15 August at Albert Park in intense heat and humidity, formed part of a 'double header', as a soccer match was played on an adjoining field. This led to a great crowd of over 6,000 watching the game, won easily by Morrison's men, 22-0, the widest margin of any game they played. Confirming the residents' love of all sports, the rugby field again had a concrete cricket pitch bang in the middle. During 'lemons', two pipers played several laments. Morrison and his fellow Scots must have felt at home.

That night at a banquet the mayor of Durban pointed out that such tours 'brought various parts of the Empire into closer contact'. At the same time, he admitted that Durban was 'Association' land (soccer) and that the game of rugby had been a 'revelation' to him. He invited the team to return and promised a more even contest. Thereafter the pipers were again brought in to entertain the guests. They were welcomed 'enthusiastically and uproariously' by the Scottish members of the team!

On the Sunday, the team were driven around the city, taking in the view of the bay from the Berea. They had tea with the mayoress before spending the afternoon at the Point Yacht Club where the commodore, Frank Chiazzarri, put his steam launch at their disposal. The team was sad to depart by train for Johannesburg on Monday morning.[7]

Back to the Reef

In years to come, the South African rugby hierarchy would ruthlessly exploit the differences between the coast and the Highveld, sending visiting teams back and forth between the two extremes (and toss in games contrasting the desert and verdant areas too). Teams would accordingly not be able to acclimatise. It was intended to give the Springboks a vital edge, especially towards the end of a game, when exhaustion began and the thin air on the Reef made itself felt. It is unlikely that this was the intention in 1903, but the endless train travel in itself must have been tedious for Morrison's team.

If that was the case, it did not show. On Wednesday 19 August, they defeated a Witwatersrand side 12-0 at the Wanderers. One of the smallest crowds of the whole tour watched the game as the sky was heavily overcast and the 'wind blew cold and raised an intolerable dust'. The Wanderers field had recently been dug up and carefully prepared and was thus in much better condition, and softer, than it had been previously, which might have encouraged the tourists. *The Sportsman*'s correspondent noted a change: they had played well. He used words and phrases like 'dash', 'outplayed', 'quicker' and 'excelled in the loose'. Jim Gillespie had taken over the kicking duties from Frank Stout and did well, but more importantly, there was some aggression in the team and the backs were looking more confident. There was hope.

That night they were invited to His Majesty's Theatre to watch *The Messenger Boy* and on the Thursday night the squad were the guests of honour at a ball held in the Wanderers Hall, together with 500 invited guests. Once again, dancing went on until the early hours.

On Saturday 22 August, Transvaal brought them down to earth. They lost 4-14. Only Skrimshire troubled the scoreboard with a drop, while for Transvaal, Jimmy Sinclair crossed the line twice (both converted by A. Molloy) and Charlie Jones kicked a penalty. Jack Orr, who John Hammond had briefly met in 1896, acted as referee.[8] The team now had four days to rest before facing the combined might of South Africa on the 'new', softer, Wanderers Ground.

First Test

Today, playing rugby on your home ground is seen as a huge advantage. In 1891 the visitors from England seemed to be the crowd favourites. By 1903 in South Africa, despite the political divisions that applied, the crowds watching were solidly behind the local teams, who also knew the local conditions. However, there was one great disadvantage that applied to the local Test team. Players were largely drawn from the local team hosting the match. They were expected to provide the backbone of the national team. A few other players were invited from further afield to close the gaps if the local team showed weakness in a particular position. This was not calculated to produce the strongest possible team.

Accounts of the build-up to the match read like modern reports. Spectators streamed into Wanderers on 26 August 1903 from across the whole Transvaal, from Potchefstroom in the west, Pretoria in the north, Carolina in the east and the Orange River Colony in the south. Some even travelled up from East London and Durban.

For the Wanderers Test, it was no surprise that Transvaal provided seven of the South African team. Their captain, Dr Alexander Frew, who had played for Diggers and Transvaal locally, had already played three times for Scotland. It was to be his only match for his adopted country. Dr Frew, however, selected shrewdly. He chose most of the backs from the Western Province, the forwards from Transvaal and put the Griqualand West half-back pairing of Powell and Dobbin together.

Mark Morrison and John Hammond had an easier task. The forwards were led by Morrison, Tedford, Stout, and William Cave, who had consistently played together. The half-backs were Gillespie and P. S. Hancock of Richmond and England, who would be playing together for the eighth time on the tour. The backline contained Skrimshire, Collett, Davidson and E. M. Harrison, who by now had played together more than a dozen times. Louis Greig of Cambridge, who had played well against Transvaal, was also selected.

The referee was W. P. Donaldson. He was an international player and had captained Scotland. Dr Frew was thus the odd man out when the three met for the toss. He was the only man present who had played for, but not captained, Scotland! Frew won the toss and elected to play with the breeze (and sun) at his back in the first half. Kick-off was a rather late 4.30 pm.

All accounts of this Test, except one, tell the same story. Dr Frew's South African team began slowly, and the Home Unions' side made most of the attacks that were repulsed. Against the run of play, Barry 'Fairy' Heatlie unleashed a kick of great length that drove the English back into their own half. Frew then broke away with the ball and it was passed via Powell to Japie Krige, who, true to form, sped down the middle of the field, evading tackles. He then put in a chip kick that the visitors fumbled. 'Uncle' Dobbin fell on the ball over the line for the first try. Heatlie converted. The local side led 5-0.

Gillespie and Hancock now combined to carry the ball into the South African half, from where Gillespie put in a good long kick that Joe Barry collected on his try line. The local team weathered this storm by scrumming the ball out of the danger zone and Dobbin cleared the ball further downfield. Alexander Frew, following up well, fly kicked it further downfield and won the race to touch down behind the visitors' line. Heatlie converted the second try from an acute angle and after just fifteen minutes, the South Africans led 10-0.

The Sportsman's correspondent noted that these reverses 'put the Englishmen on their mettle' and 'from now on they played a magnificent game'. The half-backs, Gillespie and Hancock, were using the boot highly effectively and with Skrimshire backing them up, most of the play took place in the local team's half. Just before half-time Skrimshire produced a moment of individual brilliance. He took possession and then 'doubled back' according to *The Sportsman*. Barry Heatlie, thirty years later, recounts that Skrimshire started off on the halfway line where he 'feinted to drop at goal ... suddenly he elected to run and burst magnificently through our ranks to score'.[9] Gillespie converted, and at 'lemons' it was 10-5 to South Africa.

The one account that contradicts all the others is by none other than Barry Heatlie – who played in the game! He incorrectly records that Great Britain dominated the first half and that South Africa had to play catch-up in the second.[10]

The second half saw the local team having to defend from the kick-off. Soon Morrison's men levelled the scores, thanks to another piece of individual brilliance. Joseph Wallace of Ireland charged down a clearance kick by Charlie Jones and, collecting the bouncing ball, flicked it to Robertson Smyth who put William Cave over for a try which Gillespie converted: 10-10.

The account of the match in *The Sportsman* makes exciting reading. As it neared its end, both sides had opportunities to score, both used long, raking kicks to win ground and drive their opponents back to their try lines. The scrumming was hard and relentless. When Mr Donaldson called time on the contest, a 10-10 draw seemed like a fair reflection of events.[11]

The forwards had played each other to a standstill. It was in the backs that the South Africans had let themselves down. Whereas Morrison's backs had been poor in the preceding matches, during the Test they had risen to the task magnificently. Clever kicking had won them territory, and they had used their possession well. South Africa's three quick backs, Krige, Barry and Van Reenen, had hardly seen the ball at all.

That night there was a banquet in the Masonic Hall with a 'brief' toast list, according to *The Sportsman*. After the toast to The King, only the Chairman of the TRU, John Hammond, Mark Morrison, Dr Frew, the Chairman again and a Mr R. Goldman proposed toasts! When Morrison spoke, he regretted not having given a 'better exhibition', to which the guests shouted 'No, No!' He paid compliments to both Johannesburg and the Wanderers pitch, which he declared the best they had played on, which evoked cheers. Hammond once again mentioned how important it was for South Africa, as England did, to fully embrace the amateur code and have 'nothing to do with them' (the League). This drew cheers. Dr Frew struck a conciliatory note, indicating whilst they were 'a little lucky in making a draw, he thought they would have been unlucky to have been beaten'. The town police band played popular selections and the exhausted players all left for bed at 10 pm.[12]

Bloemfontein and Sanna's Post

On Thursday evening, the team left Park Station for Bloemfontein, the capital of the Orange River Colony (ORC). Their travails with local transport continued. It was only once they were well outside Johannesburg that it was discovered there was no bedding in their carriage. The team accordingly spent a cold, uncomfortable night made worse when, at 5.30 am, the carriage caught fire due to a 'heated axle' and they had to abandon it hastily.

They finally reached Bloemfontein just before lunch. After a wash and brush up, they had a 'sumptuous' lunch. Thereafter, they

BOER TACTICS AT SANNA'S POST

By early 1900, British forces had invaded the Orange Free State from the Cape and had succeeded in capturing Bloemfontein. Field Marshal Lord Roberts, commanding all British forces, planned to use Bloemfontein as his staging point to prepare for the invasion of the ZAR and the capture of Pretoria. Once this was achieved, he was certain, all Boer forces would surrender.

OFS forces under the brothers Piet and Christiaan de Wet, who were to prove two of the OFS's most capable and resourceful commando leaders, decided not to attempt stopping Roberts' forces in pitched battles and instead used their very mobile commando forces in hit and run tactics. Sanna's Post, located 40 kilometres to the east of Bloemfontein, was to be the first such example of these new tactics.

Christiaan de Wet was determined to capture the Bloemfontein waterworks and thus disrupt the vital supply of water to the city. Brig.-Gen. R. G. Broadwood's forces, based on the Basutoland border further to the east, had begun to move westwards towards Bloemfontein and De Wet realised he could accomplish two tasks at once by trapping these forces at the same time. Without informing anybody in his commando, he led them on a fast, cross-veld ride during the night and by dawn on the morning of 31 March 1900, half his forces were lying quietly in wait, concealed along the banks of the Koornspruit (Corn River) in the vicinity of Sanna's Post and the waterworks. The other half of his force, under his brother Piet, were sheltering behind nearby hills further to the east. Broadwood's force, unaware of the situation as they had not employed scouts to ascertain if enemy forces were present, walked into De Wet's trap.

Piet de Wet's artillery opened fire at about 6 am. Broadwood's forces, exhausted by their long march, were taken by surprise and confusion reigned. Broadwood did exactly what Christiaan de Wet had anticipated and sent his forces westwards, away from the firing initiated by his brother Piet. Broadwood also ordered 'Q' and 'U' batteries of the Royal Horse Artillery (RHA) to move towards the Koornspruit to cover his retreat away from Piet de Wet's firing, not realising he was asking them to set up where Christiaan de Wet was waiting for them.

As wagons and men began to enter the Koornspruit riverbed, Christiaan de Wet's men silently began taking them prisoner. Major Taylor, in command of 'U' battery realised too late (his guns were already in the riverbed) what had occurred but managed to raise the alarm. This allowed Major Phipps Hornby of 'Q' battery to wheel his guns and move away from the Koornspruit, evade capture, and take refuge close to the nearby railway station. Every gun of 'U' battery, bar one, was nevertheless captured, with the Boers simply shooting the horses as they tried to climb back out of the banks of the Koornspruit.

A fierce battle erupted and 'Q' battery, unlimbered, began to fire on the Boer forces in the Koornspruit. Broadwood sent the Household Cavalry and the Burma Mounted Infantry south to attempt to outflank the Boers in the riverbed. 'Q' Battery under Major Hornby fired continuously, but Boer marksmen hidden along the banks of the river had their range, and casualties mounted rapidly: 'At first three men were loading, laying and firing the gun, then two, then in some cases only a single man. One gun was being worked by Lieutenant Peck alone.' When Boer forces began to outflank 'Q' battery, Broadwood ordered their retreat.[13]

Just ten men of 'Q' battery remained by this stage. The two remaining officers, Major Phipps Hornby and Captain Humphreys, led the retrieval of the guns. They called for volunteers from nearby infantry. Five officers volunteered, as did Captain Maxwell of Robert's Horse, a Cape unit. These men removed the guns one by one under withering fire, so fierce that as they walked out towards the guns, 'the storm of bullets was so violent that they pressed their helmets down on their heads and bent forward as if they were meeting a heavy wind'. Only one gun was left behind, no horses to pull it clear being left alive. [14]

Such was the bravery shown by these few men that when they eventually brought the guns to safety behind a depression, infantry along the way, despite it being 'to court death to show a hand ... in a spontaneous outburst of admiration, rose to their feet and cheered the gallant survivors'. The retreat was covered by men of the New Zealand Mounted Rifles under Major Robin.[15]

Broadwood and Roberts, alarmed by the loss of life, with 155 of their men being either killed or wounded and over 400 taken prisoner of war, ordered a further retreat. The waterworks were left in the possession of De Wet. The disruption of the water supply to Bloemfontein caused an outbreak of enteric fever that was to kill over 2,000 soldiers and inhabitants over the following months. The Boer commandos realised how successfully they could operate and the battle at Sanna's Post encouraged them not to give up hope. The war would not end with the capture of Bloemfontein, or Pretoria.

Leo Amery concluded that Sanna's Post once again showed, 'As so often has been the case in our military annals, a disaster was saved from disgrace by the behaviour of the soldiers.'[16] Lord Roberts decided that such conspicuous bravery would be rewarded in a different way. Four Victoria Crosses were awarded to members of 'Q' battery, voted for by the remaining men of the unit. The RHA still has a battery named 'Sanna's Post'. Maxwell also received the Victoria Cross for his part in the battle. He and Humphreys had attempted to pull the last gun back to cover themselves.

were driven around the city to view its charms and that night a ball was held in the Ramblers Hall. The following morning saw them visiting the Bloemfontein waterworks, followed by the nearby battlefield of Sanna's Post.

This battlefield would have provided the team with an interesting and tragic insight into the South African War.

That afternoon at 4.30 pm, Morrison's men confronted a team representing the ORC at the Ramblers Ground in the middle of Bloemfontein. The wind that had prevailed in the morning had died down and conditions were pleasant. The large crowd was entertained by the band of the 2nd Worcestershires before the contest.

The Sportsman's correspondent, who had followed the team throughout the tour, considered this contest the 'very worst one the English have played' with the tackling of the backs 'dreadfully weak'. The team showed no 'finish'. Possibly this was a reaction to the Test three days previously, or the field which, once again, was extremely hard. Morrison's men narrowly won the contest 17-16 with the ORC team scoring four tries, including two in the last few minutes, both of which the kicker, J. McDonald, failed to convert. A banquet was held that evening in the Ramblers Hall and the team departed for Kimberley at 9 a.m. the next morning.[17]

Back to Kimberley and the Second Test

Despite Kimberley being just 165 kilometres from Bloemfontein, it took the team the whole of Sunday to cover the distance, the train only arriving early on Monday morning. On the Wednesday afternoon, for the third time, the tourists faced Griqualand West. They had lost their previous two games to this team, but this time were victorious 11-5. Their cause was helped by the fact that the two Griqua centres were severely injured, with R. Bishop leaving the field of play with a broken collarbone and his partner, J. Gartnell, being 'lame' for much of the meeting. Arthur Tedford scored the only try of the second half to put the contest beyond doubt.

Two more battlefields were on the team's itinerary: first Magersfontein, south of Kimberley, on the Thursday, and on Friday, Carter's Ridge. Magersfontein would have been especially poignant to the Scottish members of the party, for it was there that the Highland Brigade, under Maj.-Gen. Andrew Wauchope, suffered over 160 casualties (including Wauchope himself) during 'Black

Week'. During the week 10–17 December 1899 British forces suffered three devastating defeats, here and at Colenso and Stormberg.

On Friday evening the team attended the opera *Cavalleria Rusticana* that was being performed at a Kimberley theatre by a touring Italian Opera Company.

The second Test, played on the Kimberley Athletic Ground on 5 September 1903 with the South African team led this time by Jackie Powell of Griquas, ended in a 0-0 draw. Alfred Tedford, who after all was a forward, recorded three decades later how 'dreadful' the British Isles backs were. He was amazed that Morrison's men had managed to 'hold on' for the draw.[18] One reason was possibly that whereas Morrison had made just two changes (Robert Neil replacing Edward Harrison at full back and Edward Walker in for Ian Davidson on the wing), the South Africans had made eight changes. Three of those were in the backline, where both centres from the first Test, Krige and Van Reenen, did not play. Amongst the forwards, Dr Frew could not travel south to play, and Barry Heatlie had to return to Cape Town from Johannesburg as quickly as possible to be with his wife for the birth of their second son.

It has been suggested that Krige, and possibly Van Reenen, were so unhappy with the game plan in Johannesburg and being starved of the ball, that they had made themselves unavailable for selection.[19] At the heart of the selection conundrum always faced by the local captain was the question of availability and getting men around the country. We have seen how slowly transport moved. This team consisted of eight players from the local union, Griqualand West.

Tedford thought that Patrick Hancock had played well behind the scrum and inevitably Reg Skrimshire's name came up. He went over and scored, only for the referee, Percy Day, to decide that there had been a knock-on in the run-up and thus disallow the try. The Test series remained wide open. All would rest with the final game of the tour at Newlands.

Final Test
On Thursday 10 September, the tourists drew 3-3 with Western Province in the penultimate match of the tour. Fittingly, tries

apiece were scored by the two brilliant centres opposing each other on that day: Japie Krige for the hosts, Reg Skrimshire for the 1903 tourists.

Hard grounds and harder games had taken their toll and on the eve of the Test only sixteen of the original British tour party were fit enough to be considered for selection. Even John Hammond began to speculate that he might have to play for the team. In fact, the team that was selected was identical to the second Test team. Only Robert Neil of Scotland had to play completely out of position at full back.

Nature intervened and it began to rain. On Friday 11 September, the heavens opened over Newlands. It rained steadily until 11 a.m. on Saturday and then after a brief respite began to rain again in the afternoon. The tourists were delighted – they were used to playing on wet fields; the South Africans were not. By early afternoon Newlands was 'practically under water'.[20] Suggestions that the game might be postponed were rejected by Morrison, who inspected the pitch and found it fit for play. This pleased the crowds who, despite the rain, had begun to congregate outside the ground from early in the day.

The South African captain was Barry Heatlie once again. Two other Western Province players, Anderson and Jones, had selected the South African team with him and only four non-Western Province players made it into the team. McEwan, Botha, Ferris and Nel all played for Transvaal. Heatlie himself, in recalling this Test years later, conceded that the South African penchant for selecting basically local teams to represent the country was not at all wise.[21] He also recalled the most controversial selection – of his school friend Paddy Carolin as half-back – which was not Carolin's normal position. It was to prove a wise selection and Carolin would go on to make his mark on South African rugby. Heatlie once again demanded that the South African team wear the Old Diocesans RFU bottle green jerseys worn in 1896. The local outfitters could still supply him with enough to clothe his team.

The crowd of 6,000 (the largest for the three Tests) that had braved the weather was delighted when Heatlie led his team out onto the field on 12 September 1903 at Newlands and when Patrick Hancock kicked off 'sharp to time', there was much cheering. The field was very muddy, and the rain continued to fall during the contest. The wind blew strongly across the ground. The conditions militated against running rugby. If ever there was a game of halves, this was it. The first half was a hard slog, with the South African side defending continuously. Perhaps the key was in the wind, as in the newspaper accounts it was conceded that when the second half started it 'favoured' Heatlie's men, which would suggest that they would then have been playing with Table Mountain at their back and thus the northwester too. An early break by the Scot, Jim Gillespie, could have led to a try, but the pass to Skrimshire went awry. Then the South Africans dribbled through and Ferris narrowly missed the touchdown as the ball rolled over the dead ball line.

Now came the moment of the match. After 'tight play' Hancock kicked the ball into touch, but well inside the British Isles half. From the resulting line out the No. 8, Charlie Brown of Western Province, broke through and passed to Willie McEwan, who caught the pass well and in turn passed to Joe Barry, who dotted down in the corner. It was the only international try he ever scored, but what a try. Not a hand had been laid on him and the *Cape Argus* called it a 'splendid' effort.[22]

Both teams now upped the pace. Morrison dribbled through the South African line, which was open once he passed Van Reenen at full back, but Japie Krige 'nipped around and although slung over the line, saved daringly'. A 5-yard scrum resulted, but Hancock, in trying to get through, was penalised and the local side could kick for touch. The South Africans slowly drove the tourists back down the field and whilst the crowd was 'cheering like mad' the *coup de grace* was delivered. Tommy Hobson, the little half-back, grabbed the ball from the back of the scrum and swerving inwards linked up with his storming prop, Allan 'Oupa' Reid, who crossed the chalk to score a try in the only international he ever played. Heatlie converted.

Hugh Ferris nearly added a third try, but slipped and Loubser, after a 'daring save' was even applauded by the British team. In the dying stages of the game Morrison received a bad kick in the face, but remained on the field. More open play took place with both 'PO' (Pieter Albertus Ryno Otto) Nel at one side and then Tedford on the other, nearly scoring. Finally, 'no side' was blown and the *Cape Argus* reporter indicated that considering the conditions it had been a 'capital game'.[23]

Morrison and his men sportingly joined the excited crowd in cheering the South African side off the field.

In 1896, the first Test victory on Newlands had heralded the arrival of South Africa on the rugby scene. The 1903 series victory ushered in a new era in South African rugby. The confidence this first series win inspired can be seen in the results that were to be achieved by Paul Roos' 1906 tourists to the British Isles. It would be more than half a century before South Africa would again lose a series.

Reflections: South Africa Not Finished Yet

The poor weather limited the celebrations at Newlands. There was to be a celebration of a different kind later that night by the players, or at least some of them. The *Cape Argus* reported on this in the Monday edition. It appears that members of both teams, but primarily the tourists, congregated at the Opera House in Cape Town late on Saturday night, where their actions were called 'disgraceful in the extreme' by the newspaper and required the summoning of a police sergeant and no fewer than 25 constables to prevent 'an outbreak'. It is not clear what the outbreak might have been. The *Cape Argus* was furious and fulminated against the tourists, asking if the visitors were 'under the impression they are visiting a country of barbarians' and pointing out that they were 'supposed to be representative of the Rugby game at Home'.[24]

By Wednesday, the rowdiness had been forgotten and the team gathered in the York Room of the Theatre Restaurant for an early lunch, as they were travelling home on the *Kinfauns Castle* that night. The mayor was present, as was the president of the WPRFU. To save time, no speeches were given, just a simple toast to 'The King'. The mayor did however ask their indulgence in allowing him to propose a second toast of 'Long life and health to our visitors'. On that happy note the lunch adjourned at 2.15 pm. Morrison and his men were accompanied to the docks by members of the WPRFU and South African players and seen on board their vessel.

When the *Kinfauns Castle* docked in Southampton two weeks later, Mark Morrison gave interviews to journalists awaiting the team's arrival. He was very complimentary about the hospitality that had been extended to them during their stay and prophetically warned that a combined South African team (if it did indeed tour Great Britain a few years hence) would 'fully extend' the Home Union sides. Rugby, he concluded, was making 'great headway' in southern Africa, especially in 'Dutch' areas. When asked about the highlights of the tour, his mind went back to the day the team had visited the battlefields of Magersfontein, where so many of his 'gallant' fellow Scots had paid the highest price, and the bravery of Q Battery at Sanna's Post.

Finally, he was asked what he thought of the South African countryside. This, he believed, had been the 'last place created and ... it had not been finished yet'! The team disembarked and headed to their homes 'absolutely brimming over with recollections which must live as long as life lasts'.[25]

1903 TOURING PARTY
Manager – John Hammond

Backs
Gilbert Collett (England)*
Ian Davidson (Ireland)*
John Gillespie (Scotland)*
Louis Greig (England)*
Edward Harrison (England)*
Patrick Hancock (England)*
Alfred Hind (England)
Robert Neil (Scotland)*
Reg Skrimshire (Wales)*
Edward Walker (England)*

Forwards
Mark Morrison (Capt.) (Scotland)*
David Bedell-Sivright (Scotland)
William Cave (England)*
Thomas Gibson (England)*
J. C. Hosack (Scotland)
William Scott (Scotland)*
Robertson Smyth (Ireland)*
Frank Stout (England)*
Alfred Tedford (Ireland)*
James Wallace (Ireland)
Joseph Wallace (Ireland)*

* Played in at least one Test match

4

THE 1910 BRITISH ISLES TOUR: A UNIFIED SOUTH AFRICA FOR THE FIRST TIME

Dr Tom Smyth[1] led the fourth British Isles tour of southern Africa from June to September 1910. The squad comprised twenty-eight players and two managers: William Cail of England and Walter Rees of Wales. Twenty-six matches were planned, the most played by a touring party to date.

Both Cail and Rees were steeped in rugby. Cail had been involved in the drafting of the laws of the game in the late 1880s and was a former president of Northumberland union. Rees had been a courageous player in his day and was described as a 'tactful' man.

Six players from Ireland, including Tom Smyth, and six from Scotland, were joined by nine English players and seven Welshmen. Seven players in the squad played for Newport RFC in Wales. During the tour, Tom Richards, an Australian then residing on the Reef and playing for Transvaal, joined the squad. He qualified as he had previously played for Bristol RFC in England.

The team arrived late in May after sixteen days cooped up on board ship, to be met on the quayside by enthusiastic crowds. Their first meal in Cape Town was an official lunch with the mayor. The president of the South African Rugby Football Board (SARFB), Billy Simpkins, addressed this gathering and advised the visitors to 'put their shoulder to the wheel' and prepare for a 'hearty' welcome wherever they played.

The team's arrival coincided with the proclamation, on 31 May 1910, of the new Union of South Africa. Comprising the four formerly separate colonies of the Cape, Natal, Orange River and Transvaal, it could be argued that Tom Smyth's team were the first to face a truly South African side.

By the time the lunch started, Simpkins and Cail had already had a slightly acrimonious first meeting. The planning of the tour had been done via cables between the SARFB in Cape Town and the Rugby Union in London, but via a third party in Britain, W. P. Donaldson. It was now realised that there had been a misunderstanding about the tour itinerary. Cail and Rees had objected to playing matches in the weeks prior to the Test matches. It became apparent that Donaldson had failed to cable their objections to the SARFB, who, assuming silence meant agreement, had gone ahead and arranged matches in those weeks. They had also levied fees on the provincial rugby unions hosting those games.[2]

Cail pointed out that the International Rugby Football Board did not allow teams to play in the week before a Test match and accordingly lodged his opposition to the itinerary as it stood. Simpkins explained the SARFB's position and the fact that they had agreed to fund a much larger touring squad, including two managers, to compensate for the length of the tour. In the end the two men agreed to see 'how things went'. Their failure to resolve the matter at this stage would have an impact on the tour in the weeks ahead.[3]

Early Victories

Learning from previous tours, Smyth's men boarded the Union ship *Gaika* after just a day in Cape Town and voyaged along a stormy Cape coast to Mossel Bay. There they could train in peace and find their feet out of the spotlight. Their first game was on 11 June against the local side, South-Western Districts, which they easily won 14-4. Tom Smyth, fittingly, scored the first of their four tries that day. Newspaper reports indicated that although the field had been in good condition, there was still a lot of dust present during play, which surprised the visitors. The South-Western Districts forwards had held their opponents ominously easily. It was the visiting backs who had won the day. Smyth and his men boarded RMS *Saxon* the day after the match and returned to Cape Town.[4]

Smyth's squad had acclimatised at the Cape for over two weeks before they ran out on to Newlands' turf on 15 June for the second tour match. They triumphed 9-3 against a Western Province (WP) Country team. Over the next week, at the same venue, they beat WP Colleges (11-3) and drew with WP Town (11-11).[5] These matches were a prelude to the WP match on 25 June. As Paul Roos's successful Springbok team, which had toured the British Isles in 1906–07, had mainly comprised Western Province players, Cail viewed this match as the 'fourth Test'. Their backline was especially feared.

Keen rugby observers and journalists had questioned some of the selections in the British Isles team, but the first four matches had surprised them. Smyth's team was combining well. In the match against the WP Town team, *The Sportsman*'s correspondent was complimentary. However, he suggested that the half-back pairing of George Isherwood and Jack Spoors had struggled and might yet require reinforcing.

The Sportsman suggested that whilst WP liked to win their matches 'at the same time they like to feel that the men who come from afar are players worthy of their steel, and that it is an honour to be beaten by them'.[6] A full house at Newlands watched Smyth's forwards grind the local pack down. His backs, combining well, made the WP backs look out of sorts. Half-time came, however, with neither side having been able to score.

Shortly after the resumption, Charles 'Cherry' Pillman capitalised on a mistake by the WP full back, D. C. Jackson, and 'snatched' the ball away from him, and after chipping it over the backline scored the only try of the match, which he converted himself. Late in the day, Jackson converted a penalty, but that was the only score WP managed. Smyth's men were victorious 5-3. WP had not been defeated for thirteen years. Correspondents following the team were impressed and suggested that the result 'greatly enhanced the reputation of the Britishers'.

Watching the game and reporting for *The Athletic News* was the sports editor of the local *Cape Times*, Leslie A. Cox. Born in

England in 1871, Cox had moved to Cape Town in the early 1890s. He had served in the South African War and seen considerable action. Cox had been one of the sceptics, unsure that Smyth's men would be able to meet the challenge presented in southern Africa. Now he waxed lyrical. The British Isles forwards, especially their loose forwards, had dominated the exchanges in this 'magnificent struggle' and he described the 'tornado-like rushes of the loose-limbed winging forwards' that kept the WP pack at bay. He also pointed out that as the rain started midway through the game, the WP wing, E. T. Stegmann, had been injured and carried off the field (knocked unconscious by a kick to the jaw); both the rain and the injury were advantageous for the tourists. Accordingly, the local team, already weakened by the withdrawal of their captain, W. A. 'Billy' Millar though ill health on the morning of the match, now had to move a forward out of the scrum to cover for the 'crocked' Stegmann. Cox was also impressed with the play of the two capped Welsh forwards, Harry Jarman and Phil Waller, whilst their full back, Stanley Williams of Newport, played a blinder. However, all concurred that the wing forward, Cherry Pillman – 'we have never seen his equal' – was the find of the tour.[7] Cox also noted Pillman was the best-groomed man on the field!

After a brief celebration, Smyth's men followed the paths already trodden by previous teams and headed for Kimberley. To Cail and Rees's dismay, they left four players in Cape Town to recover from their injuries. James Kerr of Scotland had damaged his knee badly (he would not participate in any other match during the tour as a result); Dr Robert Stevenson, another Scot, had strained ligaments and would sit out the next seven matches; Mel Baker of Newport had damaged his ankle and would sit out eight matches; and Ken Wood of Leicester was in hospital with an infected throat.

The Reckoning: 'The Great North Road' and Transvaal
After a lengthy train journey, the British Isles team faced Griqualand West on Wednesday afternoon. The Griqua forwards, led by the 'giant' Springbok Klondyke Raaff, their backs well marshalled by the Springbok scrum half, 'Uncle' Fred Dobbin, were fleet of foot

and used to the gravel playing field. They won 8-0. Leslie Cox described the field as being like the 'Great North Road', but instead of macadam there was 'hard Kimberley grit'. When shown the enclosure before the encounter, some of the British team thought they were being pranked! Newspapers reported in the following week that British players had dug out stones the size of their fists from the field. These reports were strongly denied by the Griqualand West Rugby Union.

Pillman was rested for this game and his absence was felt by the visitors. Contributing to their downfall were the many disputes that arose with the referee, James Leck. Cox felt there was too much 'talking at the referee', a practice that was dealt with in South Africa 'with a very strong hand'. Leck was the referee who had taken control of Currie Cup finals since 1906 and was thus 'capable'. Cox provides a clue as to who was doing the talking when he accredited the on-field disputes to 'the Irish temperament' which is 'hard to restrain'. Three Irishmen played that day against Griquas: Alex Foster out on the wing, hardworking Oliver Piper in the forwards, and the captain – Dr Smyth!

In front of 15,000 spectators, which saw a record gate for rugby games in South Africa of £1,800, Griquas, Cox felt, deserved to win 'from start to finish'. One of the tourists confided in Cox that playing on that ground they 'would beat us every time'.[8]

There was no let-up in the schedule and three days later, after more train travel, the British Isles faced Transvaal on the 'dusty' Wanderers field. This time, more than 15,000 watched the contest and receipts were even higher than the Kimberley encounter. At the same time as Smyth's team was touring southern Africa, a team from the Football Association was following the same route. The previous week, they had played on the same ground, but correspondents noted that the crowd (and receipts) were larger for Smyth's team, thus confirming the popularity of the 'carrying game' in the Transvaal.

The Transvaal team, led by their 'big, fast, brawny, clever' forwards, did not give Smyth's men a chance. By half-time they led 13-0 and won 27-8, at that time a substantial margin. Cox felt that although the margin was a wide one, it did not represent the 'character' of play which was 'keen'. For Transvaal the wing, 'Hudie' Hahn, and tight forward, Dougie Morkel, scored most of the points and impressed the South African selectors. One of those selectors was R. W. Stanton, who refereed the match. On the British Isles side, Pillman converted Dyne Fenton Smith's try and put over a penalty. Cox was disappointed in the results of these two games. He felt Smyth's men had 'lost all the honour and glory that had accrued to them' from their early victories.[9]

Pretoria and Protest

After the Transvaal defeat, the team desperately needed a victory. They achieved this in the next match in Pretoria, defeating the local team 17-0 and scoring four tries in the process. Watching the match was the recently appointed first Governor-General of the Union of South Africa, Herbert Gladstone, 1st Viscount Gladstone, together with the new Union Prime Minister, General Louis Botha and General Lord Methuen, General Officer Commanding-in-Chief, South Africa. After the match the Prime Minister's wife held an 'at home' for the team. The team members were individually introduced to Louis Botha and spent time in his 'striking' presence that evening.

After the Saturday defeat by Transvaal, the team had been expected to travel to Pretoria for the Tuesday match, then to return to Johannesburg where, on Thursday, they were to face a Transvaal Country Club team before the mighty Transvaal for a second round on Saturday. Four matches in eight days: it was too much. The team was travelling so much they found that they could not even wash and dry their 'much worn' rugby jerseys.

William Cail now lodged an official written protest with the SARFB concerning the fixtures his team were expected to fulfil. The SARFB, while acknowledging the letter, still 'succeeded in avoiding giving a definite decision'. Cail's protest went together with his indication that the next fixture, due to be played two days later, on Thursday 7 July, in Johannesburg against the Transvaal Country Club team would not be honoured.

The 1891 touring team arrived in South Africa with limited knowledge of what awaited them. The following two tours saw

Johnny Hammond, who had played in the first tour, fulfilling a vital role, first as captain (1896) and then as manager (1903). He knew what the team would be facing and could prepare them effectively. Hammond's premature death in 1907 had robbed the tourists of his wise counsel. While Cail would have been party to the drawing up of the itinerary, he did not possess first-hand knowledge of the distances they would be required to travel and under what circumstances. He had also not experienced the playing conditions that existed in the Union.

News spread about the protest. By Thursday morning, no answer from the SARFB had been forthcoming. The Country Club team members were dismayed. This was their one and only chance to face the famous tourists. Cail and the team relented after holding a meeting with the Country Clubs team, which was attended by members of the Transvaal Rugby Union. The match went ahead on the Thursday afternoon. Speculation in the press had led to public confusion about the fixture and just 300 spectators were present.

Smyth and his team took out their frustrations on the hapless Transvaal Country Clubs team. They thrashed them 45-4, scoring eleven tries, the biggest win of the tour. Pillman converted six of the tries (including one he scored) and Reg Plummer scored a hat-trick of tries. Late in the game Plummer crossed the try line for the fourth time, but then passed the ball to his Newport teammate Jack 'Ponty' Jones (who had previously played for Pontypool, hence the nickname), allowing him to score his first try of the tour.[10]

The 'return' Transvaal match, in front of over 10,000 spectators on Saturday 9 July, saw the local team score thirteen points in the space of six minutes. This included tries by both the speedy Transvaal wingers. The first, after fourteen minutes, saw Bob Loubser dot down far out, and Dougie Morkel converted well. From the restart Hahn, on the opposite wing, received the ball from Toby Louw who had made a good break. Hahn avoided Maurice Neale of England and jumped through a despairing Stanley Williams' tackle to score. Morkel converted again. Four minutes later R. H. Williamson crashed over far out, but Morkel missed the conversion. Those present anticipated another 'sweeping' victory for the home team.

Smyth's men rallied and fought back. Pillman put over a penalty from an acute angle and at half-time they trailed 13-3. Late in the second half, with Transvaal on the attack deep in the visitors' half, Morkel put in a cross kick. The ball was intended for Hudie Hahn but bounced awkwardly. Dr Charles Timms of Edinburgh, playing centre, collected it on the first bounce and evaded a couple of defenders. He passed the ball to the 'rotund' Oliver Piper who put in a 'terrific' sprint. When he was about to be 'collared' he in turn passed to Tom Richards, recently added to the squad, who went over for the try. The crowd loved it: 'The spectators in the stands and the four corners of the ground rose and cheered the effort for quite thirty seconds.' *The Sportsman*'s correspondent thought it one of the best tries seen at the Wanderers ground.

The second half belonged to the British Isles side and they pressed relentlessly, but it was to no avail. The final score was a 13-6 victory to Transvaal. *The Sportsman* thought 'The better side had lost.'[11]

The managers, Cail and Rees, had still not received an official response from the SARFB to their request for fewer games to be played. There were more 'discussions' after the second Transvaal match. Cail and Rees proposed that if the South African Board was not prepared to sacrifice matches, they should consider a request to postpone some matches. This would allow the team to have a full week to rest prior to each of the three Test matches.

The itinerary had placed a heavy burden upon Cail's team. The greater number of matches they were required to play meant they had to criss-cross the Union on slow trains. After playing a match they were required to entrain immediately for the next destination. As the tour had progressed, Cail had found it harder to maintain the fitness of the squad. Playing on the extremely hard fields had resulted in numerous abrasions, some of which did not heal cleanly or quickly. Writing decades later, Alex Foster of Ireland recalled this aspect of the tour:

Our list of casualties and minor injuries was always heavy. Elbows and knees were skinned in spite of elbow-guards and reinforced kneecaps; you were lucky if the wounds did not fester; and even if the scabs were healthy, you would burst them next time you bent the limb if they had already not been knocked off by people passing you in the train.[12]

After the Transvaal match, Mel Baker, the Newport wing, was found 'under the X-rays' to have broken his foot. Stanley Williams was crocked, as was Maurice Neal. Amongst the forwards Dr Robert Stevenson and Edward Crean were injured, whilst Dr Edward Ashby and Dr William Tyrell were seldom selected. This meant a greater burden for those who were picked.

Down to the Coast for Some 'Rest'

On the Sunday after the second Transvaal match, the team took the train to Pietermaritzburg. En route they viewed some of the South African War battlefields, and the town of Ladysmith that had been besieged in 1899–1900. There was little time for sightseeing however, as on Wednesday 13 July they faced a Natal team on the Pietermaritzburg Oval. Cox noted that Cail had selected a weaker team to allow his 'scarred and battered warriors a much-needed rest'. As Natal was meant to be one of the weakest teams they would face, it seemed a wise move. Unbeknownst to Cail, in the years since Mark Morrison's men had visited this part of the country and beaten 'crude and raw' teams representing Durban and Pietermaritzburg, now they faced a Natal team representing the whole colony. The hosts threw themselves into the fray and by half-time the score was 8-8. With five minutes to go the local lads led 16-13, having scored three tries. In the dying moments, Ken Wood of Leicester dotted down to level the scores and Pillman converted with an excellent kick to win the game for the visitors by two points.

The following day, 14 July, the SARFB finally held a meeting in Cape Town to discuss the request from Cail and Rees to reduce the number of matches in the tour, or at least to rearrange the itinerary to allow them a rest week before the three Tests. Delegates felt that the Board had leant over backwards to accommodate the British team. Realising that the tour would be onerous, they had agreed to a larger touring squad. They had also agreed to meeting the costs of hosting two managers, Cail having indicated that, for personal reasons, he would not be able to spend the entire tour in Africa. In addition, almost as soon as the team had started the tour, they had requested further players be sent out. Eric Milroy, J. Webb and E. G. Handford had joined the squad from the Britain, whilst the Australian-born Tom Richards had already been drafted locally. In all these cases, the SARFB had quickly agreed to their inclusion and was covering the costs associated with hosting them. They felt that Cail had two fifteens at his disposal, including seventeen internationals he could call upon.

The SARFB decided that to cancel any of the matches would constitute a 'breach of faith with the public'. The lack of response from England to the proposed itinerary in April had been viewed, and was still viewed by the Board, as acceptance of the situation. The only compromise offered was to delay the 'return' game against WP due to take place prior to the third Test at Newlands. This would, ironically, lengthen the tour and still not provide the week gap Cail desired. It would also mean that the last Test would be played on Tuesday 6 September. The midweek games before both the first and second Tests were confirmed.

Members of the press were now following this story carefully. As a result, the British team management first heard the result of the discussions in Cape Town through the press when they arrived in Durban on the morning of 15 July. The SARFB had not managed to contact Cail and Rees to inform them of the decision.

The press travelling with the team could see first-hand the problems under which Cail and Rees were labouring. Their initial reaction had been simply to expect the British Isles team to accept their lot as previous teams had, but now there was growing sympathy. Journalists also realised that if there was no agreement, there was a possibility that the tour could be abandoned.

On Wednesday 16 July, the British Isles team again faced Natal at Lord's Ground in Durban. This time Cail 'paid Natal a high compliment' and put virtually his full international team onto the field. Natal played the first half with the strong wind at their backs. They opened the scoring after eight minutes and even though Ken

Wood dotted down for the visitors, 'Natal now showed what they were capable of and took charge of the game.' By half-time they led 13-5.

With the wind in their favour in the second half, Smyth might have expected his team to put some points on the board. The British Isles half-back pairing of Jack Spoors and George Isherwood had been viewed by some as a weak link in the team since their first appearance. Now with time ticking away, they proved unable to crack open the Natal defence.

Verbally rallying his men during a short break in play, Tom Smyth, in a stroke of genius, moved Cherry Pillman into an 'extra back position'. Pillman used his boot to 'drive' the Natalians back until Stanley Williams could get within range of the posts and pop over a goal from a mark, 8-13. Shortly thereafter Alex Foster swept in for a good try after clever backline play, 11-13. With the British backs now playing 'brilliant' football, it comes as no surprise to read that the semi-injured Mel Baker crossed for a try, 14-13. Finally, Pillman 'with fine opportunism went over with a great solo effort, kicked the goal, and so completed the success of his team 19-13'. This rousing game had thrilled the crowd. The pluck shown by Smyth's men in the last quarter was 'something to be remembered', Cox conceded. Pillman's contribution in the backline was impressive and crucial. It would not be the last time this rangy wing-forward played there on this tour.[13]

Leslie Cox took stock. The forthcoming game against the Orange River Colony marked the middle of the tour. Ahead of Cail and Rees's charges lay a further fourteen games and, possibly more daunting, even longer distances to cover by train. First, they faced a lengthy rail trip from Durban to Bloemfontein and then two games in Kimberley on gravel. Thereafter, a total of six full days (there and back) in the train to play a Southern Rhodesian side in Bulawayo. Upon their return to the Union, they would first face a Witwatersrand side on the Tuesday and then South Africa in Johannesburg four days later in the first Test. To add to the tour management's woes, they had also just heard that a further two players, Crean and Neale, would be remaining in Durban for treatment.

Cox compared Smyth's team to that of Mark Morrison in 1903. By this stage Morrison's men had lost eight of their eleven games, whilst Smyth's men had won eight of the twelve and drawn one. This tour was 'by no means bad'. At the same time, Cox had altered his views of the 'complaint' that Cail had laid at the door of the SARFB, and from whom they had still not heard officially. Cox suggested that unless there was some dialogue, the international matches might indeed be cancelled, and local games substituted. This, he felt, would be 'repugnant'. His report would have been read with alarm by the office bearers of the SARFB. Cox had realised Cail and Rees had no further options to explore. The tour was in jeopardy.

On to the ORC – and a Final Letter From Cail

When the British Isles team arrived at the station in Bloemfontein, there were hundreds of locals present to greet them. Notwithstanding the losses suffered on the field and the growing match controversy, South Africans were very keen to make sure that the team felt welcome.

The Orange River Colony (ORC) match was played in front of a crowd of 3,000 on a lovely sunny day. The Rambler's Ground was in prime condition having had 50,000 gallons of water lavished on it in the preceding days.

The *Rand Daily Mail* compared the weights and ages of the two teams. They reported that the average age on both sides was twenty-three, but the average British player weighed 80 kilograms against the 77 kilograms of the ORC side. The British forward pack averaged 85 kilograms against their opponents' 77 kilograms.[14] So the meat was in the British pack, though the ORC backs must have been bigger than their opponents.

Once again, the tourists started slowly and by half-time were behind 0-3. Early in the second half 'Ponty' Jones made a clean break and then passed to Tom Smyth who scored, Pillman failing 'miserably' with the conversion. Arthur McClinton of Belfast was one of the enigmas of the tour. He played full back as understudy to the brilliant Stanley Williams and during the whole tour was only called into the line of duty eight times. He had already made some good stops of forward rushes in this match when, shortly after his captain's try, he collected the ball and from inside his own half put over a magnificent snap drop. Those four points put his team ahead for the first time. All the play was now in the ORC half. A clearance kick from the ORC full back then went straight to Smyth who scored his second try, which Pillman converted. A late try by the ORC team meant victory to Smyth's men was by a margin of three points, 12-9.

That evening, while the team were being entertained to a dinner in the Rambler's Hall, Cail wrote another letter to the SARFB. He again expressed his dismay at the handling of the situation by the SARFB and indicated that his team would not be playing matches in the weeks leading up to the first and third Tests and 'possibly' the second Test too. It is not clear why he did not ask for a clear week before the second Test. It was perhaps that he felt the games to be played in the Eastern Cape (the second Test was due to be played in Port Elizabeth) would not be as strenuous. Cail's ambivalence about this match would again cause further confusion later in the tour.

The tourists travelled on to Kimberley. On Saturday 23 July, and the following Wednesday, the British Isles team played matches on the local 'gravel patch'. They lost both games: first to Griqualand West 3-9 and then the Cape Colony 0-19. Both matches produced exciting, fast-paced rugby. In the Griqualand West contest, the game was in the balance until the hosts scored a try in the last minute to assure victory. Pillman scored the lone try for his team and, although completing the match, was injured and would miss the next six contests. In the Cape Colony match, the margin was a wide one, yet the visitors acquitted themselves well. It was felt that they were harshly treated by the referee, R. W. Stanton. 'Every time the visitors had an opportunity of getting away, some infringement took place.'[15] They could not however, avoid the fact that in the two games, eight tries had been scored against them and they had only crossed their opponents' line once.

On the same day of the Cape Colony match, the SARFB held an 'emergency' meeting in Cape Town to discuss William Cail's

Bloemfontein letter. By now the press in South Africa was openly speculating that the tour might be abandoned with the concomitant loss of face for South Africa. The SARFB had also received a cable from the Transvaal Rugby Union urging a compromise. The 'voluminous' correspondence was again reviewed, and this time common sense prevailed. The SARFB decided to cancel the Witwatersrand game prior to the first Test. In its place a match between 'South Africa' versus 'Rest of Transvaal' would be played. The Western Province game scheduled to be played between the second and third Tests would now be played after the third Test. In both cases this would give the British Isles team a free week before the Saturday Test match. Nothing was proposed about the game scheduled to be played in the week prior to the second Test. The crisis had been averted ... for now anyway.

William Cail and the team left Kimberley three hours after the Cape Colony match ended on Wednesday night. The news of the SARFB backdown only reached them when they arrived in Bulawayo at 9.10 a.m. on Friday 29 July. The original plan was for them to play Southern Rhodesia on the Saturday afternoon and then return immediately to Johannesburg. Instead, Cail decided the team needed a complete break. First though, they had to face the local side.

The Southern Rhodesian side were up for the battle against their prestigious visitors and within a few minutes their scrum half, F. W. Wunder, had crossed for a try. Two quick tries by Reg Plummer and William Tyrell, of Queens University and Ireland, righted the ship, but then the Rhodesians scored a further try. Just before half-time Arthur McClinton again put over a 'fine' drop goal from far out. In the second half the British Isles scored eleven unanswered points to win the contest 24-11.

After the match, the British teamed entrained again, but this time for a break at the Victoria Falls. More than two decades later, Alex Foster, in recalling the tour, listed this stop as his best memory. 'The stupendous sight of the Victoria Falls and her boiling gorge below ... have left a clear imprint upon the mind.'[16] On their return to Bulawayo they attended a dinner. The Southern Rhodesian captain,

H. O. Coker, turned to Tom Smyth and William Cail during his speech and asked them to see that future tours included more games north of the Limpopo River: 'Remember us,' he pleaded, 'we have not had fair play from the strongest centres of South Africa.' Smyth agreed: 'You have not.' Coker had struck a chord. Later that evening, despite the hour, over a thousand people were present at the Bulawayo station to send the team on their way.

Next stop was Johannesburg and the first Test match. As the match against Witwatersrand had been dropped from the schedule completely, the visitors could prepare adequately for the encounter. The 'business end' of the tour was at hand: provincial games were important, but performance in the Tests defined a tour. The whole squad knew this.

First Test

Fifteen thousand excited fans packed the Wanderers ground on a clear, bright Highveld winter's day to watch the first Test, refereed by R. W. Stanton on 6 August 1910. Ponty Jones led the British Isles, as Smyth felt he 'was not up to form' and dropped himself. Mel Baker, 'the Newport comet', was again injured, as was William Roberston. Douglas Morkel of Transvaal led the Springboks.

The opening exchanges saw both teams move the ball down their backlines and put in good long touch kicks. Jones, leading by example, was especially fierce in his tackles. Archie Marsberg, the Springbok full back, was slow in responding to some of these kicks, but Jack Spoors was 'never able to get his backline into effective order'. In fact, Spoors' passing was downright poor, and Jones was repeatedly having to 'tidy' up in the backline. Stanley Williams at full back was his usual sure self and stopped good runs by both Springbok wings Hahn and Loubser, bundling them out into touch. Midway through the first half the Springbok 'threes' again sped downfield behind a kick. Williams bravely tackled the centre, Jack Hirsch, who had collected the ball and, in the process, broke Hirsch's leg. The seriousness of the injury was evidently not apparent to the team at this stage and Morkel temporarily moved Arthur Williams, of Griqualand West, out of the scrum to play on the wing.

No replacements were allowed, and the Springboks were thus at a considerable disadvantage, but it did not seem to affect them. A few minutes after Hirsch's departure and after a period of sustained pressure, Ken Wood fumbled a poor pass from Spoors. Douglas Morkel collected it and 'got the ball travelling' and Hirsch's erstwhile centre partner Dirkie de Villiers went in for the first try. Morkel was unable to convert.

The British Isles 'revenge' was swift, and it was initiated by their captain. Ponty Jones took yet another wayward pass, this time from Wood, one-handed, and the ball was subsequently 'sent to Foster for his glorious run home'. Marsberg was found wanting as Alex Foster sped past him, but he did manage to force him to dot down far out. Stanley Williams failed with the conversion and when half-time was called, the teams were equal at 3-3.

During the break, the news that Hirsch would not be returning to the fray was passed to Douglas Morkel. He decided to move Loubser onto the wing and put himself at centre. Williams was moved back into the scrum, where he preferred to play. Early in the second half, Jack Spoors broke well and chipped the ball over the Springbok backs. Marsberg had again been caught out of position, however Spoors knocked on with the try line at his mercy.

There were 'glorious dashes' by both Hahn and Loubser, but the extra man advantage enjoyed by the visitors saw them dominate territory. Their finishing, however, left much to be desired.

Against the run of play, De Villiers kicked downfield, and Williams hastily had to seek touch. Morkel, using his experience as a forward to his advantage, took the quick line-out and 'dashed' over the try line with Stanley Williams 'vainly hurling all his weight on the giant to throw him over'. Dirkie de Villiers was unsuccessful with the kick. The Springboks now led 6-3.

Shortly thereafter, Freddie Luyt, who was combining well with Dobbin, broke around the edge of the scrum, catching his opposite number George Isherwood napping, and scored the Springboks' third try. Morkel converted and the local team led 11-3, against the run of play.

The British Isles team continued to dominate the exchanges and it was no surprise when Ponty Jones put over a drop to reduce the deficit to 11-7. The gap was further narrowed when Isherwood picked up a bouncing ball and fed his fellow half-back, Spoors, who ran in a good try far out. Williams failed with the conversion. The Springboks now led by one point, 11-10.

The play that followed was 'helter skelter' across the whole field and had the crowd on its feet. After some hard forward scrumming, a brilliant double-play made the game safe for the Springboks. Morkel, who popped up everywhere during the second half, emerged from a scrummage with the ball and 'lightly' put in a cross kick. Hudie Hahn made a 'spectacular spring' to collect the ball in the air and then made ground to score. Morkel failed to convert, thus leaving the score 14-10 in favour of the hosts.

Both sides knew it was a few minutes to the final whistle and gave their all. It was 'sheer war' and despite sweeping moves, 'bustling' play and much excitement amongst the huge crowd, 'no-end' was called to a great cheer from the local supporters. The Springboks were victorious 14-10.[17]

Such were the travelling demands on Cail's men that it was understood they would be entraining the same night for the Cape. It was only after the match that they heard they would only be leaving the next day. Accordingly, the great rugby gathering at the Carlton Hotel, where the visitors were staying, was abandoned and a crowd of 'rugby men' attended a show at the Standard Theatre where 'many boxes were engaged'.

The South African win, despite the disadvantage of playing two-thirds of the match one man short, was impressive. All the Springbok backs had played well, except for Marsberg, who was too slow and who had kicked poorly. For the British Isles team, Jones and Williams in the backline and Piper in the forwards had played well, but the result of this match might well have been different if Smyth and, especially, Pillman, had been playing.

The Eastern Cape and Border

The next day Cail and his charges headed towards the coast and softer fields. Before they reached East London, however, they had to play one more match against North Eastern Districts on a rock-strewn 'field' in one of the smallest Karoo 'dorps' any British Isles rugby team would ever visit: Burgersdorp.

Burgersdorp, a station on the railway line between Johannesburg and East London, had barely 2,000 inhabitants in 1910. It served as a focal point for the local, sparsely populated, farming area. No fewer than twelve of the fifteen British Isles players who had played in the Test match played again in this match. Jones led the visitors in the continuing absence of Smyth. They started well. First Maurice Neale crossed the line and then shortly afterwards Ponty Jones dotted down, with Stanley Williams converting to make the score 8-0.

The local side fought back, however, and shortly before half-time Young scored an unconverted try. At the break, the score was 8-3. Midway through the second half Pocock scored for the Districts side and Young converted to level the scores at 8-all. Stanley Williams hit the poles with a penalty and there were close calls for both try lines, but no further scoring. The Reuters correspondent covering the game thought the visiting forwards 'indolent' and the local team were 'in the game' as much as their esteemed visitors. Once again, the passing amongst the British backline was poor.[18]

Added to the loss in the first Test, the morale in the team cannot have been high. Their captain was injured, as was their star player. Cail and Rees now realised that during the earlier negotiations they should have also demanded a week's break before the second Test to be played on 27 August. Accordingly, they addressed a request to the SARFB asking for the cancellation of the game to be played on Tuesday 23 August against Midlands. Once again, the SARFB declined their request.[19]

At 6.35 am, on the morning after the hard game against North Eastern Districts, the team boarded the train, reaching the coastal city of East London that night at 11 pm. The following day (Friday 12 August) the press, who once again followed the 'bickering' between the two rugby bodies closely, were able to carry a dramatic announcement. William Cail had decided to cancel the remainder of the tour! The team would return to Cape Town and embark on the first mail ship available for Southampton.

Negotiations began at once, both in East London and Cape Town. Cail acceded to the local team's entreaties once more. The match against the Border team went ahead, but as a 'charity' game and not as a 'fixture'. The British Isles team played in their club jerseys to emphasise their unhappiness. The uncertainty reduced the crowd who watched, but there were still over 3,000 present to see the visitors win 30-10. They ran in eight tries, which included a hat-trick by Maurice Neale. Their score could have been much higher, but Stanley Williams only succeeded with one conversion.

If William Cail thought his decision to return home would force the hand of the SARFB, he was wrong! Over the weekend after an 'emergency meeting' at their offices in Cape Town, an unequivocal reply came back. The Board, through its representative Louis Smuts, 'appealed' to Cail to continue with all the planned fixtures. Smuts continued: 'We have met you in every possible way and reasonably expect you to cooperate.' Smuts ended with a facetious comment that would have stung: 'You must have fully twenty men fit.'

The press was aghast. They suggested that Messrs Simpkins, Smuts and the SARFB did not know Cail 'as the Transvaal Rugby Union did' and should, accordingly, not have been so hasty as to issue the 'ultimatum' they had. Louis Smuts objected to the press using the word 'ultimatum', indicating that it was simply a 'carefully worded message'.[20]

The earlier crisis had been resolved by the Transvaal Rugby Union cancelling a contentious match, and now the Eastern Cape Rugby Union came to the rescue of the tour and offered to cancel the Midland game. Instead, the planned Wednesday game against Eastern Province would be played on the 20th, thus leaving the week before the Test free for the visitors. The SARFB grudgingly accepted the EPRU offer, cabling Cail that they still could 'not recede from attitude previously taken up'.

Cail, in daily touch with the pressmen travelling with the team, would have read the comments published in the *Rand Daily Mail* of 15 August. It was suggested that he and Rees were not blameless, having followed a path 'conspicuous by the absence of those courtesies which are essential in the amicable solution of difficulties'. Cail and Rees accepted the EPRU offer. The tour continued.[21]

An exhausted, depleted, and dispirited British Isles team clambered aboard yet another slow train and headed inland to play a second game against Border, this time in King William's Town.

The 'return' Border game in King William's Town was, as the British Isles had found to their cost on this tour, 'strenuously contested from start to finish'. It started sensationally when the local hero, Johnson, crashed over for a try in the fourth minute, which he then converted. The visitors fought back via tries by Timms, Jones and Neale and midway through the second half led 13-5. In the dying moments of the contest, first Sprenger and then Leighton scored tries for the local team, with Fuller converting the second try to earn Border a 13-all draw.[22]

Cail and his charges moved on to Port Elizabeth and on Saturday 20 August defeated Eastern Province 14-6. The crowd, aware of the situation for the visitors, 'cheered them to the echo when they ran onto the field'. Once again, the game was a 'keen' one. Cail now had two of his best players back: Tom Smyth and Cherry Pillman. Pillman was played outside George Isherwood at half-back and Jack Spoors moved into the centre position. The changes worked. First Alex Foster sped through for a good try and then Isherwood put Foster away for his second try shortly thereafter. Isherwood seems to have got a 'second wind'. He had played well in both Border matches and did so again in this match.

Spoors also responded well to his change of position, putting the speedy Newport winger Mel Baker in for a try after a good break, whilst Arthur McClinton played well at full back. But it was Pillman's play that was a revelation. He made innumerable openings and was 'shining' in his position. Having not played the previous six matches, it is also surely the case that he was well rested. Dr Tom Smyth, once again captain after missing the previous five matches, played well too.

Second Test: Cherry Pillman's Game

The team could finally rest until the Test match. It was at this stage that William Cail, as arranged months previously, took leave of the team to travel to Cape Town and catch the mail ship home to Newcastle, leaving Walter Rees in charge. On his way home, Cail was interviewed in Cape Town. There were, he concluded, 'no soft games in South Africa' and no pack of forwards they had met were weak. He also pointed out the huge difference in playing on coastal and inland fields.

The South African selectors named their team for the second Test. It was, suggested the *Rand Daily Mail*, a 'curious' team, containing no fewer than eight Western Province players, who, the correspondent pointed out, had been beaten by the tourists. There was no place for either Douglas Morkel or Bob Loubser. Other changes were Billy Millar at eighthman, Clive van Ryneveld in place of Uncle Dobbin at the base of the scrum and Percy Allport at full back in place of Marsberg. The *Rand Daily Mail* concluded that 'the Springbok team will scarcely carry the confidence of Rugby followers generally'.[23]

The British Isles team was remarkably similar to that selected for the first Test. Tom Smyth played in place of Oliver Piper in the forwards and Jack Spoors replaced Ken Wood in the centre. The only great change was that Cherry Pillman, normally 'wing-forward', played at fly-half.

There were but three scores recorded during the second Test, played on 27 August 1910 at Port Elizabeth on a lovely cool, but sunny, day in front of 7,000 spectators on a grassy, well-conditioned, Crusaders Club pitch that 'gladdened the hearts' of the visitors.

The first points came three minutes from the half-time whistle. Robert Stevenson had been heavily 'grassed' during a tackle and had to leave the field to have a cut above his eye sewn up. This did not stop the British Isles attacking and Spoors was held up just short. The Springboks cleared the ball and Dick Luyt sent Hahn away down the touchline at 'terrific' speed. Stanley Williams saved the day, but in bundling Hahn out into touch, became 'temporarily disabled'. During this time, with just thirteen able British players on the field, Wally Mills, Bob Loubser's replacement, scored far out after clever play by Dick Luyt. Luyt, however, missed the conversion. At half-time, the score was 3-0 in favour of the Springboks.

The second half saw both Williams and Stevenson return to the fray, but the Springboks were on song. Hahn first put in a scintillating run and then a few minutes later De Villiers broke through the British line, but Billy Millar, with the try line at his mercy, knocked the pass on. The British forwards were holding their own and after good work by Jarman and Smyth, Ponty Jones found touch in the Springbok's half. From the resulting scrum Pillman got possession and put a kick over the advancing Springbok backs. It bounced awkwardly for Percy Allport at full back, and Jack Spoors collected the ball and scored. Pillman failed to convert, hitting the upright.

Two minutes later, with twelve minutes left for play, the decisive moment arrived. Cherry Pillman almost 'bullocked' his way over the try line, according to the Springbok captain Billy Millar, before passing to Maurice Neale who scored midway between the poles and the touchline. Pillman converted. The British Isles team held off all further attacks and the final score was 8-3 in their favour.

The comments on the match all focus on the brilliance of Pillman, who was declared the 'hero of the match'. He played a game he 'apparently invented himself' and was here, there, and everywhere. The packs of forwards matched each other. It was the Springbok backs, and, specifically Dirkie de Villiers, who were singled out for allowing the British Isles' backs to carry the day.

Billy Millar, recalling the Test two decades later, was certain who had won it for the visitors:

I assert confidently that if ever a man can have been said to have won an international match through his unorthodox and lone-handed efforts, it can be said of the inspired black-haired Pillman I played against on the Crusader's ground on August 27, 1910.[24]

Millar also paid tribute to George Isherwood, who 'played the game of his life', and combined well with Pillman.

There was general amazement at the result. The poorly performing (Billy Millar diplomatically called them 'inconsistent') British Isles team had 'put one over' the Springboks. For the first time, the latent provincialism that would blight the selections of many a Springbok team in years to come was revealed. How was it possible, asked many in Kimberley, Johannesburg, and Pretoria, that both Griqualand West (with no men in this Springbok team) and Transvaal could hammer the tourists, yet the national team could not?

The *Rand Daily Mail* summed up the game by decrying the South African belief in their 'innate superiority' that was now shattered and must forever be put aside. The Springboks had been defeated by a 'much cried down' team who used a forward as their fly-half![25]

To Cape Town and the Last Test

The British Isles team made two player changes to their winning combination. The major move was to send Cherry Pillman back into the scrum at the expense of Tom Richards. Spoors moved back to fly-half, Ken Wood came into the centre and Mel Baker replaced Alex Foster on the wing. On the Springbok side there were five changes. Crucially, Douglas and W. H. 'Boy' Morkel came into the forwards. Wally Mills had played his one and only game for the Springboks and had scored a try but had to make way for Bob Loubser. Amongst the forwards, A. C. Lombard, Toby Moll, Cliff Riordan, and W. A. G. Burger were dropped for N. J. Crosby and H. J. Reynecke. The team now had nine players from WP and six from Transvaal.

Billy Millar, reminiscing about the game, recalled he did not think that 'so much interest could be engendered for a mere game. All South Africa seemed to have gone football mad ... it was clearly manifest which was our national game...'[26]

The day of the third, and deciding Test, was sunny and cool. There had been rain in the previous days, but the field was dry and firm. The size of the crowd was estimated to be between twelve and fifteen thousand. Newlands was packed. Dr Tom Smyth kicked off at 4.19 p.m. on 6 September 1910.

Initially the teams contested fiercely, but no one gained much advantage. There was one penalty attempt by Morkel, but it went wide. Ten minutes into the game the tourists suffered what Millar later termed 'an incalculable loss', when the 'grand' full back Stanley

Williams of Newport pulled a muscle in his back and had to leave the field. Williams had already stopped several rushes, but now he had got close to the scrum and when it wheeled, three 'green garbed men' fell on him. No replacements were allowed, so the tourists were always going to struggle with only fourteen men. Minutes later, Fred Luyt, playing at fly-half, ran past his opposite number Jack Spoors and put Gideon Roos away for an easy try, which Morkel converted.

The British Isles held on grimly until half-time, but shortly after the resumption of play, Luyt went down the blind side and scored after the Springboks had camped close to the tourists' try line for some time. Douglas Morkel converted to make it 10-0.

The loss of Stanley Williams was to prove crucial in the match and effectively, the series. Added to that was the fact that the altered Springbok pack, led by the two Morkels, was dominating their opponents. 'There were no two ways about it; the British forwards were not in it. They seemed lifeless.'[27]

It was at this stage that Springbok full back Percy Allport sealed the game and the series for South Africa. The British forwards had finally broken through the South African line after being pinned in their own half for some time. Allport picked up the ball from in front of the British forwards and then, according to Millar, who must have seen dozens of Springbok tries from both on and off the field by the time he wrote, twenty years later, '...scored a spectacular try which will never be forgotten'. Allport dodged a forward 'only to find a phalanx of forwards atop him. He swerved, and, finding a clear field got into his stride ... he sped for the line to the accompaniment of a tumultuous roar.' The defence was slow in reacting, and with no full back in place 'Allport just managed to fling himself over the line as the enemy closed with him.'[28]

As can happen in these situations, some players throw caution to the wind when on the losing side and the *Cape Argus* carefully recorded that some 'undesirable play now ensued, both sides being somewhat vigorous'. Cox, writing in *The Athletic News* more than three weeks after the Test had been played, was much more outspoken. Bob Loubser had been lying on the ground with the ball in play 20 yards away, when 'three Welshmen' proceeded to kick him in the ribs. Cox reported that Loubser 'shouted as each kick was administered', whilst the crowd 'howled' their displeasure. Billy Millar, alerted by the crowd, spun around, and went to Loubser's defence. He, too, had to be cautioned by referee R. W. Stanton. A penalty was awarded to the Springboks, which Morkel converted. Cox was outraged by the whole incident, pointing out that 'If rugby football is to maintain its hold on the public and the young manhood of the country it is essential that such tactics should be exposed.'[29]

Further points accrued to the Springboks via a try by Reynecke, converted by Douglas Morkel. Spoors scored a try, the only time the tourists could cross the line, and Cherry Pillman converted. The Springboks were worthy winners 21-5. The match and the series were theirs.

A Sad Conclusion

Three days later, on the same field, the delayed game between WP and the British Isles team was played. The local team avenged their defeat early in the tour, winning 8-0. Finally, Smyth and his men took the mail ship back to Southampton, arriving in late September, ready to prepare for their home season. Four members of the tour party had decided to remain in South Africa.

On his arrival at Southampton, Rees was asked about the conduct of the team members off the field, as there had been persistent rumours in 'colonial' newspapers of excessive behaviour. Rees called these reports 'bunkum' and indicated that it would be hard to find a 'finer set of fellows'.

Leslie Cox, the most outspoken correspondent with the team, penned an overview of the tour, pointing out that if future tours were to be successful, the strongest possible teams had to be sent to confront the three southern hemisphere rugby countries. He lamented the 'disastrous' 1910 tour and trusted that the rugby authorities would not send another team 'for many a long day to come'. [30]

It would indeed be long enough – fourteen years before a British Isles team would again set foot in Africa. The reason for that break had nothing to do with decisions taken in London or Cape Town, but rather an event that took place on 28 June 1914 in Sarajevo.[31]

1910 TOURING PARTY
Managers – William Cail and Walter Rees

Backs
Mel Baker (Wales)*
Alexander Foster (Ireland)*
Noel Humphreys (England)
George Isherwood (England)*
Jack Jones (Wales)*
Arthur McClinton (Ireland)
Eric Milroy (Scotland)
Maurice Neale (England)*
Reg Plummer (Wales)
Jack Spoors (England)*
Charles Timms (Scotland)
Stanley Williams (Wales)*
Ken Wood (England)*

Forwards
Tom Smyth (Capt.) (Ireland)*
William Ashbey (Ireland)
Edward Crean (England)
#Frank Handford (England)*
Harry Jarman (Wales)*
Charles Pillman (England)*
Oliver Piper (Ireland)*
James Reid-Kerr (Scotland)
#Tom Richards (England)*
William Robertson (Scotland)
Dyne Fenton Smith (England)*
Robert Stevenson (Scotland)*
William Tyrrell (Ireland)
Phil Waller (Wales)*
#Jim Webb (Wales)*

Replacements
* Played in at least one Test

Charles Timms (1884–1958)

Charles Gordon Timms was born to Scottish parents on the Mount Heese Station in the state of Victoria, Australia. He and his brother Alec attended Geelong College and both excelled in all sporting codes.

Timms studied medicine at the University of Edinburgh and during his time there played rugby for the university. He was selected for the 1910 British Isles tour of South Africa, being one of the small number of players chosen who had not represented his country.

During the tour he played in just eleven of the twenty-four matches and was not one of the stars of the tour. He scored three tries from his position in the centre against Pretoria, Transvaal Country, and Border.

When war broke out Timms joined the Royal Army Medical Corps and was promoted to the rank of captain. He was attached to the 7th Battalion Royal Fusiliers. In July 1917 Timms was awarded the Military Cross (MC) for showing 'conspicuous gallantry' under 'incessant shell fire' as, 'quite regardless of personal danger', he attended to the wounded.

In the same month he was awarded a second MC when he continued to tend to the wounded and evacuate them from the frontlines, despite being 'nearly surrounded by the enemy'. Timms was awarded the MC on two further occasions, in both cases going forward almost into enemy lines to treat and rescue the wounded. Only three other soldiers in the entire British and Allied forces were awarded this tally of Military Crosses.

After the war Timms returned to Africa. He worked in central Africa and was based in the Protectorate of Somaliland when he was awarded the OBE in 1936. Three years later, when war broke out, aged fifty-five, he volunteered and once again served his country. (See *The London Gazette*, Nos 30188, 30183, 31119 & 31158)

5

THE 1924 BRITISH LIONS TOUR: COVE-SMITH'S BLUES

In the aftermath of the Great War and the Spanish flu pandemic which followed, it took rugby authorities nearly six years before they could organise the first post-war tour. The huge loss of life and economic disaster these events had entailed, for Britain and its colonies, was still weighing heavily on society. In the years between the world wars, just three Lions tours were to take place: to South Africa in 1924 and 1938, and to New Zealand in 1930.

The 1924 British Isles team to South Africa was captained by Dr Ronald Cove-Smith. Cove-Smith's squad was managed by Harry Packer who was born in England, but had played seven times for Wales. The touring squad included thirty-one players, the majority coming from England and Scotland. They ranged in age from nineteen to thirty-two, with the group of forwards being a full five years older, on average, than the backs. The average height of the squad was 5'11". Their colours would be 'all blue'.

Several key Home Union players could not afford to spend over three months away from home, notably Wavell Wakefield of England and A. L. Gracie of Scotland. The Admiralty also refused leave to players selected from their ranks. The loss here was of H. W. V. Stephenson, the 'best all-round three-quarter in the United Kingdom'. The tour party included four uncapped players.

Officially named the British Isles Rugby Union Team, this was the first team to be called the British Lions. The team travelled out on the *Edinburgh Castle*, arriving in Table Bay five days before the first match against Western Province Town and Country, played at Newlands on 12 July 1924.

Cove-Smith described his charges as 'a team of pals' and 'a level lot', but conceded that they were 'not the best that could be sent'. Harry Packer indicated that the team was full of 'fine sporting spirit'. Admitting that they had little first-hand knowledge of the local game, they dismissed reports that had circulated in the British press that South African rugby was 'down and out'. Instead they indicated that they were 'not at all afraid of any of the half-backs, full backs or forwards South Africa can put on the field'.[1]

The voyage to Cape Town had allowed the men to get to know each other well. Cove-Smith saw to it that the team exercised on deck every morning at 7 o'clock sharp. Members of the team were all-conquering in the deck games. To the amazement of their teammates, Arthur Young and Norman Brand performed high dives off the top deck of the liner while she re-coaled at anchor in Madeira!

When the *Edinburgh Castle* hove-to in Table Bay a welcoming flotilla of small boats soon surrounded it. On board these craft were not only representatives of the South African Rugby Football Board (SARFB), but other sports too, including tennis, soccer and even lawn bowls. On board one vessel was J. D. de Villiers, the president of the local referees' society, who was to accompany the team for the duration of the tour as the SARFB's representative.

A dinner attended by local dignitaries was held that night to welcome the team. Cove-Smith spoke, according to *The Sportsman*'s correspondent, 'poetically' of the 'spirit of brotherhood and good fellowship' that his team represented. He then described their arrival that morning and his first sight of Table Mountain 'in the half light, which lit up the crags and crannies ... grim and awesome'.[2] He declared his team ready to face the local teams cast in the same vein.

A Difficult Start

Even before the first match was played, a British Lion was seriously injured. After training and a long run on the second day in Cape Town, the team practised on a very wet Newlands ground on the eve of the match to be played there. Part of the practice was set aside to get used to the knee guards they would be wearing to play on the extremely hard grounds they would encounter. During this time one of the three full backs in the squad, Wilfred Gaisford, damaged his knee badly. His tour had ended before it began.

The match against Western Province Town and Country was played in front of 15,000 spectators on a sunny day. Speedy wing Bill Wallace of Northumberland scored the first try of the tour in the thirteenth minute, but Dan Drysdale missed the conversion. Fierce play followed until the twenty-seventh minute when Japie Krige, despairing of beating a 'defence that resolutely refused to be beaten', put over a drop goal. Three minutes later J. du Toit did manage to score an unconverted try and W. P. Town and Country led 7-3 at half-time. Just thirteen minutes into the second half Tom Holliday was heavily tackled and had to leave the field with a broken collarbone. Another unconverted try by Bill Wallace was not enough to save the day for the visitors. The game was lost 7-6.

Tom Holliday was playing centre when injured, although his position for his club was at full back. It was in that position that he had been chosen for the squad. Harry Packer had lost two of his three full backs in forty-eight hours. He called for a replacement for this position. Robert Henderson, the Scottish forward, also injured his knee during the practice and would not be able to play for several weeks.

Getting Going

Three days later, the Lions were back at Newlands facing the Combined W. P. Universities team. The visitors won this match 9-8. Arthur Young played superbly at scrum half and he had a hand in all three tries scored by the team. The first of these saw him beat his opposite number Dawie 'Pally' Truter (who would play twice for the Springboks in the series) and then send out a perfectly timed pass to his fly-half, Vince Griffiths, who scored. It was a 'glorious try, start to finish' according to those watching.[3] Further tries were scored by Tom Voyce and Ian Smith. Dan Drysdale at full back, who defended his line bravely and confidently, missed all three conversions.

Playing at fly-half for the Universities team was the University of Cape Town student Bennie Osler. With several South African selectors present he intercepted a 'wild' pass using his speed and then put in a neat cross kick which D. P. de Villiers collected and ran in to score.[4] Osler had just played himself into the Springbok team.

That night the team departed by train for Kimberley. Interviewed amongst the throngs seeing them off, Cove-Smith conceded that his team was still a bit 'sticky' and needed to improve.

In past tours the Griqualand West teams, playing on gravel pitches, took a fearsome toll on visiting teams. This time Dan Drysdale captained the Lions and his men thumped them by 26 points to nil. In the process they scored eight tries (Bill Wallace crossing five times). Just one try was converted by Doug Davies. Kimberley was experiencing a poor time financially, but a large crowd was still present at the contest. Emphasising the fact that this was still a mining town was the news that the Griqualand West wing had to be replaced on the morning of the match. He had blown his thumb off in a mining accident the previous day!

The Lions now spent twenty hours on the train to Salisbury (now Harare) in southern Rhodesia. During a stopover in Bulawayo, they had an impromptu game on the station with locals who had flocked there just to see the team pass through.

The Scot, Niel McPherson, led the Lions to an easy 16-3 victory over Rhodesia. Many of the spectators, standing on planks balanced on buckets, and sitting in their cars with the windshields lying horizontal to avoid reflecting the sun's rays, did not see much. The dust stirred up by the players lay heavily upon the field. The dam that supplied Salisbury with water had recently burst. Sir Charles Coghlan and his cabinet adjourned the parliamentary sitting to attend the match, having hosted a lunch for the team in the Meikles Hotel.

'Mercian', reporting for *The Athletic News*, was unimpressed by the referee C. F. Cranswick's, interpretations of the laws. For example, Steele, the local scrum half, 'gave the dummy' several times prior to putting the ball in at scrummage time. This ruse, Mercian pointed out, was never attempted by even the 'wiliest' of Welsh and English 'scrummage workers'![5]

To Packer's dismay, the news now came though that Kelvin Hendrie's injury sustained against Griqualand West was more serious than first thought (he would miss the next seven contests). In the Rhodesian match, Andrew Ross, the Scottish forward, was tackled as he kicked the ball, resulting in his tearing ligaments and muscle. He would play no further role in the tour.

On the Witwatersrand

The team left Salisbury station on Friday at 12.45 p.m. and arrived in Johannesburg on Monday at 4.34 am. After spending that night at the Carlton Hotel, their base on the Reef, they travelled to Potchefstroom where they defeated Western Transvaal 8-7 on Wednesday 30 July.

On Saturday 2 August, back in Johannesburg, Cove-Smith led his team to a 12-all draw with the powerful Transvaal team on the Wanderers ground. Transvaal were the reigning Currie Cup champions and in the previous two years had swept all before them. Their team had matured out of all recognition from the teams that represented the union in the early decades of their existence. There were still four miners playing, but more than half the team now came from Pretoria and also included three university students.

E. H. D. Sewell, the experienced British journalist, author and, in his younger days, accomplished professional cricketer and powerful rugby player, was following the tour. He contributed an article to the *Rand Daily Mail* on the morning of the Transvaal match. Not wanting to venture into the 'treacherous realms of prophecy', Sewell nevertheless provided a knowledgeable summing up of the respective strengths of the two teams. This, he concluded, was to be the 'severest' test the British team had yet faced on tour. The rarefied atmosphere and their 'thick-and-thin patriotic' supporters would assist Transvaal, but the British forwards alone carried more than 70 international caps between them. The Transvaal pack, most of whom had never seen the game played outside of South Africa, would have to 'rout' the visiting pack to have any chance, he thought. He did sound a word of caution. If the British pack did win the forward battle, they would have to use their possession wisely.

Sewell drew upon his lengthy experience of watching important games of rugby. He recalled the New Zealand-Wales clash of 1905, the Newport-South Africa clashes of both 1906 and 1912 and finally, the match between England and New Zealand at Crystal Palace in 1905, when England won the scrums and New Zealand the game, scoring five tries in the process. What the team did with the ball obtained from the scrum was all-important: 'That's the rub,' he concluded.[6]

On a beautiful Highveld winter's day, the match started with a bang. Herbert Waddell of Scotland, preferred to Vince Griffiths at fly-half, much to E. H. D. Sewell's chagrin, put over a drop after just two minutes. Transvaal responded with a try by Van Druten which was sensationally disallowed by the referee. Two minutes after that, Waddell broke through the Transvaal line to score a good try, which Tom Voyce converted. Nine points in nine minutes to the Lions.

A 'stern forward battle', as Sewell had predicted, now evolved and shortly before half-time Bosman converted a penalty to leave the half-time score 9-3 in favour of the tourists. Van Druten scored a try early in the second half after a 'clever piece of play' that saw him chip the ball over the advancing backline, collect it and score under the posts. Bosman converted. N. Hudson, playing centre for Transvaal, then put the local team into the lead for the first time, with a 'brilliant piece of opportunism', putting over a drop from far out.

Roy Kinnear was having a splendid game at centre and he broke through only for Rowe Harding to spill the last pass from

Reg Maxwell. Kinnear broke through again a few minutes later, and this time Harding held onto his pass to dot down. Voyce missed the conversion. The score was now tied at 12-all.

The visitors launched attack after attack, but Transvaal stood their ground, displaying fine 'fighting qualities'. The last ten minutes of the match were played at great pace and had the crowd on its feet. Just before full time Bill Wallace squandered the Lions' best chance when he held onto the ball with four teammates outside him and the line open. The score remained 12-all at full time. It was a 'creditable' performance by the Lions *The Athletic News* decided, and a fair result.[7]

The First Test Looms and Losses Mount

Cove-Smith's charges had by now played six games and lost just one. They had been together as a team for over a month and although there had been injuries, they had more than held their own. Now, however, the tour took a turn for the worse. The match following the draw with Transvaal was played against an Orange Free State Country XV in the small town of Kroonstad in the mielie (corn) growing belt of the Union.

The Lions gave a disappointing exhibition that was 'spiritless'. Possibly underestimating their opponents, they lost a dour, hard battle 6-0. Three days later they lost again, this time to Orange Free State on the Ramblers ground in Bloemfontein.

This match started sensationally for the visitors with Kinnear breaking through the middle, corkscrewing out of a tackle, and passing the ball to Wallace who dotted down after just two minutes. The conversion was missed. For the rest of the half there was no further score from either side. For almost the whole time the local side offered no attacks, only 'sheer grim dogged defensive work'.[8]

Early in the second half D. S. Hill converted a penalty for Orange Free State to level the score. The host's centres were both at Bloemfontein's Grey College and were '17 or 18'. They both played well. With the score level late in the game, one of them, Jimmy Wansbury, finally broke through the Lions line on his own 25-yard line and after making good ground passed to his schoolfellow, Sarel Marais, who scored. The Orange Free State 6-3 win was greeted with incredulity by their supporters.

Dan Drysdale, who had captained the Lions on the day, was injured late in the game and was no longer on the field when the try was scored. Once Wansbury broke through, the absence of a full back must have made his task easier. Drysdale suggested it was the 'prettiest' try scored against them on the tour and suggested the two schoolboys might play for the Springboks one day. The South African selectors agreed, and both were called up to play in the trial match prior to the first Test.

The tourists now took the long train trip down to Pietermaritzburg where, on Wednesday 13 August, they played Natal and drew 3-all. To rest players for the Test, just three days away, Packer had to chop and change his line-up. Stan Harris was drafted in to play full back and had an awful game. Herbert Waddell was forced to play as a forward. Ian Smith saved the day for the Lions, scoring a breakaway try from deep inside his own half.

Packer was desperate to find additional fit players and it was suggested that T. E. S. Francis, a Cambridge 'blue' who was in the Union, might be drafted, or D. Cunningham of Ireland, who lived in the Cape. Harold Davies of Wales was already in the Union, having arrived on the latest mail ship, but would not be travelling to Durban. He would meet the team in Johannesburg on the eve of the second Test. The Irish fly-half W. A. Cunningham was also on his way. These reinforcements were urgently needed.

On their way to Durban a fire broke out in one of the railway carriages. Fanned by the rush of wind, the conflagration spread. Tom Voyce acted swiftly. He sprinted through the train and managed to alert the driver, who halted the locomotive. This allowed the train staff to put the fire out. The fire had started, it was later confirmed, in the compartment of 'four well-known players playing cards'. A cigarette had been carelessly discarded. The press was unimpressed. The deteriorating record of the tourists and this event led some to muse that the Lions should spend less time on 'feting and entertainments' and more time 'preparing and practising'.[9]

The press was also reporting that scouts for the League club Wigan were in the Union and having success in signing up players to join the paid ranks. Wigan already had three South Africans in their squad, led by former Springbok A. J. 'Attie' van Heerden who had been in the 1921 Springbok team that toured New Zealand. Now the 6'2" Van Rooyen of Steynburg (sic) was going to move to Wigan and two other players, Burger of Transvaal and Van der Spuy (also referred to as Van der Sparoy), had agreed to move. The amateur game was under attack in the Union.[10]

First Test: An Optical Delusion

The match of 16 August 1924 at Kingsmead Cricket Ground was the first rugby Test to be hosted in Durban. The match referee was L. D. Oakley, president of the Griqualand West RU, and the match was played on a well-grassed field.

The injuries to the Lions squad had continued to grow. During the Natal match Young had been injured and Waddell had a 'twisted groin'. Waddell was still selected for the Test, with Herbert Whitley his half-back partner. Waddell and Whitley had only played together once on the tour. Drysdale was pronounced fit and he was selected at full back. The pack of forwards, including Cove-Smith as captain, was much the same as had faced Orange Free State a week earlier.

The problems facing the Lions management have been documented. The Springboks also had their problems. The last Springbok Test had been played in New Zealand nearly three years previously. The great distances and slow communication in the Union meant it was hard for the local selectors to evaluate players. Dr Pierre 'P. K.' Albertyn was chosen to lead the Springboks. Two of the five selectors had never seen him play rugby! Members of the Lions squad probably knew his style of play better than the selectors, as he had played rugby at a high level while studying in England. Back in the Union, he played for the unfancied small union of South Western Districts. His appointment was met with 'amazement' by most South Africans.[11] He himself was 'flabbergasted'.[12] It was a brave choice by the local selectors.

Phil Mostert of Western Province was asked to lead the Springbok forwards. He was joined by four fellow forwards who had faced New Zealand in the 1921 team: Nicolaas du Plessis, Theuns Krüger, Mervyn Ellis and Alf Walker. There was thus a good blend of old and new in the pack. This pack, however, was lighter than the famous 1912 Springbok pack and there were murmurings that Cove-Smith and his men would prove too strong for them. The Springbok backs were a different story. Only Walter Clarkson of Natal had played for the Springboks previously. Six out of seven were winning their first cap. There were three Natalians in the team: Walker, Clarkson, and Cecil 'Bill' Payn. Western Province provided the most, five players, including the new fly-half, Bennie Osler.

Both teams stayed at the Federal Hotel in Durban and on the eve of the Test, the two captains attended a short ceremony where two trees were planted at the 'International Ground' to celebrate the first Natal Test. Every seat in the ground was sold and by the time the teams walked out at Kingsmead on the Saturday, a 'delightful' day, there were more than 10,000 spectators present.

Headlines after the match said it all: 'Disappointing Test'. The forward battle that was expected did take centre stage, but the disappointment was linked to the preponderance of kicking, instead of ball carrying attacks, by both sides.

The first points came after eighteen minutes, via a superb long-range drop goal from Osler, the first of the 108 points he would score for his country. By this stage, the tactics used by the South Africans were plain to see. Osler and Albertyn, who continually played at inside centre, focused all their attentions on poor Waddell, Osler's opposing number. Time and again Waddell got the ball and the two men together. Both Springboks were very quick, with Osler especially having 'lightning quickness off the mark'.[13] The disruption to the Lions' backline was complete. 'Mercian', reporting for *The Athletic News*, noted that Uncle Dobbin, now retired from the game and a South African selector, had been to most of the tour games. It is possible that this idea was his.

The Lions' poor backline passing and constant Springbok pressure finally paid off towards the end of the first half. However, the Springbok try was to prove controversial. Clarkson broke away and raced down the right-hand side of the field. Desperate defence was required and Smith, the Lions left wing, was left facing two charging Springboks, since Aucamp was outside of Clarkson. As Clarkson flung out the pass to his wing, Smith attempted to intercept it, but only succeeded in knocking it backwards. Aucamp collected the ball and scored the try.

Most of the spectators, sitting close to the field and on low stands, thought that Aucamp had knocked the ball on and assumed his effort would be disallowed. However, Mr Oakley, closely following the play, had no hesitation in awarding the try. Some in the crowd were unhappy. Osler was unable to convert and the score at half-time was 7-0 to the Springboks.

The Sportsman's correspondent 'PHF' (P. H. Francis) was careful in his reporting. His initial reaction, seated as he was far from the incident, was to assume the knock on had occurred. After the match he interviewed Cove-Smith, Smith, Aucamp and the referee. All were certain: the try was fair. It was, he suggested, an 'optical delusion' that Aucamp had knocked the ball on.[14]

If the first half had belonged to South Africa, the second belonged to the Lions. As locals had feared, the cohesive and experienced British pack slowly began to assert themselves. Whitley, the smallest man on the field at 9 stone 9 lbs , at the base of that pack, was playing bravely and well. Waddell, however, was still 'off his game' according to the *Rand Daily Mail* and did not 'combine well' with his backline according to *The Sportsman*.

After twenty-three minutes of play in the second half, the Lions scored a try under the poles. There is some confusion as to who scored it. *The Athletic News* correspondent suggested it was Herbert Whitley, but in official records it was credited to Freddie Blakiston.[15] The conversion was missed.

Uncapped Reg Maxwell, playing in the centre, was having a torrid time, like Waddell. Albertyn, his opposite number, was playing the game of his life. His shrewd positional play and generalship was crucial to the Springbok cause on the day. Maxwood went to ground late in the game and was led off the field in considerable pain. His shoulder blade muscles had been badly torn. He, too, would play no further part in the tour. The best player in the British backline was Drysdale. Osler peppered him with high kicks and he fielded them all fearlessly; in one instance close to his try line he was hit so hard by the Springbok forwards as he claimed the ball that he was 'nearly knocked into the stand'.[16] Despite a 'ceaseless struggle' between the packs with Brand, MacPherson and McVicker (who had a broken nose) to the fore for the Lions, the final whistle sounded with the score 7-3 in favour of the Springboks.

The emphasis on kicking and not running the ball was deprecated in the press. Albertyn's unobtrusive yet brilliant play earned him good reviews. There was agreement that the Test had not been one to savour. The *Rand Daily Mail* summed the contest up thus: 'In the first half South Africa scored their seven points and were worth every one of them; in the second half Britain scored three points and were worth twice as many.'[17]

Both teams now entrained for Johannesburg where the second Test would be contested. The Springboks had a week to recover. The Lions had to face the Witwatersrand team on Wednesday afternoon on the Wanderers ground. That ground would also host the Test.

Second Test: In the Ascendant

The Witwatersrand match, watched by 7,000, was lost 10-6 by the Lions. Such was the number of their injured players, they struggled to put a complete team onto the pitch. This midweek game saw a superb performance by the second-string Transvaal full back, 'I. B.' de Villiers, who scored all the local team's points via a long-range penalty and lengthy drop goal and a further penalty. Ian Smith 'shot' past four defenders to score the lone Lions try.

Tom Voyce missed the conversion but converted a penalty. Once again, the Lions half-backs played below par.

It is noteworthy that four members of the Lions squad played in the first Test, the Witwatersrand game and then again in the second Test. They were Ian Smith on the wing and three forwards: Doug Davies, Doug Marsden-Jones and Niel MacPherson, who captained the Lions in the Witwatersrand match. Packer changed but three of his players for the second Test, all backline players. Harold Davies of Wales, the first replacement called for, who played his first match against Witwatersrand, replaced the injured Maxwell. Young came in at scrum half for Whitley and, on the wing, Rowe Harding replaced Wallace.

The *Rand Daily Mail* suggested 'IB' should replace Jackie Tindall as Springbok full back in the Test. The South African selectors were shrewd and realised that, since his impressive contribution in New Zealand with the 1921 team, he had slowed down considerably. Instead, they brought in young Nico Bosman. Clarkson had been injured in the first Test and he was replaced by Jack Bester to partner Albertyn. Pally Truter became the new scrum half as Willem Myburgh was getting married.

The Lions team was not too down in the dumps. On the Tuesday afternoon the South African Party Woman's Club had organised an afternoon tea for the team. Hosted by the Governor General's wife, Mrs Patrick Duncan, and Mrs L. Blackwell, the function was well attended by many 'girl helpers'. There was impromptu dancing, and the 'tea' went on until darkness fell.

Saturday 23 August was a very warm day in Johannesburg. Officially 15,000 attended the second Test, but entry controls were lax, and it was suggested that a further 5,000 could possibly have been present, from all corners of the Union. The former Oxford 'blue' V. H. 'Boet' Neser refereed the match.

During the first Test the referee, Mr Oakley, had found it hard to distinguish between the bottle green and dark blue jerseys (both teams also wore dark shorts). When the Springboks appeared on the Wanderers field, their jerseys had a gold band about an inch wide sewn around the middle below the badge.[18]

The first half saw a hard-fought forward battle with neither side dominating. Mr Neser awarded numerous penalties, not allowing the game to flow. One of the penalties was conceded in front of their poles by the Lions, easily converted by Osler. E. H. D. Sewell felt the awarding of this penalty unfair, as both sides had been guilty of 'foot up' and Mr Neser only decided to see this close to the Lions poles. At half-time South Africa led 3-0.

Early in the second half, two things occurred in a short space of time that changed the momentum of the match. Firstly, Roy Kinnear came 'swinging through the centre in great style' and beat the defence. He passed to Freddie Blakiston, who 'kept the yard lead' and scored a try under the poles. Mr Neser adjudged the pass to Blakiston forward. Harry Packer was furious. It was, he suggested, 'as fair a try as was ever scored'. Secondly, a few minutes later Dan Drysdale, who had once again been giving a polished performance at full back, injured his leg. He became a passenger and Robert Howie had to withdraw from the scrum to cover for him. The South African pack began to steamroller the Lions.

Ken Starke went over and shortly thereafter Phil Mostert, with two defenders clinging to his back. Osler converted the second try and the Springboks led 11-0. The 'spirit to win' had understandably left the tourists, and South Africa piled on the agony. First Jack van Druten, and then, just before the final whistle, the Springbok captain, Albertyn, both scored. Osler failed with both conversions. The final whistle saw the Springboks win by the large margin of 17-0.

Apart from Drysdale's injury, Brand had to have fluid drained from his injured knee after the match and would not play again on the tour. Young, Kinnear and Smith all had minor injuries. The pressmen all gave the same verdict. The *Rand Daily Mail* suggested the Springboks had 'overwhelmed' Cove-Smith's men; *The Sportsman* felt the Springboks had been 'flattered' by the score but had 'overrun' the Lions; *The Athletic News* that 'the Africans had assumed ascendency in all departments'. Criticism of the referee was voiced, and Mr Neser would not take charge of a further match on the tour. *The Sportman*'s correspondent was the most outspoken: 'Refereeing in South Africa is, well, hardly of a high-class standard generally.'[19]

A *Purple Patch Before the Third Test*

There was no let-up in the demands on the visitors. Four days later they lost 6-0 to a Pretoria team. They only had fifteen fit men available to select. Roy Kinnear had to play as a forward, Davies at full back. After this match, the team attended a dance in the city hall, where Mr Edgar Adler's Syncopated Orchestra entertained the large number of guests. The mayoress wore a 'charming frock of peacock blue charmeuse embroidered in silver, with hip draperies of georgette, peacock-blue crepe de chine with a girdle of ostrich feathers'.

Thereafter, the Lions headed south to Kimberley. On 30 August they beat a strong Cape Colony team on gravel. Bill Cunningham of Ireland met the team there and was immediately included at fly-half to give the 'overworked' Waddell a break. Cove-Smith pointed to this game as being important to him, breaking the series of losses the team had endured. Further good wins against North Eastern Districts and Border followed in early September, but in the run-up to the third Test, they lost to Eastern Province 6-14. To attempt to rest the first-string players for the Test, there were some odd selections for this match. For example, the forward Tom Voyce played wing. The good news was Drysdale returned from injury.

The Lions and South Africa both made changes to their teams for the third Test at the Crusaders Ground, Port Elizabeth, on 13 September 1924. The Lions half-backs were Whitley and Cunningham and Vince Griffiths moved into the centre. In the forwards, Brand was replaced by Voyce. Marsden-Jones and Hendrie were injured and were replaced by McVicker and Henderson. On the Springboks side, local man Jack Slater replaced Aucamp on the wing, Pierre Albertyn got his third centre partner in a row, this time Sas de Kock replaced Jack Bester and Dauncie Devine took over at scrum half. Payn and

Mostert were replaced by 'BV' Vanderplank and Paul la Grange among the forwards.

Billy Millar refereed the third Test and did a good job of it. This time the talking point of the contest was not the rugby, but the weather. Port Elizabeth is not known as the 'windy city' for nothing. The wind howled across the field. The result was that it was extremely hard to kick or even pass accurately. Both sides fell back on strictly 'orthodox' play. It was a 'hard, gruelling game'.

After eighteen minutes, Cunningham scored an unconverted try. Seven minutes later Van Druten replied. Van Druten's try should have been converted by Osler, but the ball toppled over and Voyce was then able to prevent the conversion attempt. The score at half-time was 3-all.

The second half was no different. The Lions missed two penalty chances. One of these was right in front of the Springbok poles: 'It was not to be; Drysdale must have had the left boot on the right foot for he missed the easiest of kicks.'[20] Cunningham and Whitley comprehensively outplayed Devine and Osler, but the Lions failed to avail themselves of chances that were presented. Albertyn once again marshalled his men well and the closing stages were 'fought out desperately'. He recalled the Springboks defending like 'demons' in their own twenty-five for much of the half. 'The game was a disappointing one from everybody's point of view – spectators, Britons, and Springboks alike.'[21] Cove-Smith, recalling the match in later years, understandably saw matters in a more positive light, as a 'ding dong forward battle … a hard, well fought tussle with many points of good technique'.[22]

Almost on the final whistle the local wing, Slater, broke through and, against the run of play, looked like he would go over and clinch the game, but Stan Harris put in a wonderful tackle and saved the day. The 3-all draw meant that the Springboks had won the series.

Fourth Test and the Last Leg
On their way to Cape Town and the last two contests, the Lions faced, and defeated, Pierre Albertyn's South Western Districts side

in a fast-paced game 12-6 in the small Karoo town of Oudtshoorn. Bill Cunningham now left the team as he had to return to his job in Johannesburg and Arthur Young departed via mail ship back to Britain.

On the Friday before the fourth Test at Newlands heavy rain fell overnight. The first spectators were already at Newlands gates at 6.45 am, while it was still dark. Mr Robeck, the Newlands groundsman, expected 20,000 spectators, but in the end only 18,000 attended, a new record nevertheless for Test matches played at the ground.

The fourth Test, a 'cracker' of a game, was played on 20 September 1924, at Newlands, Cape Town. Cove-Smith was a fan of Newlands. 'What a pleasing ground is this Newlands after a scorching tour on sun-baked pitches...'[23]

The WPRFU organised food and music to keep the spectators happy, although the jazz music planned could not be played until the 'horns' of the loudspeakers had been emptied of rainwater! Ginger beer and cakes were sold to the crowd and 10 gallons of milk had been delivered while it was still dark to provide warm tea and coffee for the masses. This was needed by those assembled, as by midday 'the nor'westerly wind was pouring dark and heavy rain clouds through the gap between Table Mountain and Devil's Peak.' On the four corners of the field yellow and green flags fluttered.

Herbert Waddell, back in at fly-half, kicked off at 4.10 and Springbok pressure was applied from the start, with the Springbok captain Albertyn missing scoring by inches when he was held up. Osler missed a drop goal attempt. Albertyn's centre partner, Bester, opened the scoring when Kenny Starke on the wing flipped him an inside pass at pace to send him over with ease. Osler was doing brilliant work handling the wet and muddy ball and after twenty-seven minutes of the game he sent the ball down the backline again. When it got to Starke, instead of running as he was expected to do, he took a drop goal from 50 yards out, with the wet ball, and put it over. Years later Albertyn was to recall that surprising drop as being 'magnificent'. Tom Voyce put over a penalty late in the half for the tourists. Half-time saw South Africa ahead 7-3.[24]

Thirty seconds into the second half, while some spectators were still enjoying their half-time ginger beer and cream cakes behind the pavilion, Kenny Starke charged down the clearance kick from the kick-off and scored to make it 10-3. But there was still a lot of rugby to play. Harris, on the wing, put in a strong run and was only just brought down by Bosman at full back. Then Theuns Krüger, the Transvaal hooker, received a 'nasty jar' and had to leave the field. Now with South Africa fielding only fourteen players, the Lions began to fight back.

Quick thinking by Cove-Smith and Rowe Harding sent Harris over to narrow the deficit to 10-6. Kenny Starke had not finished, however. Albertyn intercepted a pass, flicked it on to his partner Bester, who put Starke away for an unconverted try. Voyce replied quickly for the tourists but finally Slater, the Eastern Province winger, sealed the game with the last try for the Springboks, who ran out 16-9 winners. Clem Thomas recalls this match as being an 'absolute cracker of a game ... the perfect game of rugby football'.[25]

On the Thursday after the fourth Test, the Lions ended their tour on a high note, beating Western Province 8-6. Dan Drysdale, however, did not have a happy end to his tour as he was knocked out cold and carried off the field. Cove-Smith led the team for the last time in this, his thirteenth match, and scored the last try of the tour and then converted it himself. In the tour as a whole the Lions had only managed to convert ten of the forty-five tries they had scored. Cove-Smith was making a point!

Tom Voyce, a forward, was the top scorer on the tour with 37 points. To tour South Africa and win you need a good goal kicker to take advantage of the conditions. In the Test series, South Africa had scored 43 points to their opponents' 15. All told, the Lions had won nine and lost nine matches with three drawn contests.

In his recollections Cove-Smith noted the difficulties of a rugby tour of South Africa. The long distances on cold trains, playing at high altitude and then on the coast, and then back at altitude, the excessive hospitality, the heat, and the hard fields and harder teams made up of big men. Though he ended his recollections of the 1924 tour by stressing that 'The success of such a tour, however, cannot be merely measured by the points garnered or lost, but more by the points of contact that can thereby be established between men of different upbringing and outlook.'[26]

Cove-Smith's generous memories of the tour were reflected in the team send-off from the docks in Cape Town. A great crowd accompanied the team to the mail ship and, as the vessel pulled away from the dockside, cheers rang out.

Home

The *Edinburgh Castle* reached Southampton on 13 October. Cove-Smith and Packer gave interviews to local pressmen before disembarking. Cove-Smith admitted that he was bringing back a 'lot of crocks' and some who would not play rugby again during 1924. He singled out, on the Springbok side, Frank Mellish, Phil Mostert and the 'wily' Pierre Albertyn for their solid abilities and Jack van Druten for his speed around the field. It seemed to the Lions that Van Druten had played as both a forward and a back! Cove-Smith felt that the 1924 vintage of Springboks was not, however, as good as that of 1912.

Cove-Smith singled out seven players in his squad who had been the 'stalwarts': all were forwards. Of those he mentioned, three – Blakiston, Davies and McVicker – had played fourteen of the matches, and one, MacPherson, fifteen. He might have mentioned the wing Harris who also played fifteen times, and the 'overworked' Waddell and Rowe Harding who both played fourteen times amongst the backs. Cove-Smith concluded that the squad's weakness was at 'halves and centre'.[27]

Both Packer and Cove-Smith were closely quizzed about South African refereeing. They were diplomatic. The problems, they felt, were merely differing 'interpretations', nothing more. 'We have no grumble,' Cove-Smith stressed, suggesting it was 'newspaper guff'. He was also indignant when asked if they had 'neglected fitness for social entertainment'.[28]

The *Athletic News* correspondent was not impressed by aspects of the tour. It was, he concluded, 'not so much a rugby tour as hard labour'.[29] The schedule of twenty-one games was also 'overcrowded' and should be reduced. He had to concede that when the Springboks had toured Britain in 1912, they had played twenty-seven matches and the 1906–7 visitors had played twenty-nine games, but these teams had slept in 'comfortable hotels every night', whereas the Lions had spent many nights on trains. He agreed with P. H. Francis, who concluded that the tour had only been a 'qualified success' and had offered a number of lessons if other such visits were to be considered.[30]

As the 1924 Lions tour neared its end, the All Black tour of England, Wales, Ireland, and France was just beginning. On the same day the Lions and Springboks faced each other in the third Test in Port Elizabeth, the All Blacks won their first tour game against Devonshire. The All Black 'Invincibles' under Cliff Porter would play thirty-two matches on this tour – and win every one.

Cove-Smith would score a try for England against the All Blacks in the Test at Twickenham and eight other 1924 Lions would play in the three Home Union Tests against Porter's men. Scotland declined to host the All Blacks on this tour.[31] If one includes the Scots who played internationals in the 1925 Five Nations Tournament (which they won), then two-thirds of the 1924 Lions squad played at the very highest level in the months following the completion of the tour. This disproves the suggestions that Cove-Smith was asked to lead an under-strength team to the Union.

Author Clem Thomas in *The History of the British Lions* quotes Rowe Harding's thoughtful conclusions on this tour. After dealing with the difficulties of touring in South Africa and dismissing the suggestion of 'dissipation' having anything to do with the results, he pointed out that every player on such a tour had to be 'first class'. He also took a dim view of the attitude of the British rugby authorities, who, he felt, treated the colonies with 'condescension'. New Zealand, and to a lesser extent South Africa, had become, whilst operating within the bounds of amateurism, far more organised and professional in their preparation of their rugby players and teams. These attitudes were to be reflected in the outcome of tours and Test matches in the 1920s and 1930s.[32]

1924 TOUR SQUAD
Manager – Harry Packer
Ronald Cove-Smith (Capt.) (England)*
A. Frederick Blakiston (England)*
J.H. Bordass (England)
Michael Bradley (Ireland)
T. Norman Brand (Ireland)*
James Clinch (Ireland)
#William Cunningham (Ireland)*
#Harold Davies (Wales)
Douglas Davies (Scotland)*
Dan Drysdale (Scotland)*
Wilfred Gaisford (England)
Vincent Griffiths (Wales)
W. Rowe Harding (Wales)*
Stanley Harris (England)*
R. G. Henderson (Scotland)*
Kelvin Hendrie (Scotland)*
Thomas Holliday (England)
Robert Howie (Scotland)*
Roy Kinnear (Scotland)*
Douglas Marsden-Jones (Wales)*
Reginald Maxwell (England)*
Niel MacPherson (Scotland)*
Jim McVicker (Ireland)*
William Roche (Ireland)
Andrew Ross (Scotland)
Ian Smith (Scotland)*
A. Thomas Voyce (England)*
Herbert Waddell (Scotland)*
William Wallace (England)*
Herbert Whitley (England)*
Arthur Young (England)*

Replacement
* Played in at least one Test

The 1891 British Isles touring team to South Africa.

Above: The first match of the tour,
British Isles *vs* Cape Colony, 9 July 1891
in Cape Town.

Right: The 1891 British Isles tour
captain, W. E. Maclagan.

Travelling by horse cart was common for the early British teams.

The second Test at the Eclectic Cricket Ground in Kimberley, 29 August 1891.

The 1896 British Isles touring team to South Africa .

Right: The 1903 British Isles tour captain, Mark Morrison.

Below: The 1903 British Isles touring team to South Africa.

Bottom: British team for the third and final Test in Cape Town, 12 September 1903.

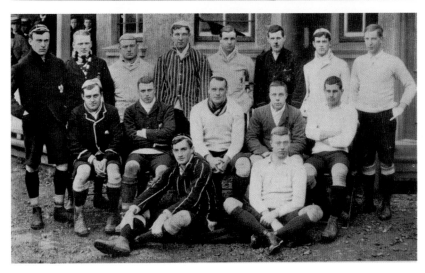

Above: The 1910 British Isles touring team to South Africa. Captain Tommy Smyth fourth from left, second row.

Left: The 1910 tour Souvenir issue.

Below: Action from the final Test at Newlands, 1924. A British player is collared by Spingbok Alf Walker.

Above: The Springbok team for the third Test in Port Elizabeth, 1924. The captain, Pierre K Albertyn, third from left, middle row, had come straight from the famous Guys Hospital to captain South Africa.

Right: The 1924 tour Souvenir issue.

Below: Line-out action from the first Test, Ellis Park, 1938. The Lions scrum half waiting for the ball is Jimmy Giles. The Springboks' No. 9 is hooker Jan Lotz and No. 10 prop Fanie Louw.

Sam Walker leads the Lions onto the field in the last Test in Cape Town.

Springbok scrum half Danie Craven on the break in the first Test.

Above left: Haydn Tanner played scrum half in the second Test in Port Elizabeth. One of the greats of Welsh rugby, he played for Wales from 1935 to 1949.

Above right: First Test, 1938. Lions vice-captain Viv Jenkins kicks for touch from a penalty.

The 1938 British Lions of Sam Walker on board the *Stirling Castle*.

The 1955 British Lions touring team.

Cliff Morgan scores, first Test, Ellis Park.

Dickie Jeeps is tackled by Salty du Rand. First Test, Ellis Park.

Above left: Centre Jeff Butterfield was one of the stars of the 1955 British Lions.

Above right: Cliff Morgan leads the Lions onto the field in the third Test, Pretoria, in the absence of Robin Thompson.

Right: Big Welsh lock Rhys Williams was one of the stalwarts on the 1955 South African tour.

Below: The 1962 British Lions touring team.

Bottom: Springbok centre John Gainsford scores in the first Test, 1962, drawn 3-all.

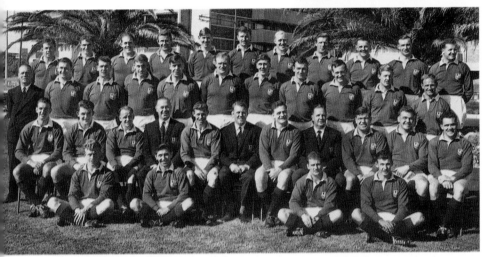

Above left: Mike Campbell-Lamerton in action against the Southern Universities at Newlands.

Left: Lions No. 8 Alun Pask scores vs WP, 1962.

Below: The 1968 British Lions touring team.

Above right: Dawie de Villiers kicks, first Test. Jan Ellis behind him, Jim Telfer on the ground.

Right: Peter Stagg wins line-out ball for the Lions ahead of Frik du Preez, first Test, Pretoria.

Below: John Pullin knocked out cold in the third Test, Newlands.

Left: Lions captain Tom Kiernan scored 35 points with the boot for the Lions in the Test series.

Below left: Lions prop John O'Shea is about to be sent off vs Eastern Transvaal at Springs, 1968. Referee Mr Bert Woolley and Lions flanker Mick Doyle try to restrain him.

Below: Roger Young, Gareth Edwards and Jeff Young before going down into a Witwatersrand mine.

J. P. R. Williams on the run vs Western
Province, Newlands, 1974.

Mervyn Davies
in action for the
Lions, first Test,
Newlands, 1974.

The Battle of Boet
Erasmus, third Test,
Port Elizabeth, with
Bobby Windsor,
Hannes Marais and
J. P. R. Williams in
the thick of things.

Lions captain
Willie John
McBride
leads the way
vs Orange
Free State,
Bloemfontein,
with Fergus
Slattery and Ian
Maclauchlan in
support.

The Lions
of 1974 had
plenty to laugh
about: Phil
Bennett, Roger
Uttley, Bobby
Windsor and Ian
McGeechan in
the second Test,
Pretoria.

A triumphant
Willie John
McBride
celebrates the
series victory
after the 3rd Test.

Above left: 1980 British Lions captain Bill Beaumont.

Top right: Lions flanker John O'Driscoll in action vs Northern Transvaal.

Above right: The 1980 Lions front row of Graham Price, Peter Wheeler and Fran Cotton.

Springbok flanker Rob Louw and Maurice Colclough having a bit of a scrap, with Peter Wheeler, Graham Price, John O'Driscoll (No. 6) and Theuns Stofberg, Louis Moolman and Kevin de Klerk standing by.

Above: Alan Bateman and Neil Back in action vs Emerging Springboks, Wellington.

Below left: 1997 British Lions captain Martin Johnson.

Below right: Rob Kearney scores, second Test, 2009.

6

THE 1938 BRITISH LIONS TOUR: THE END OF AN ERA AND THE BLUE JERSEY

The rumblings of war were becoming ever louder across the world when Sam Walker led his team of twenty-nine British Lions onto the *Stirling Castle* in Southampton on 21 May 1938 for the voyage to South Africa.

Two months previously the Rugby Football Union had announced the names of the players who had been selected. Several players had been unable to make the tour that would mean being away from home for more than four months. Among those men were three of the Home Union captains: Peter Cranmer of England, Cliff Jones of Wales, and Wilson Shaw of Scotland. Ulster and Ireland captain Sam Walker was asked to lead the team. Major Bernard Hartley, a former England player and the Army representative on the RFU, was asked to manage the side. H. A. Haig Smith, secretary of the Barbarian Football Club, was his deputy.

The squad contained nine players from England, eight each from Ireland and Wales and four from Scotland, and was a mixture of experience and youth. Five of the players had never been capped for their countries. Fifteen of the squad were backs and just fourteen forwards were selected. Bearing in mind the Springbok reputation for dominating the forward battle, the intention of the Lions to play a fast-paced, open game using their backs was clear for all to see.

The task the Lions faced in 1938 was a monumental one. The Springboks had not lost a series since 1896, when Johnny Hammond had led the team from the British Isles to victory. During 1937 the South African team had travelled to Australasia where they had defeated Australia twice and then won the Test series 2-1 in New Zealand. The team the Lions would face was thus a proven and battle-hardened one. On the Springbok side, only two players were no longer available for the series: the captain, Philip Nel, had famously confirmed his retirement from the game by hurling his boots into the ocean en route back to the Union, and the centre Louis Babrow was studying abroad.

Arrival and Early Games in the Cape

The *Stirling Castle* drew into Cape Town harbour at dawn on 4 June. South African rugby officials and players, led by their president Theo 'Sport' Pienaar, went on board and many interested bystanders were present to welcome the team. Press representatives conducted interviews and the team left the vessel to attend a luncheon hosted by the mayor of Cape Town, William Foster. In response to the welcoming speeches, Hartley indicated his team would 'do their utmost' during the tour.

In the afternoon, the squad had the opportunity to stretch their legs and put in some practice on the Green Point Track field, located near the harbour. During the practice two of South Africa's most experienced forwards, 'Boy' Morkel and Phil Mostert, were invited by Walker and Hartley to coach the forwards in the 3-4-1 scrumming method employed so successfully by the Springboks. The Home Union teams employed the 3-2-3 scrum, and it required the adapting of body and feet positions to be able to maximise their scrumming abilities.[1]

The team then returned to the *Stirling Castle*, which set off around Cape Point and headed east along the South African coast. After a brief stop in Port Elizabeth, the team arrived in East London harbour on the morning of 7 June. After seventeen days of travelling, the team could finally disembark. They had four days to lose their 'sea-legs' and prepare for the first match against the team from Border on Saturday 11 June. Joining the team in East London were Dick Luyt and Mac Strachan. Luyt, an ex-Springbok, had been appointed by the South African Rugby Union to act as the liaison officer for the team and Strachan would act as their baggage master for the duration of the tour. Both tasks were demanding.

The South African Rugby Football Board (SARFB) was providing a weekly allowance to each player and this was distributed by Luyt. He was also required to deal with the media and make sure that the social arrangements ran smoothly. Strachan had to ensure that over 150 suitcases and other items of personal baggage were conveyed safely between hotels, railway stations and ships and that everything arrived on time and in good order.

There was a great deal of interest in the early games, as the players were almost all unknown to the South African public. John Sacks, writing in the *Rand Daily Mail*, cautioned his readers to hold off on their opinions of the team until at least six weeks had passed. Only in the week preceding the first Test, he felt, would the true nature of the abilities of the squad be fully revealed. Early 'setbacks' should, accordingly, not be taken too seriously.[2]

The Border team had been carefully chosen for the first match. They were bound to be competent, but were not in the top echelon of local provincial teams. They fielded three Springboks in their ranks. Over 10,000 spectators, a new record for East London, were present when Walker led his team out in their blue jerseys, white shorts, and blue stockings with green piping. The initial exchanges confirmed what many had believed would be the Lions' playing style: they moved the ball wide quickly and players tried to exploit any gap in the Border defence. Twice Lions players crossed the try line in the early exchanges, and on both occasions the referee called them back for an infringement. Playing at full back, Vivian Jenkins, elected vice-captain on board the *Stirling Castle* by the team, missed two attempts at goal. After this disappointing start for the Lions, as often happens, the team under pressure scored first via a penalty when Walker went offside. Border led 3-0.

The Lions responded well and after quick backline movements Ernest Unwin scored a try. Walker took over kicking duties, but also missed the conversion. A few minutes later Jeff Reynolds put Unwin through for his second try, which Jenkins converted. The lack of cohesion of the Lions was now becoming clearer to see. First, Roy Leyland dropped a pass with the try line at his mercy, and then a clearance kick did not find the touchline but a Border player, and the local team scored a converted try. The half-time score was 8-all. Duncan Macrae scored the match-winning try early in the second half, which Jenkins failed to convert. The Border fly-half, Kopke, missed four attempts at goal during the second half. The final score was 11-8. It had not been a convincing win for the Lions.

Walker's men now began to get a taste of what touring in South Africa was like. That night over 1,000 attended a function at the Colosseum Tea Room. Just two of the touring team were married men and the large number of young ladies present testified to the popularity of the men wearing Lions blazers!

Sunday was a rest day and on Monday morning the team set off on the first of many train journeys. It took over twenty-six hours for the train to reach Kimberley, where they were to face Griqualand West on Wednesday afternoon. Major Hartley was so dismayed upon learning of the length of the trip that he asked Dick Luyt to contact the Griqua authorities and cancel all social arrangements prior to the match.

Leaden skies and an icy wind met the team in Kimberley. They also met an unsympathetic referee. Early in the match the Griquas scrum half broke around the blind side and passed to his schoolboy winger Jannie Engelbrecht. Engelbrecht appeared to have been forced out short of the try line, but the three points were confirmed by the referee. The conversion went astray. Jenkins missed two penalty attempts before Walker, and then Ivor Williams, crossed for tries. Jenkins converted one of the tries to leave the half-time score 8-3 in favour of the visitors.

The second half belonged to the visitors, who managed three tries and a penalty by Walker. Of the five Lion tries just two, however, were converted and Walker employed no fewer than four kickers, including himself. The final score was 22-9 to the Lions, with Griquas scoring a try on the stroke of full time.

A dance and banquet were held in the City Hall after the game. The following morning the Lions left Kimberley for Cape Town. Once again, the trip would take over a day to complete, thus leaving the squad one day to prepare for the game against Western Province Town and Country at Newlands. At each station where the train halted, the players would alight and walk about to stretch their legs. On one occasion some Lions players even ran up and down passing a leather cushion from the carriage.

This first match at Newlands did not go well for the Lions. They went down 11-8 in front of 25,000 spectators. Yet commentators were impressed by the skills the team exhibited. The Lions threw the ball about and Reynolds was especially incisive, making numerous breaks. But once again, penalty kick after kick was missed, some from easy positions. Jenkins had been slightly injured during practice and Charles Grieve was at full back in his place. He played well under pressure but missed crucial kicks.

Piet Bayly, a local selector, thought the Lions unlucky to lose and declared that 'In a month's time they will take some beating.' Phil Mostert was impressed they were using the scrum formation he had taught them with such success and predicted that when the team 'settled down' the public could expect 'great things' from them.[3]

The organisers of the tour could have helped the Lions' cause by having them play Western Province on the Wednesday following this match, but instead sent them over 400 kilometres through the Karoo to face South Western Districts in the small town of Oudtshoorn. The match itself, watched by just 3,500 spectators, was no great rugby spectacle. The local team spent their time disrupting play and the Lions, playing a very second-string side, did not combine well. The result saw the visitors run out 19-10 winners. Of the five tries the Lions scored, only two were converted.

The team visited the nearby Cango Caves during their stay in Oudtshoorn. There was a power failure during the tour of the caves and the team stumbled about in the pitch darkness for some time. Two players, Duncan Macrae and Eddie Morgan, became separated from the team. 'Heartrending Welsh and Scotch howls coming in unison from the depths of the darkness behind us ... yelling for succour' led Robert Alexander to them! [4] As they left the caves, Ivor Williams fell in the darkness, landing awkwardly on his knee and injuring himself. He would miss the next three matches.

On the return journey to Cape Town, their train incorrectly entered the siding at Buffelsjachts Rivier (Buffalo Hunting River) in the middle of the night. To the train driver's horror, a passenger train was already stationary in the siding and only his prompt application of full brakes averted a serious crash. Passengers were thrown from their bunks and luggage flew around compartments. The two trains became entangled, but passengers, including some of the team, disembarked and were able to disentangle the bumpers, allowing the trains to continue on their respective ways.

On Saturday 25 June the match against Western Province, holders of the Currie Cup and a side packed with Springboks, was the first major test for Walker's men. The Lions were hammered. Walker himself had to withdraw just minutes before kick-off due to an injury to his hip and the Lions looked 'ragged' to the onlookers. They held on grimly until half-time when the score was 8-3 to the local team. In the first ten minutes of the second half, Western Province scored three tries. At 21-3 the cause was lost, but the Lions rallied, and Jimmy Giles took the play to their opponents. He broke well to allow Macrae to score a try. The one positive of the match was the kicking of Vivian Jenkins. In the first half he put over a penalty from 40 yards and in the second half, one from 45 yards. The final score was 21-11 to Western Province.

Northwards

The first five matches of the tour had seen the Lions beaten twice. They now climbed aboard the train in Cape Town and headed for the Transvaal, Orange Free State and Rhodesia. They would play nine matches between the end of June and the end of July, and would win eight and lose just one, to Transvaal, at Ellis Park.

During this period, the Lions scored their biggest win of the tour (against Rhodesia) and saw off the powerful Northern Transvaal team, which included the Springbok captain Danie Craven, 20-12. They defeated Western Transvaal (26-9), Orange Free State (21-6), Orange Free State Country (18-3) and Cape Province (10-3). They also faced down Rhodesia twice (25-11 and 45-11).

Their only stumble was in the first of two games against Transvaal on 9 July when they lost 9-16 in front of a crowd of 30,000 at Ellis Park. This match, a fierce encounter, saw the teams locked at 3-all at half-time. Early in the second half, wing Bill Clement injured his knee badly and had to leave the field. The Lions still held on and at 6-all there was everything to play for. Then Jeff Reynolds, who had been the outstanding back in the tour party, injured his ankle and limped off, followed by Basil Nicholson who was concussed. The Lions finished the match with just twelve players on the field. Even so, they continued to attack to the end and were the last to score.

On 30 July, the eve of the first Test match, they gained their revenge against Transvaal. With Jeff Reynolds back, having sat out the intervening four matches, they won 17-9. This win prompted John Sacks to compliment the Lions on their forward play, it being of an 'exceptionally fine standard', and suggest that the Springboks had better beware.[5] It was Transvaal's first defeat of the season and the first time since 1896 that a team from the British Isles had defeated them.

During this period of the tour, the entertainment and travelling went on continuously. The trip to Rhodesia saw them travel in the train for two full days, but also allowed them to visit the Victoria Falls. During the short time they were able to stay there, they crossed into Northern Rhodesia to view the Falls from a different angle and went on a game cruise on the Zambezi River.

If the Lions were in danger of being 'killed by kindness' by their hosts, as the *Western Mail* alleged in an article of 29 July, the players were also laying their bodies on the line during every contest. Against Orange Free State Country in dusty Kroonstad, George Comey at fly-half instead of Jeff Reynolds, was repeatedly subjected to 'smashing tackles' by his opposite number, Brotherton, and the full back, Kruger. Against Rhodesia, the Lions found the opposing backs lining up as close to the advantage line as was possible, 'perpendicular to the scrum'. It made passing harder, but once through the line, the gap could be fully exploited. In the game against Northern Transvaal, the Lions' last line of defence had to withstand a stream of high kicks which saw them receive man and ball at the same time. Players were injured, but Hartley and Walker managed the squad well. Right up to the first Test there was still no clear 'A' and 'B' side. Selection for the Test side was wide open. Every member of the squad hoped to make the Test team and played accordingly.

A Difference of Opinion

In one area Hartley and Walker seemed to have differing opinions. After the game against Western Transvaal in Potchefstroom, Major Hartley, speaking at the dinner that evening, indicated that his team had come to South Africa 'purely to play the game for the game's sake. [The] actual result of matches was of secondary importance.'[6] At the function after the loss to Transvaal, Hartley stated that 'no one minds who wins, and it is the way one plays on the field that a person conducts himself throughout life'. These noble sentiments went down well with the South African press and those in the room who applauded loudly. However, one suspects that Walker and his men might have had a different opinion. At the same Transvaal function when it came to Sam Walker's chance to speak, he was unequivocal: he had heard it said that the British Lions did not mind losing. He wished to 'assure this gathering that members of the team possessed of a will to win'. At another function in Johannesburg, Walker drove home the message. The Lions 'wanted to win every game they played'.[7]

On the South African side too, there were those who cautioned against an increasingly belligerent attitude to rugby. John Sacks was dismayed by the stream of letters he was receiving at the *Rand Daily Mail*. Springbok supporters were critical of local players and their tactics, both in matches against the Lions, but also in Currie Cup matches. He pointed out that not only had the decade seen the Springboks defeat all the Home Unions, but also Australia and New Zealand – away! Sacks had toured Australasia with the Springboks and had seen first-hand the more open and adventurous rugby they were prepared to play. South Africans, he claimed, had a new hobby: 'criticising players ... running down' the local players ... denying that South African teams played 'bright' rugby. He wondered what would satisfy these critics. Ironically, it was the open, fast rugby that Walker's men played that Sacks thought contributed to these letters. The Springboks played a 'dull' type of game according to many supporters. They did not like it.

Sacks was full of praise for the 'brilliant' Lions who were both 'likable' and 'clean living and conscientious in training' in a way that it would be hard for other teams to equal, but he suspected that the Springboks would triumph and show the locals what they had missed and why they were wrong. Sacks was understanding. During the 1930s the Springboks had played fourteen Test matches, but only five in South Africa, and those in the early part of the decade. What, he speculated, would the keen New Zealand fans make of it, reading these letters of criticism of the Springboks? [8]

South African administrators were also dismayed by the attitude of local crowds. At the team function after the Northern Transvaal game in Pretoria, Professor H. B. Davel, president of the union, pleaded with South Africans to take a step back as he felt they had 'forgotten how to play the game for the game's sake'.[9]

The convincing victory over Transvaal on 30 July was a tonic for the Lions. They now had a week to prepare for the first Test at Ellis Park on 6 August. The tough end of the tour was to hand....

First Test

The Lions management had one great advantage over the Springbok selectors: their whole squad was in one place and they knew who was uninjured and playing well. The Springbok selectors decided to have a trial match to help them select the team, on the Thursday before the Test. Players and press were horrified, and an amendment was soon made. The trial would only be twenty minutes each way, and players would be 'moved around'.

Potential Springbok players from Western Province, travelling to Johannesburg by rail, disembarked from the train when it stopped in Kroonstad to stretch their legs. When the train departed, they were at the other end of the platform and left behind. They had to hire a taxi and race to the next stop to rejoin the train. On Thursday evening, the Springbok team was announced. Twelve of the players had played in the last Test against New Zealand the year before, two others had been in that touring squad. The only new face was the centre, Piet de Wet of Western Province.

On the Lions side, twelve of the players who had been victorious over Transvaal the previous week were picked. Bunner Travers, the Welsh hooker, could not be considered for selection as he was suffering from concussion and his place was taken by Bob Graves. There were two uncapped players in the team: Gerald Dancer and Bill Howard. Jeff Reynolds and Jim Giles, playing together for the seventh time on tour, would be the half-back pairing who would have their work cut out opposing Craven and Tony Harris. The centre pairing of Macrae and McKibbin would be playing together for the fifth time on the tour.

Ellis Park was designed to take 30,000 spectators. Reports differ on how many people descended on the stadium on 6 August 1938, the day of the Test, but one thing was certain: it was full to bursting point. Spectators, mainly children but also adults, spilt out onto the field itself. The kick by Duncan Macrae to begin the match went out on the full and the players were called back to the centre line by the referee, A. M. Horak, for a scrum. The ball never emerged from the crowd and a new one had to be called for! Police began to try and shift spectators back from the field and Mr Horak stopped the match until the field itself was clear. For the next eighty minutes young and old kept moving onto the field and Mr Horak and the touch judges had to keep moving them back. It was suggested that 36,000 were present, but some felt the number was closer to 40,000.

Both teams began cautiously and first Russell Taylor of Wales and then Gerry Brand of Western Province kicked penalties for their sides. Vivian Jenkins made the Springboks pay for an infringement, putting over a 40-yard penalty. The Springbok forwards were, however, beginning to take control of the match and Tony Harris was using the ball well. After a break by Harris, who fed Lochner, the wing Dai Williams cut inside and went over for the first try. Brand converted. The hosts led 8-6.

With the Lions pinned in their own half for most of the time, the crowd was amazed when, after Mr Horak awarded them a penalty, Jenkins indicated he would attempt a kick at the poles. From 8 yards inside the Lions half he not only put the ball through the uprights, but it went 'sailing over' with room to spare. The spectators, used to long kicks at goal on the Highveld, were nonplussed. It was the locals who were meant to kick prodigious distances!

Shortly before half-time, to intense excitement, Dai Williams crossed for a second try, only to be recalled by Mr Horak for an infringement. Seconds later, however, the Springboks were not to be denied and Fanie Louw, the powerful prop, hacked the ball through and won the race to the line to score a try which Brand converted to leave the half-time score 13-9 in favour of the Springboks.

Shortly after the second half began, the Springboks sealed the match. A penalty awarded on the halfway line saw Craven call Brand forward and indicate he must kick at poles. Brand quietly declined, feeling it was too far. Craven reminded Brand of a penalty he had converted years previously, when playing for Gardens club against Craven's Stellenbosch University team, and he suggested a drop attempt. Craven recounts Brand shrugging and taking the kick which went 'hoog en reguit, en lank trek die bal pale toe... Dis oor en die menigte word mal' (the ball travelled high, straight, and long... It was over and the crowd went mad).[10]

Shortly thereafter, Tony Harris cut through the 'thin blue line' and dotted down. Brand converted and at 21-9 the Lions had a mountain to climb. Jenkins did his best and converted another long-range penalty that brought the Lions within nine points. Just before the final whistle, Williams scored his second try after a fluid Springbok backline movement. Brand converted and the Springboks were victorious at 26-12.

Craven enjoyed the moment to the full. Aware of the criticism of the Springbok's traditional style of play, he suggested that now the local supporters could 'in werklikheid ondervind wat hulle in hulle verbeelding saam met ons in Nieu-Seeland deurleef het' (experience for themselves what they had imagined we had achieved in New Zealand). The crowd loved every minute of the game and Craven became philosophical in his account. Describing Brand's conversion of Williams' second try, he recounts how the full back had to shorten his run-up, as the crowd could not physically retreat out of his way. Brand and Craven, the players, stood together and became part of the crowd. 'Ons was deel van die toeskouers en ons praat oor en weer.' (We were part of the crowd and spoke back and forth.)[11]

The conversion was destined to be Gerry Brand's last act as a Springbok. Injured in the run-up to the second Test, Brand had played the last of his sixteen Tests and thirty further matches in the green and gold, contributing 293 points in all. 'It was a fitting way for him to end his Test career.' [12]

The British press were dismayed by the result. The *Sunday Mirror* recorded that the crowd had 'howled' on the Springboks, but Walker was generous in his post-match comments. 'They were much too good for us.'[13] Craven singled this Test match out in his reminiscences recalling it a 'Pragtoets', a splendid match, for him and his team.[14]

The Game Reserve and to the Coast Between Tests

On the day following the Test, the Lions again boarded the train. They journeyed on President Kruger's railway eastwards over the escarpment and down into the 'Lowveld' on the Union border with Portuguese East Africa (Mozambique). The Kruger Park, the 'game reserve', was their destination and they spent the next five days enjoying the peace and tranquillity of the bushveld, evenings under the stars around braais (barbeques), and viewing the wild animals that abounded there. Ironically, the one wild animal they would not be able to see was the Springbok (Antidorcas Marsupialis Marsupialis), whose natural habitat was restricted to the open plains of the Highveld. Major Hartley and Haig Smith decided to remain in Johannesburg with the injured players.

The city of Durban had been very unhappy that they had been denied a rare home Test match. As a result, the South African rugby authorities allowed the city to host the innocuous-sounding Northern Provinces match. This team was made up of players from all the Transvaal provinces, Orange Free State and Natal. A week after the first Test, the Lions thus had to face a team that included six Springboks and was brimming with talent. The Lions lost to them by an even wider margin than the Test, 26-8, and conceded four tries in the process. The *Rand Daily Mail* was unimpressed with the visitors' performance. Injuries and the resting of players and some playing out of position had not helped their cause. The bounce of the ball had also favoured the local team on the day. They had been 'routed', Sacks concluded.[15]

In the next four matches, all against coastal provinces, the Lions were victorious and so restored hope to their cause. They first defeated Natal (15-11), then Border (19-11), North Eastern Cape (42-3) and finally, on 27 August, Eastern Province (6-5). The team must have been happy to travel between Durban and East London on board the *Arundel Castle*. They had travelled nearly 8,000 miles on trains, occupying almost fifteen days of the tour.

By the time the Lions squad assembled in Port Elizabeth on the eve of the second Test, eight of their squad were *hors de combat* either temporarily, or for the remainder of the tour. The Lions team for the second international match showed no fewer than seven changes, the Springboks just two.

Second Test: The 'Tropical' Game

The Crusader ground in Port Elizabeth was the venue for the second international match of the tour. Careful planning in reaction to the crowd scenes in the first Test saw 20,000 spectators seated in an orderly manner. The teams had something else to confront in addition to each other. Heat!

The Port Elizabeth temperature for early September hovers around a pleasant 20 degrees Celsius. On the day of the Test, 3 September, it was over 35 degrees by the time the teams took the field. There was no cooling breeze. Despite the intense heat, the match, controlled by referee J. J. Strasheim, started at a furious pace.

The Lions, aware of their need to square the series, did most of the attacking and the South Africans had to defend desperately during the first twenty minutes. Russell Taylor missed an easy penalty and as the half wore on, the Lions' pack began to tire. It was Tony Harris who initiated the first score when he broke away while still in his own half. Big Ferdie Bergh received the ball in the movement and passed to flanker Ben du Toit at the perfect moment. Du Toit dotted down behind the posts and Turner converted.

Just before half-time, the fierce-tackling John Aspey, the Springbok flanker who had replaced the injured Ebbo Bastard, crashed into Jeff Reynolds and both had to leave the field with head injuries. Aspey soon returned, bandaged, to the field. Reynolds did not. While the Springboks enjoyed a numerical superiority, Craven carried the ball downfield and Flappie Lochner went over to score. Turner again converted. Half-time saw the Springboks ahead 10-0.

Reynolds reappeared at the start of the second half, wearing both a bandage and a scrum cap, but early in the half Basil Nicholson had to leave the field in discomfort. Now the Springboks were in full flight and moving the ball wide to exploit their advantage in numbers once again. After yet another sniping Craven break, new cap Johnny Bester went over. Turner failed with the conversion, but converted two further penalties. Just before the final whistle Reynolds collected a dropped ball and put Laurie Duff away for the Lions lone try. Grieve failed with the conversion. The final score saw the Springboks ahead 19-3. They had won both the match and series.

The after-match function at the Elizabeth Hotel was a rip-roaring success and couples danced well into the sultry night. Not one member of either team who had played that day attended. They were all in their rooms sleeping!

Danie Craven had played in mud, driving rain, freezing weather, waterlogged pitches, even snow on one occasion. The heat in Port Elizabeth in this Test was, for him, the harshest condition he ever faced on a rugby field. He and Sam Walker agreed on this matter. According to Craven, anyone who played in that Test would tell you: 'Nooit weer'. (Never again.) [16]

Third Test: The 'Most Stirring'

Both teams boarded the *Windsor Castle* and set off for Cape Town and the third, and last, Test, to be played a week later at Newlands. The sea trip was so stormy that the vessel could not enter Cape Town harbour but had to heave to in Table Bay. Craven noted that most of the Springboks were thoroughly seasick. This journey is also remembered for another reason. During a shipboard conversation, it is alleged that A. F. Markötter, South African selector and shrewd rugby observer, discussed with Sam Walker the relative merits of players on both sides. During the conversation Markötter scribbled down the names of the best forward unit he believed the Lions should field. When the Lions team was announced a few days later, there was surprise at the changes in the scrum. It was alleged in some quarters that Markötter's list had been followed to the letter.

The Lions returned to their hotel on the Atlantic seaboard, the Springboks were accommodated in the St James Hotel on the False Bay coast. They did not like this beautiful, but quiet and isolated location and after two nights moved to the Metropole Hotel in Long Street. Craven was not in favour of the move, pointing out that in the bustling city centre the team were never together, there were too many interruptions, but he was outvoted.

There was nothing resting on the game but honour. It turned out that honour made for a good rugby game.

On 10 September Danie Craven, captaining South Africa in his last Test match, won the toss and decided to play with the stiff wind that was blowing down the ground, since the Newlands groundsman had advised him that the wind would shortly die down. The groundsman was to be proved wrong. It would be a costly mistake.

The Lions, wearing their blue jerseys for the last time, showed from the first minute that they were not going to give an inch and it was they who opened the scoring when the winger Elvet Jones dotted down. Craven was dismayed and later recorded that Walker's men exhibited 'Wellington-gees' (the spirit of the Duke of Wellington).[17]

The Springboks hit back quickly, with the centre Freddy Turner intercepting a pass by 'jumping' into the path of the ball and scoring a try that he converted himself. The Springboks led 5-3.

The Springboks used the wind well. A Dai Williams cross kick found his fellow wing Johnny Bester, who dived over, and Turner converted. 10-3 to the Springboks. The Lions were struggling when the hooker Jan Lotz barged over just before half-time for a try, but it was not converted. At half-time the Springboks led 13-3.

Observers noted Sam Walker gathering his men around him in the middle of the field during the break, while Craven did not. South Africa had never surrendered a lead of ten points in any Test match. Walker was seen to be exhorting his troops in what observers suggested was 'language that must have been plain'. The Lions now had the wind, which had picked up speed, at their backs. The Springboks continued attacking, but the two Georges, Cromey and Morgan, the Irish half-backs, who were used to playing at windswept Lansdowne Road, kept the South Africans in their own 25. Then the Springbok defence cracked, and it was Walker himself who barged his way across the advantage line, allowing 'Beef' Dancer, playing prop that day, to score. Harry McKibbin converted. The Springboks still led 13-8.

The Lions pushed back downfield with wind-assisted kicks and after a penalty for 'hands in', McKibbin added three points. The Springboks now led 13-11. Thereafter followed a period of forward mauling in the centre of the field, before Cromey broke away at speed and beat the defence, passing to the flank Robert Alexander, who went over with three South Africans trying to bring him down. The conversion was unsuccessful. The Lions now led 14-13.

The Newlands spectators, realising they were witnessing a special contest, rose to the occasion and the cheering was almost continuous. An easy penalty taken by Freddie Turner for a Lions infringement meant the locals took the lead again, 16-14. The Lions continued to keep play in the Springbok half and when Harris missed touch with a kick, Charles Grieve collected it and steadying himself, put over a drop from 40 yards out. The Lions were back in the lead, 18-16.

The last minutes of the game were played at a furious pace and the final break was engineered by the big Lions forwards. Jock Waters, Walker and finally Blair Mayne, 'now playing like men inspired', set off down the field 'sweeping despairing tacklers aside' and it was the Scot Laurie Duff who crashed over for the try. The conversion was missed, but the game was won. Lions 21, Springboks 16.

Or was it? The Springboks mounted a last attack, knowing the whistle was imminent and the crowd, on their feet for the previous ten minutes, cheered them on. Craven broke and put Bester away, who passed to Dai Williams who scored. The referee, however, ruled the Craven pass forward and called them back for a scrum. The Lions heeled it and kicked the ball out. It was over! The Lions were victorious after all, 21-16.

The spectators flooded onto the field. Two Springboks, Ben du Toit and Lukas Strachan, hoisted their fellow forward Sam Walker onto their shoulders and carried him off the field. In retrospect Walker would label that moment 'the biggest thrill of my career'.[18]

The Last Days of the Tour

On the eve of the Test, his last, Danie Craven had been inundated for requests for interviews. In one of them he had indicated that the Springboks, fresh from winning the rubber, would not change their game plan and would 'attack from start to finish in carefree fashion'.[19] It was revealed after the match that some Springbok players had suggested to him at the beginning of the second half that the team should 'close up' the game and play more conservatively. He declined their request.[20] The result was seven tries in all, and John Sacks called it the 'most stirring Test ever seen in South Africa'. Later in the same article he went further: it was the 'most sensational in Test history'. Even the referee agreed. Nic Pretorius indicated that it had been the fastest game of rugby he had ever controlled.[21]

Craven was generous in his praise of his opponents: 'It was a very enjoyable and terrifically hard game. The British side deserved all they got, and we have no complaints whatsoever. The better side won.' Walker, too, was generous in his praise for both his opponents and his teammates at the after-match function that took place at the Del Monico restaurant. When it was time for Walker to speak, those present chanted 'We want Sam, we want Sam!'[22] Sacks gave a sober assessment of the contest. The victory for the Lions, he suggested, was a good one for South African rugby as it tempered the 'frightening conceit' that some locals were beginning to exhibit about the land's rugby abilities.

The Lions played one more match at Newlands, losing to a Western Province Country XV four days later. It was a sad end to what all agreed had been a special tour. South Africans showed their appreciation when the tourists departed on the *Athlone Castle,* coming out in their thousands to bid them farewell. Major Hartley, surveying the large crowd from the deck, told a reporter that the players had memories they would 'cherish all [their] lives'.[23]

Events in Europe were gathering momentum and it would be eleven long years before Newlands would again echo to the cheers of spectators witnessing an international match. For many players on both sides this match would prove to be their last international. One, Robert Alexander of Ulster, who scored one of those vital Lions tries, would not live to play any international rugby again. He would lose his life during the invasion of Sicily.

When Sam Walker recalled the tour more than twenty years later, it was to the last Test at Newlands that his thoughts went:

The second half [of the Newlands Test] is one that will never be forgotten by anyone who was privileged either to play in it or witness it, for the British Lions played like men inspired... To this day my most treasured rugby possessions are a blue no. 14 jersey and a tattered pair of shorts, both unwashed and still retaining traces of mud from a famous ground to associate as it were, a truly Homeric struggle between two great rugby teams... That epic game made all my efforts well worth while.[24]

The End of an Era
As the *Athlone Castle* headed out of Table Bay with the Lions on board, those witnessing her stately progress did not realise it represented the end of an era. The next Lions touring party would not arrive by ship in Table Bay in 1955, but via aeroplane. They would also fly between destinations in the Union and the endless train journeys would be but a memory. Stadiums had also improved beyond recognition by 1955, and the fields were all well grassed, though they might be harder than those in Great Britain. The Lions would also play in red rugby jerseys with white shorts and blue stockings edged with green.

Certain aspects, however, remained unchanged. The altitude was still a factor to be considered and touring teams continued to struggle with itineraries that saw them move back and forth from coast to Highveld. The teams that the Lions faced continued to contain uncompromising players keen to show their prowess, the balls continued to bounce uncomfortably high and fly great distances, but the welcome continued to be sincere and heartfelt.

William Wotherspoon had initiated a sturdy tradition on 9 July 1891 at Newlands ground. Forty-seven years later it was still thriving. The Second World War would see a suspension of formal rugby contacts. Informal contacts in North Africa, Italy and in prisoner of war camps across Axis counties would continue between the rugby-playing countries of the British Empire. Then once again, when the war clouds had dissipated, formal rugby traditions would be renewed and expanded, and friendships rekindled.

1938 TOUR SQUAD
Managers – Jock Hartley and Jack Haig Smith

Backs
Vivian Jenkins (Vice-Capt.) (Wales)*
Charles Boyle (Ireland)*
William Clement (Wales)
George Cromey (Ireland)*
James Giles (England)*
Charles Grieve (Scotland)*
Elvet Jones (Wales)*
Roy Leyland (England)
Duncan MaCrae (Scotland)*
Henry McKibbin (Ireland)*
George Morgan (Ireland)*
Basil Nicholson (England)*
F. Jeffrey Reynolds (England)*
Haydn Tanner (Wales)*
Ernest Unwin (England)*

Forwards
Sam Walker (Capt.) (Ireland)*
Robert Alexander (Ireland)*
Stanley Couchman (England)
Gerald Dancer (England)*
Peter Duff (Scotland)*
Charles Graves (Ireland)*
William Howard (England)*
Robert Blair Mayne (Ireland)*
Morgan Morgan (Wales)*
A. H. G. Purchas (England)
Albert Taylor (Wales)*
William Travers (Wales)*
John Waters (Scotland)*
Ivor Williams (Wales)

* Took part in at least one Test match

7

THE 1955 BRITISH LIONS: HONOURS EVEN

In 1955, the British Lions toured for the second time following the Second World War, and for the first time to South Africa. Their African journey was preceded by their tour to New Zealand and Australia five years earlier, when they came away with a draw and three losses to the All Blacks and wins in both Tests against the Wallabies. Captained by Ireland's Karl Mullen, these 1950 Lions were for the first time officially known as the 'British Lions' rather than 'British Isles', also playing in a redesigned jersey. Travelling by ship, they stopped off at Ceylon to play the national side in Colombo for their biggest win of the tour (44-6). None of these players were selected for the 1955 tour of South Africa. There was disappointment amongst Welshmen that the speedy Ken Jones didn't make it and Irishmen lamented the omission of their star fly-half, legendary Jack Kyle.

First choice fly-half Cliff Morgan from Wales, however, came back as one of the true stars of the tour:

At that period Lions tours were four or five years apart; you needed to hit the top at just the right time to be included once, and you had to have a long international career to be asked a second time... It was an offer you could not refuse, a chance and challenge to play the best rugby in your life. I felt that once I had been a Lion I would have done everything I could in the game. I looked at the company I would be keeping. The other nine Welshmen in the team I knew well, of course, but the buzz I got was from the thought of playing with Jeff Butterfield as my centre and Tony O'Reilly on the wing.[1]

The 1955 Lions played twenty-five matches on their tour of South Africa, Rhodesia (now Zimbabwe), South West Africa (now Namibia) and East Africa, winning nineteen, losing five and drawing one. Their wins included two Test wins against the Springboks to draw the series 2-all. They won the first Test by a single point and the third by three points and lost the second and fourth matches by wider margins. The tour kicked off on a disappointing note with the tourists losing 6-9 to Western Transvaal in Potchefstroom, while later on tour they were also beaten by Eastern Province (0-20) and Border (12-14). Their only draw was with Eastern Transvaal (17-all).

The squad was captained by the twenty-four-year-old Robin Thompson of Ireland, whose appointment was initially criticised because of his comparative youth. The team manager was Jack A. E. Siggins, formerly of Belfast and Ireland, and the assistant manager Danny E. Davies, a former Cardiff player. It was a team that had a lot of fun from the time they were fitted for their blazers. 'At least it gave us a good laugh because all the sleeves were too long, the shoulders too wide, and everything had to be altered,' said Cliff Morgan.

That broke the ice, and that evening we came to the decision that we were going to be a singing team. I was appointed choirmaster with first call on the hotel piano, and every day for a week we practiced English, Scottish and Irish songs in English, Welsh songs in Welsh and, in four part harmony, *Sarie Marais* in Afrikaans, which we thought would go down well with the people over there.[2]

The team was to have all hotel and travelling expenses paid, plus 2 pounds 10 shillings pocket money a week each, provided they could produce chits showing how it had been spent.[3]

While the last Lions party to visit South Africa in 1938 travelled by sea each way, the 1955 Lions were booked to go by air. On 10 June, they flew on a BOAC Argonaut, 'a rather ponderous aircraft', as Cliff Morgan recalled, via Rome, then Cairo, Nairobi and Livingstone on the African continent, before arriving at Johannesburg five and three-quarter hours late. The touring team was amazed at the large crowd that had come to welcome them. As reward they practically sang their full repertoire from *Sosban Fach* to *Sarie Marais* while cheered on by the enthusiastic South African fans.[4]

The first game the Lions played, on 22 June, was against Western Transvaal – led by Springbok lock Johan Claassen – in Potchefstroom and the tourists lost by 9 points to 6. Tries by Morgan and Pedlow were not enough to beat the Western Transvaalers' two drop goals (full back Jack van der Schyff and fly-half Pieters) and a penalty (Van der Schyff). Time and again the Lions would move upfield against Western Transvaal but then be driven back, 'fifty, sixty and seventy yards at a time'. The Lions encountered several South African characteristics in this game which amazed them. Sand tees on which to place the ball when kicking at goal were allowed on account of the concrete-like grounds; the huge forwards; and the fact that Potchefstroom, despite the game being on a Wednesday, came to a complete halt and spectators were seen hurrying to the ground whilst the Lions were still having breakfast! This was on account of the five 'curtain raisers' that were going to be played. 'They were going to watch over seven hours continuous rugby,' the rugby correspondent Vivian Jenkins observed with amazement. They also realised that the non-white sections of the crowd were on the side of the British team 'and cheered their tries to the echo'.[5]

The team had its first taste of railway travel in South Africa when they travelled to Kimberley. 'Railway travel in South Africa, though slow, is extremely comfortable,' Vivian Jenkins noted. 'The standard of food served, the amount of it provided, and the low cost, would have made the normal traveller on British Railways green with envy.'[6]

The ground of the Diamond City was reputed to be the hardest underfoot in the whole of South Africa, but the previous week there had been heavy rain in the city and the team was relieved to discover that it was not quite as bad as expected. In their day, the Griquas were quite a strong provincial side which had beaten both the 1903 and 1910 British Lions, but were no longer the power they once were. Two years before, however, they did beat the Wallabies 13-3, so the visitors had no reason to be complacent. The Griquas offered stern opposition in the first half especially, but the Lions ran out 24-14 winners, scoring six tries to one, including a hat-trick by right wing Haydn Morris. Morgan was brilliant, moving the *Sunday Express* correspondent to label him as the best fly-half to visit the country in the past fifty years.[7]

Next stop was Johannesburg for their match at Ellis Park against the Northern Universities, a combination of Witwatersrand, Pretoria and Potchefstroom Universities. Notable players were Clive Ulyate and Wilf Rosenberg, destined to meet the Lions in the Test series. A crowd of 60,000 turned up to see the Lions comfortably beat the students 32-6. Tony O'Reilly made his first appearance, scoring two of his side's six tries.

Locals, however, were quick to warn the visitors that it would be a different story against the Free Staters at Kroonstad, who were next. Their confidence was understandable, the *Blikore* having beaten the Wallabies 28-3 two years before. Unfortunately for the Free State fans, on the day the Lions produced their finest display of the tour against provincial opposition. Their 31-3 win was hard to believe, and many local supporters who saw the result in the stop-press of the papers must have thought it was a misprint! Free State were run to a standstill, with Jeff Butterfield playing the game of his life – paving the way for some tries and scoring a hat-trick himself. Obviously, morale was high when the team flew from Kroonstad for South West Africa and Cliff Morgan had the plane rocking with laughter with his antics.

Windhoek still had a strong element of its German heritage, and the visitors found it a most interesting place, a popular spot being the German Club. Following the sparks of the Free State match, the game – played in front of only 4,500 spectators – was disappointing, in spite of the three tries the Lions produced in their 9-0 victory. Sporting his chain of office, the mayor of Windhoek was present to see the team off at the airport, as he had been to welcome them a few days earlier. On their flight to Cape Town, they stopped over at Alexander Bay, just south of the mouth of the Orange River, and 'one of the bleakest spots on earth', but extremely rich in diamonds. Sometime later, heavy rain and low cloud in Cape Town made landing a scary event, some players exchanging wisecracks on what their next of kin would do with their £5,000 insurance money.

The match against Western Province, for years a dominant force in South African rugby, was expected to demand the best of the Lions' efforts. Captained by Stephen Fry, the Springbok captain for the Test series, the local side boasted several Springboks and future Springboks. Rugby fever ran high and on the Thursday evening before Saturday's match a queue had begun to form at Newlands for tickets. Playing in front of a crowd of 35,000, the visitors were at the top of their form, winning a thrilling match 11-3 after trailing 0-3 at the break. The forwards provided a great platform for the backs, who made some slashing breaks, especially O'Reilly playing at centre. The lively hooker Bryn Meredith scored two tries and centre Davies another; Western Province, in spite of their impressive backline, could only reply with a penalty by Roy Dryburgh. Like touring sides before them, the Lions enjoyed the magnificent setting of the ground below Table Mountain, as well as the springy-turf playing surface, which facilitated attractive rugby.

From Cape Town they travelled by bus to the Little Karoo town of Oudtshoorn, then the home of South Western Districts rugby, and known worldwide for its ostrich feather industry. The province only had twelve first-grade clubs and spread across an area almost the size of England, and as expected, the Lions easily won 22-3, though not in any great style. Injuries at this stage enforced positional changes: Pedlow had to stand in at fly-half,

Baker at full back and McLeod at hooker. Left wing Sykes scored three of the visitors' five tries.

The Lions now had six wins from seven matches and one would have expected them to increase that to seven from eight with the game against Eastern Province on 16 July in Port Elizabeth, known as 'The Friendly City'. But from thirty players, only seventeen could be classified as fit to play. In the end, hooker Roe started the game injured, and O'Reilly had to play full back. Eastern Province fielded a tough pack; led by burly frontranker Amos du Plooy, the EP front row dominated and hooker Colin Kroon had an easy day against the injured Roe. The game turned out to be disastrous for the visitors. They lost 0-20 after trailing 0-9 at the break. The red-and-black jerseys scored a converted try and five penalty goals. Their performance in the front row later earned Du Plooy and Kroon places in the Springbok team for the first Test, but that would be their only appearances in the green and gold. After this showing by the visitors, many people thought the Boks would have an easy passage in the first Test – ignoring the disruption caused by all the injuries.

The team took to the air once more bound for Bloemfontein, en route to the small town of Aliwal North to play North Eastern Districts. From Bloemfontein they were transported the 140 miles to Aliwal North by bus. 5,000 spectators turned up for the match, some perched on farm wagons acting as emergency stands. Coming from only a few clubs scattered over a thinly populated area, the men from NED were no match for the Lions as expected, but at least managed two tries in their 6-34 loss. Cliff Morgan, who led the side, scored two tries, while O'Reilly with a hat-trick, Pedlow with a pair and Bryn Meredith also crossed the line.

Next up was Transvaal at Ellis Park, which fielded top players like Basie van Wyk, Des Sinclair, Piet Wessels, Natie Rens and captain Pa Pelser. Morgan was rested for this game, with Baker combining with Dickie Jeeps at half-back. All five Springbok selectors were present when the two teams faced each other in front of 45,000 spectators. On the day, the British forwards laid the foundation against a powerful Transvaal pack for a sensational 36-13 win, in which the backs ran the Transvaalers ragged. The visitors scored seven tries, with O'Reilly notching up three outstanding tries again. It was no secret that O'Reilly worked hard on his thigh muscles, which gave him an immense power surge from a standing start. 'The try scorer is the man who can keep going over a long distance and increase in speed as he goes,' the red-haired Irishman believed, 'so many players peter out after 30 yards.'[8]

Two matches against Rhodesia, one at Kitwe nearly on the Belgian Congo Border, and a second at Salisbury awaited. After a long and tiring flight from Johannesburg, a road journey from Ndola Airport to Kitwe followed and for once the players had a real taste of African dust. In spite of injury concerns over Morgan, he captained the side and came through unscathed. 5,000 spectators saw the Lions beat the Rhodesians 27-14, with left wing Sykes weighing in with a hat-trick of tries. The next game at Salisbury was a much closer affair, the visitors winning 16-12, again led by Morgan. Probably the highlight of their visit to Rhodesia was the sight of the majestic Victoria Falls where they spent a few days resting before returning to Johannesburg for the first Test on 6 August.

The First Test
Demand for tickets for Ellis Park far outstripped supply and newspapers carried stories of spectators purchasing forgeries and tickets for very high prices. The official crowd of 90,000 on that day, including most of the South African Cabinet, made it the best-attended rugby game in South Africa's history to that time.

The Test itself would be talked and written about for decades to come. 'Heroism there was, and also heartbreak: for this was surely the rugby Test of all Tests, perhaps the greatest ever played,' stated well-known rugby scribe Reg Sweet:

It was a constant round of triumph overtaking disaster, of flights against the odds. One side looked to be assured of victory, and suddenly it was no longer so... And yet it stood again on the brink of triumph in the final seconds of the match, only to lose by the odd point in 45 ... It was all emotion, bravery and brilliance, a game of rugger to go down in fable: for its spirit, too, was never once in question. And when all was said and done it was, quite possibly, the most remarkable match the game had known.[9]

The Boks and Lions took the field amidst a thunderous roar, with the second-row reserve forward, Ernie Michie, resplendent in kilt and full regalia, piping his teammates on.

The British Lions opened the scoring after twelve minutes when Butterfield received from Davies, then drew his man before passing to Pedlow who dived over in the corner. Full back Cameron failed to convert. The lead only lasted two minutes as Van der Schyff, the Springbok full back, landed a penalty from 40 yards out. The Springboks went further ahead when the British forwards were penalised for holding and Van der Schyff made no mistake from 30 yards. Their lead increased to 11-3 when Gentles broke around the scrum on the Lions 25 and passed to Fry, who sent Briers over in the corner; Van der Schyff converted brilliantly from a difficult angle.

The Lions fought back and Morgan broke free on the halfway line, before Butterfield outpaced his opponent to score under the posts. Cameron converted and when half-time arrived, the Springboks were leading by 11 points to 8. Within two minutes after the resumption the Lions almost scored but O'Reilly was tackled on the corner flag. Unfortunately, the Lions then lost Higgins, who got injured for the second time and was carried off the field. In spite of this setback, they regained the lead when Morgan brilliantly sliced through the defence to score near the posts, and Cameron easily converted. Now followed some fierce attacks by the visitors, and barely two minutes later they scored again when O'Reilly was pulled down just short of the line, but Davies picked up and went over far out. Cameron converted splendidly. Eight minutes later Van der Schyff failed to gather a kick ahead by Greenwood, and in a flash O'Reilly was in possession to touch down. Again, Cameron landed the difficult conversion. With about twenty minutes left in the game, the Lions had built a comfortable 23-11 lead.

The Springboks looked doomed. But then came an astonishing Bok revival. Gentles kicked across the line of the scrum, and with Cameron out of position, Sias Swart – South West Africa's first Springbok – collected down the left-hand touchline and went over. Van der Schyff's conversion failed, but with three minutes left, the mobile Bok prop from the Boland, Chris Koch, pounced on a loose ball some 20 yards from the Lions' try line and with determined weaving and dodging finally flung himself over the white line. Van der Schyff made no mistake with the conversion and the score read Lions 23, Springboks 19. It was not over yet; out of the blue came another Bok attack started by centre Des Sinclair, who had Gentles and Fry in support to keep the move going, and when Fry moved the ball to Theuns Briers on the wing, he beat two defenders on the touchline to score 6 yards in from the corner flag. A successful conversion would do the trick. As Van der Schyff lined up for the kick, the crowd of 90,000 fell silent. Who would want to be in the full back's shoes at that moment? Then his boot swung through, the ball sailed high … but to the left! With hunched shoulders and head hanging, the poor full back turned away in agony.[10] The image was to become one of the most published in the history of rugby photography.

Dr Danie Craven labelled the first Test as the greatest Test international match he ever saw. 'Because it was us, I like to believe him,' Cliff Morgan responded. 'And also because I know we produced great moments of rugby in a temperature of 78° in the shade and at an altitude of 5,750 feet, which left us gasping for air. To me that game epitomised what rugby and the whole tour were about – adventure, style, passing the ball and, about the most important thing in rugby, taking chances. We gave away stupid tries, I'm sure, but we went on taking risks, because when you play safe the game is impoverished. And we gained far more than we lost by that approach.'[11]

Following the first Test the Lions played and won three more games, the first in Durban against the Central Universities (won 21-14), then Boland – captained by Springbok prop Chris Koch and with quite a few players from rugged farming stock – in

Wellington (won 11-0) and a strong Western Province Universities at Newlands on the Tuesday before the Test (won 20-17). In the latter game, the home side fielded no fewer than eleven future Springboks. When they came to Newlands for the second Test, they had run up 72 tries with 19 against, so their striking power was evident.

The Second Test
The British Lions selectors made only two changes from the successful side of the first Test. Gareth Griffiths, who in the meantime had joined the squad as a replacement and had made his first appearance against Transvaal, came in for Pedlow, while Tom Reid replaced the injured Higgins and slotted in at No. 8. At the same time, Russell Robins switched from No. 8 to flank. The South African selectors had, predictably, dropped players after the first Test – five in all, including Jack Van der Schyff. Wilf Rosenberg came in to partner Des Sinclair at centre and Tom van Vollenhoven moved from centre to left wing. Roy Dryburgh came in as full back in place of Van der Schyff and among the forwards Amos du Plooy, Colin Kroon and Basie van Wyk were replaced by Jaap Bekker, Bertus Van der Merwe and Dawie Ackermann. His omission meant the end of the international road for the bald-headed Van Wyk, who had been such a vital cog in the Bok loose trio machine along with Hennie Muller and Stephen Fry during the 1951–52 UK tour and the 1953 Wallabies series.

During the Friday morning before the Test at Newlands, the Springbok wing Tom van Vollenhoven stood chatting to his teammate Wilf Rosenberg in front of the Boks' hotel. An old-timer walked up to him and hissed: 'You, what are you doing here?'

'What do you mean?' asked Tom, taken aback.

'You want to catch O'Reilly,' the old man went on, 'and you can't even catch a cold!' Ironically, it would be the day that Van Vollenhoven scored a hat-trick of tries.[12]

The tourists ran onto Newlands on Saturday 20 August as firm favourites to be the first team since 1891 to win the first two Tests in a series in South Africa. The Springboks showed composure in the first minutes of the game, but the first score was a Lions penalty by Cameron. Fierce forward exchanges spoiled most attempts at any conclusive play by the backs, but eventually in the thirty-seventh minute Van Vollenhoven scored an unconverted try from a cross kick by Sinclair to see the teams level 3-all at half-time. The South African scrum had been very solid throughout the half and had spoiled the ball going the way of the Lions, which had restrained the half-back pairing of Jeeps and Morgan.

The second half saw some of the best rugby played at Newlands before or since in any Test match. 'Newlands ground had seldom known such a day as this. It seemed not to be certain whether to sit or leap up on excited feet; and it settled for round after echoing round of untrammeled applause which must have rolled a long way up the slopes of Devil's Peak.'[13]

The 46,000-strong crowd saw an early attack by the Lions fade away and then Des Sinclair snapped up a bouncing grubber Ulyate had put through. He delayed his pass perfectly so O'Reilly had to commit to the tackle, thus allowing Van Vollenhoven to score and for South Africa to take the lead 6-3 as Dryburgh again missed the conversion.

In the next ten minutes South Africa scored three more tries. The first was a superb effort by Van Vollenhoven and it gave him his hat-trick. Gentles had broken blind against the touchline and Van Vollenhoven had only one option, his infield swerve, but it was done at such pace that Jeeps and O'Reilly were left grasping at thin air. Ulyate now took the conversion kick close to the uprights but also missed. In quick succession, Rosenberg scored on debut and immediately after the restart Rosenberg again cut the Lions midfield open and put Dryburgh in for the first try scored by a South African full back since the famous Percy Allport try on the same ground forty-five years earlier. This time Dryburgh converted and South Africa was now leading 17-3.

Ulyate was instrumental in the next try by Briers when he pounced on a loose ball and after making ground and drawing the defence put the Western Province wing away for yet another score, which made the score 20-3 to South Africa.

The Lions now finally replied via a Butterfield try created by Morgan, but new Bok flanker Ackermann responded immediately with South Africa's seventh try, which was converted for them to lead 25-6. In the dying moments the lively Bryn Meredith crossed for a consolation try and the game ended in a 25-9 victory for the Springboks, thus levelling the series.

Vivian Jenkins wrote for the British *Sunday Times* that night that 'South Africa was on the march again' and that they had been driven on by the famous 'Newlands Roar, echoing round the slopes of Table Mountain like a myriad war-drums'.[14]

After the Test the Lions attended a dance held in the tourists' honour at the Rotunda in Camps Bay. The *Cape Argus* carried photographs of the function in the Monday edition and it would seem some of the Lions were more than happy to be present this time round. Robin Thompson was pictured with the very attractive Miss Colleen Kavanagh on his arm and a kilted E. T. S. Michie seemed most attracted to Miss Jasmyne van Wyk.

Two tough encounters now awaited the tourists up North – first Eastern Transvaal in Springs and then the strong Northern Transvaal in Pretoria. Even though they drew 17-all with the Eastern Transvaalers, the Lions outscored them by four tries to two, with two tries going to left wing Arthur Smith. In defence of the Lions, it had to be said that an injury to fly-half Baker badly disrupted their line-up, and the Eastern Transvaalers took full advantage of it.

With Springboks in Van Vollenhoven, Dolf Bekker, Hansie Brewis, Fonnie du Toit, Jaap Bekker, Daan Retief and their captain Salty du Rand, Northern Transvaal was always going to be a very hard nut to crack. The Lions' hard-fought 14-11 victory deserved a lot of praise, as after only twenty minutes their captain Robin Thompson had to leave the field with a twisted knee and it speaks volumes for the remaining seven forwards that they held out against the formidable Northerns pack. Their four tries included a spectacular 80-yard sprint by Butterfield, chased by Van

Vollenhoven of all people. And no wonder that of all seven of the forwards, only Roe was not picked for the third Test.

The Third Test: Morgan in His Pomp

The Lions tour now returned to the Highveld for the third Test at Loftus Versfeld. Criticism of the 'too English' Boks under Fry resurfaced but Craven had trained his charges hard including, amazingly, a session on the morning of the game, played on a very hot day.

The British Lions went into the third Test with several major problems. Their captain, Thompson, and vice-captain, Cameron, were both injured. Their second fly-half, Doug Baker, had to stand in at full back. His selection was not without a bit of anxiety. He had left his contact lenses – which he had fitted in Hamburg – on the mantelshelf in a dressing room and a cleaner unknowingly swept it out! Management cabled a rush order to Germany, while a Johannesburg firm offered him replacements. In the end, fortunately, both pairs of lenses arrived with little time to spare but ensuring that the stand-in full back could see his way around the field.

The British Lions side for the third Test was captained by Cliff Morgan and read as follows: D. G. Baker, A. J. F. O'Reilly, W. P. C. Davies, J. Butterfield, G. M. Griffiths, C. I. Morgan, R. E. G. Jeeps, T. E. Reid, J. T. Greenwood, R. J. Robins, R. C. C. Thomas, R. H. Williams, C. C. Meredith, B. V. Meredith, W. O. G. Williams.

With 45,000 looking on, the British Lions beat the Springboks by 9 points to 6. For the Lions, Baker landed a penalty and Butterfield not only scored a try but also put over a left-footed drop goal – the first in a match of any consequence, he later admitted! For the Springboks, Roy Dryburgh kicked two penalty goals for their six points. But the star of the show was again Cliff Morgan. This is what rugby scribe Reg Sweet had to say about him:

Morgan was undoubtedly the schemer in chief, the driving force in the back division – and inevitably, the plotter against whom the most important counters had to be devised. He was hard, incredibly hard, to pin down, for he could turn within the length of a bootlace and, with a quick acceleration, be spirited away even as the trap was sprung. In the tactical role, as best exemplified by the third international at Pretoria, his ability to bring the game under personal control stamped him very closely as the foremost fly-half of his time.[15]

Sweet added:

Clifford Isaac Morgan was a man of many parts; and pluperfect at them all, so be it must have seemed to South Africa on this day that he fell heir to the captaincy of the British Isles, dictated the tactics and the course of the match, and made it certain that the Springboks could not win the rubber nor the Lions lose it. His dressing-room talk to his side before the start, so it was told, was a masterpiece of impassionate appeal to his men. He did not, it is true, go so far as it to move them to the singing of land of my fathers; his Englishmen, his Irishmen, and his Scot might have drawn the line at that! But he did appeal to them as from the heart of their homes and loved ones, the four home countries, the honour of the Lions and what you will. He hit them, someone suggested, though this was doubtless carrying it too far, with everything but the prayer book. Another thought that he had made is appeal to the emotions like a latter-day Lloyd George, and he was doubtless nearer to the mark. This, at any rate, was demonstrably Cliff Morgan's greatest day of a tour on which he had earned so much distinction. And he was clearly determined to make the most of it.[16]

Before the fourth Test, the Lions still had to face Natal in Durban, the Junior Springboks in Bloemfontein and Border in East London. They beat Natal 11-8, with tries by Pedlow, Wilson and Smith, who also kicked a conversion, while the Natalians replied with a converted try and penalty. The Junior Springboks, of which ten were to become Springboks in later years, gave them a good run for their money in front of 30,000 rugby fans, but they prevailed 15-12 after trailing 5-6 at half-time. Quinn, Sykes and O'Reilly scored tries for the Lions, all three converted by Thomas. Unfortunately for the Lions, their last provincial match against Border resulted in a 12-14 loss. It has to be said that they outscored Border by three tries (Sykes, Davies, Meredith) to one converted try. Border also scored three penalties.

The Fourth Test: A Bridge Too Far
The Springboks recovered from their third Test loss to win the fourth Test at the Crusaders ground in Port Elizabeth on 24 September 22-8 and level the series. Perhaps the tourists were beginning to feel the strain of a long, difficult tour, and the focus may have already shifted homewards as so often can be the case.

Team selection can also play a role; Reid was stood down for Thompson who had not played for a month, while the effective Davies/Butterfield combination was also broken when O'Reilly – so lethal on the wing – was moved into the centre. In addition, Morgan was nursing an ankle injury and Morgan of the third Test was not the Morgan of the fourth one.

The Lions were outscored in the Tests, but a 2-all draw in the backyard of the then unofficial world champions was not a shabby record. These Lions of 1955 are still considered one of the best Lions teams to have visited the country.

In front of 37,000 spectators, the Springboks ran in five tries, two by Briers and one each by Ulyate, Van Vollenhoven and Retief. Ulyate also added a drop goal and Dryburgh two conversions. This time it was their fly-half Clive Ulyate that had a fine game.[17] The Lions still ran the ball well and O'Reilly and Greenwood scored tries and Pedlow converted one. They led 5-3 at the break, but once the Springbok forwards got into a higher gear, the tries started to come.

The Springboks were happy with the result as they acknowledged that the Lions had been an exceptional team that had played entertaining and, at times, brilliant rugby. The *Johannesburg Star* newspaper summed up the tour as a success and thanked the Lions for 'demonstrating that the brightest football is still the best football'.[18]

The 1955 British Lions had brought great excitement to South Africa. Dr Danie Craven summed up the tour:

> For a long time yet, many of us will sigh with relief at the fact that we were able to share the rubber against opponents of their calibre. It was, I think, the finest of all our achievements, the fact that we were able to draw the series. Here was a side which might have beaten a World XV. It had no lack of outstanding players, and speed was the basis of all its attacks. There was an abundance of initiative, and the handling was outstanding. We had not previously been honoured by the presence of players of this calibre in any touring team.[19]

East Africa and Farewell

The Lions finished their tour with a match against East Africa at the Ngong Road Ground, Nairobi, winning comfortably 39-12. Manager Jack Siggins was invited by the Rugby Football Union of East Africa (RFUEA) to officially open the newly constructed RFUEA Ground at Ngong Road just prior to the Lions' last match. Legend has it that Idi Amin, who later became the infamous military dictator of Uganda, was selected as a replacement by East Africa for the match. But the story is entirely unfounded, as Amin does not appear on the team photograph or on the official team list; and replacements were not allowed in international rugby until 1968.

In his autobiography years later, Cliff Morgan wrote, 'That tour to SA did a great deal to teach me that you had to have confidence in your fellow man and faith that he wasn't going to let you down. Your life was enriched by a feeling that everybody wanted everybody else to do well, which is what made the whole experience for me.'[20]

MORGAN THE MASTER

Clifford Isaac Morgan, CVO OBE, was born on 7 April 1930 in Trebanog in the Rhondda Valley in a mining family and joined Cardiff Rugby Club straight from Tonyrefail Grammar School in 1949, playing at fly-half.

Morgan was blessed with wonderful natural balance and strength, and together with an astute line-kicking ability and stunning acceleration quickly made an impact. He also played club rugby in Ireland for Bective Rangers in the 1955-56 season, with the club being dubbed the 'Morgan Rangers' as a result. He won his first cap for Wales against Ireland in 1951, playing opposite his hero Jack Kyle. He was part of the Grand Slam-winning Welsh side of 1952 and the next year he inspired both Cardiff and Wales to historic victories over the touring All Blacks. During the British Lions tour of South Africa in 1955, in which the Test series was drawn 2-2, Morgan distinguished himself for his marshalling of a talented Lions backline. Many of the old folk in South Africa still recall it as 'the Cliff Morgan tour'. His last game of first-class rugby was for the Barbarians on 28 May 1958 in Nairobi versus East Africa.

After his retirement from the game in 1958 he found a new career in broadcasting. He will forever be remembered for his wonderful commentary on the 1973 Barbarians rugby match against the touring All Blacks at Cardiff, but his broadcasting career was far more wide-ranging. In 1960 he was invited by the BBC to join them as Sports Organiser in Cardiff and then spent two years as editor of ITV's current affairs programme *This Week*. Returning to the BBC he then produced and edited established TV sports programmes, while in radio he found a natural outlet for his love of music in presenting the BBC Radio 2 series *These You Have Loved*. In 1974 he became Head of BBC Radio Sport and Outside Broadcasts, and from 1976 to 1987 he was Head of BBC Television Sport and Outside Broadcasts, supervising coverage of major sporting events, royal weddings and other national ceremonial occasions. After his retirement from his executive post in BBC Television in 1987 he returned to radio.

Morgan was among the inaugural inductees when the International Rugby Hall of Fame was created in 1997, and for his contributions to broadcasting was honoured with an OBE and a CVO. He survived a life-threatening stroke in 1972 at the age of forty-two but made a full recovery. He died at his home in Bembridge, Isle of Wight, on 29 August 2013, aged eighty-three.

TONY O'REILLY

Sir Anthony Joseph Francis O'Reilly, KBE, AO was born 7 May 1936 in Dublin, Ireland, and was the only child of a civil servant, John O'Reilly (1906–16), and Aileen O'Connor (1914–89). He grew up on Griffith Avenue, a broad middle-class street in the Drumcondra/Glasnevin area of Dublin, and was educated at Belvedere College. From the age of six, O'Reilly was known for sporting proficiency in football, cricket, tennis and rugby union and also noted for his acting skills. He went on to study law simultaneously with University College, Dublin, and the then Incorporated Law Society of Ireland, in practice with Gerry Quinn.

Between 1955 and 1970 O'Reilly won twenty-nine caps for Ireland. His Five Nations career of fifteen years, twenty-three days is the longest in history, a record shared with fellow Ireland great Mike Gibson. He made his senior international debut, aged just eighteen, against France on 22 January 1955, and scored his four tries for Ireland against France on 28 January 1956; against Scotland on 25 February 1956; against Wales in 1959; and against France in 1963. He made his final appearance for Ireland on 14 February 1970, after a six-year absence from the national team against England. His final appearance was an eleventh-hour replacement that denied Frank O'Driscoll, the father of Brian, what would be his only chance at a Test cap.

O'Reilly toured twice with the British Lions, first on their 1955 tour to South Africa and their 1959 tour to Australia and New Zealand. He made his debut for the Lions on 26 June 1955, scoring two tries against a Northern Universities XV. He played fifteen games during the 1955 tour, scoring sixteen tries. He also played in all four Tests against South Africa, scoring two tries in the series. On the 1959 tour he played a further twenty-three games and scored twenty-two tries; he played in all six Tests, two against Australia and four against New Zealand. His total of thirty-eight tries for the Lions on two tours remains a record.

Between 1955 and 1963 O'Reilly also made thirty appearances and scored thirty-eight tries for the Barbarians. On the Barbarians' 1958 tour of South Africa, O'Reilly scored twelve tries, seven of them in the game against East Africa. He remains the Barbarians record holder for both appearances and tries. O'Reilly was a member of the IRFU Commercial Committee and was in the first class of inductees into the International Rugby Hall of Fame in 1997 and the IRB Hall of Fame in 2009.

O'Reilly went from college to work as a management consultant for Weston-Evans in Ashby-de-la-Zouch, Leicestershire, and then moved to Sutton's of Cork, selling agricultural products, coal and oil. He joined An Bord Bainne, the Irish Dairy Board, in 1962, as General Manager, and developed the successful Kerrygold 'umbrella brand' for Irish export butter. In 1969, he joined Heinz where he made his name in international business, becoming MD of the Heinz subsidiary in the UK, and moved to the company HQ in Pittsburgh in 1971 when he was promoted to Senior Vice President for the North America and Pacific region. In 1973, he became COO and President and CEO in 1979. He became Chairman of Heinz in 1987, succeeding H. J. Heinz II, and becoming the first non-Heinz family member to hold that post. O'Reilly left Heinz in 1998. During his time at Heinz, O'Reilly also held roles as a major shareholder and chairman of several companies, including Waterford Wedgwood (1995–2009) and Independent News & Media, and of a major partnership of solicitors, Matheson, in Dublin. He was honoured with the Media Person of the Year Award at the 55th Cannes Lions International Advertising Festival in May 2008.

O'Reilly sponsored and supported a wide range of charitable activities, such as the support of a Professorship in Australian Studies at UCD and of a gallery at the National Science Historical Museum adjacent to Birr Castle. The O'Reilly Foundation was set up by O'Reilly with a Board of Trustees composed of family members, and contributes to various projects with an emphasis on the education sector.

O'Reilly married his first wife, Susan M. Cameron, the daughter of a wealthy Australian mining figure, in 1962. He had six children by her, of which three boys are involved in family business interests. The O'Reillys separated in the late 1980s. O'Reilly later married Chryss Goulandris, a Greek shipping heiress well known on the racecourses of Ireland, Britain and France as Lady O'Reilly.

1955 BRITISH LIONS
Manager – J. A. E. Siggins (Ireland)
Assistant Manager – D. E. Davies

Backs
Doug Baker (England)
Jeff Butterfield (England)
Angus Cameron (Scotland)
Phil Davies (England)
Gareth Griffiths (Wales)
Dickie Jeeps (Northampton)
Trevor Lloyd (Wales)
Cliff Morgan (Wales)
Haydn Morris (Wales)

Tony O'Reilly (Ireland)
Cecil Pedlow (Ireland)
Pat Quinn (England)
Arthur Smith (Scotland)
Frank Sykes (England)
Alun Thomas (Wales)
Johnny Williams (England)

Forwards
Tom Elliot (Scotland)
Jim Greenwood (Scotland)
Reg Higgins (England)
Hugh McLeod (Scotland)
Bryn Meredith (Wales)
Courtney Meredith (Wales)
Ernie Michie (Scotland)
Tom Reid (Ireland)
Russell Robins (Wales)
Robin Roe (Ireland)
Clem Thomas (Wales)
Robin Thompson (Capt., Ireland)
Rhys Williams (Wales)
Billy Williams (Wales)
Dyson Wilson (England)

* Dickie Jeeps later played for England but was uncapped at the time of the 1955 tour.

8

THE 1962 BRITISH LIONS: THE HEAVY BOYS

By the time that the Lions had come to South Africa, the Springboks had shortly before beaten the All Blacks in a four-Test series (1960) and completed a Grand Slam of the four home unions on their UK tour (1960–61), so the visitors from the British Isles – captained by Scottish wing Arthur Smith – were well aware that they had their work cut out. A feature of the tour would be the way the British forwards held their own in the tight phases; in the loose play and in the backs they were disappointing, unfortunately. The Lions manager, commander Brian Vaughan, was a firm believer in solid forward play and reckoned that if they could match the Springboks up front, the series would be almost as good as won. Vaughan personally undertook the drilling of the forwards, and to his credit he made a good job of it. With big, heavy men in the tight positions, they scrummed very well, and solid, driving forwards, such as the legendary Willie John McBride and Bill Mulcahy, drove effectively from the line-outs. They were to discover, however, that in the faster South African conditions mobility among the forwards was quite important. Instead of a fast, roving type number eight, they chose their heaviest forward, the lock Mike Campbell-Lamerton, as anchor at the back of the scrum. The best man for the position really was Alun Pask, but he was played as blind side flanker. Sadly for the Lions, David Nash, the other number eight, contracted a serious illness that meant the end of his playing career.

Rugby scribe Reg Sweet said of Pask: '...as a blind side wing forward, [he] was surely as fine a player on the flank as any touring team had brought to South Africa in living memory. Whether defensively or on attack, his sense of positioning was to be marvelled at; and as a handling, running loose forward he was not bettered in the winter of '62.'[1]

It was clear that the composition of the British Lions side of 1962 was influenced to a great degree by the success of Wales against France in Cardiff on the weekend that the selectors met to decide on the greater part of the team for Africa. It was also suggested that the victory of the Barbarians over the Springboks the year before on the Springboks' last match of their UK tour may have shown the way. It was felt that the pattern of these matches suggested that the Lions pack could hold the Springboks at forward, and the early matches against good scrumming provincial sides like Western Transvaal and Boland confirmed this view.

Arthur Smith's 1962 British & Irish Lions needed to make a statement. Avril Malan's touring Springbok side lost just once on their 1960–61 European tour, 6-0 to the Barbarians at Cardiff Arms Park, and the Lions selectors knew that only a pack of formidable size could challenge the confrontational South Africans. Smith's forwards were the largest to ever leave Britain and boasted six forwards over 15 stone. Among them was a young Willie John McBride – on the first of his five tours – and joined by fellow behemoths Keith Rowlands, Mike Campbell-Lamerton, Peter Wright, Kingsley Jones and Syd Millar.

The tourists had few inside backs of real quality – none in the league of a Cliff Morgan or Jeff Butterfield anyway – except for Richard Sharp and Ken Jones, but Sharp sustained an unfortunate jaw fracture against Northern Transvaal before the first Test, while David Hewitt, their star centre, suffered a hamstring injury early on.

In South Africa in 1962, the ball was not the problem. It was not, of course, won in any overwhelming measure. The advantage was a slender one, but it was there. Yet there was a measure of reluctance to dare the defence in the manner that had characterised British Isles sides of the recent past... On the face of it, the Lions of 1962 made less coin than they might of the endeavours of fine forwards... In a series fought as closely as was this one, orthodox back play was not enough to tip the scales.[2]

The most experienced British Lions in the squad were undoubtedly the only two survivors from the 1955 tour to South Africa, namely Dickie Jeeps, the England scrum half, and Welsh hooker Bryn Meredith. Both were playing on their third Lions tour that would bring Jeeps's total in Tests for the Lions to thirteen. In years to come it would only be surpassed by the great Willie John McBride with seventeen. Meredith, unfortunately, had to compete with tour skipper Ronnie Dawson on the 1959 NZ tour and featured in no Tests.

For the first three Tests the series was quite close, with only eight points separating the two sides. It was only in the last Test on the bone-hard field in Bloemfontein that the Springboks ran away with it, after leading only 10-6 at the break.

The Lions kicked off their tour with a match against Rhodesia at Bulawayo on 26 May, and led only 11-6 at half-time. But after the resumption, the visitors started attacking at pace and the dykes burst for the Rhodesians. Scoring seven tries, they won 38-9, with a superb Richard Sharp at fly-half scoring two. The fair-haired fly-half had a blinder, and received a standing ovation from the sporting Rhodesian crowd of 11,000. On the negative side, hooker Stan Hodgson suffered a serious leg injury in the second half, which put him out of the rest of the tour.

Griquas on the bone-hard surface of Kimberley was another matter, though, and the local side held the Lions to an 8-all draw. Coached by the wily former Springbok back Ian Kirkpatrick, the Griquas scored two tries against the two of the Lions. The visitors were leading 5-0 at the break but were peppered with kicks which led to two tries to Griquas from akward bounces – both scored by centre Des Froneman.

Western Transvaal, known for its die-hard forward play, were now waiting in Potchefstroom – the scene of the 1955 Lions' first defeat in their very first match. But the Lions were up to the task, absorbing the bashing of the Western Transvaal pack led by the veteran Springbok lock Johan Claassen, and finishing the stronger in the end. Behind the pack, Waddell played a sound tactical game, setting his personal seal on their 11-6 victory with a neat dropped goal.

From here it was down to the coast, where they beat a Southern Universities line-up with some fine players 14-11. Meredith was not available and the replacement hooker Godwin had yet to arrive, so Sid Millar had to stand in. Behind the students' pack, scrum half Dawie de Villiers had an impressive game, which was the start of a meteoric rise in South African rugby. In the Lions' next match, against the Western Province neighbours Boland, the home side fielded a solid pack with two Springboks in the front row in the veteran Chris Koch and Melt Hanekom. But in front of 20,000 spectators at picturesque Wellington, the visitors gained the ascendancy in the second half and ran out convincing 25-8 winners. Again, Richard Sharp caused many problems with his lethal breaks. But three days later, in faraway Windhoek in South West Africa, the Lions struggled to find their feet in a 14-6 win. The match was notable in that it was the first appearance on tour of that famous Lion of all Lions, Willie John McBride, because of injury. Replacement hooker Godwin also played for the first time.

Northern Transvaal at Loftus Versfeld was always going to be a hard nut to crack, and so it proved. Fielding eight Springboks/future Springboks, with the likes of Frik du Preez, Mof Myburgh, their fiery captain Louis Schmidt, scrum half Piet Uys and Mannetjies Roux, the Blue Bulls scored three tries to the penalty goal and dropped goal of the visitors. Final score Northern Transvaal 14, British Lions 6. In mitigation, the Lions lost their mercurial fly-half, Richard Sharp, within four minutes with a fractured cheekbone following a hard tackle by Mannetjies Roux. It meant that Alun Pask had to move to left wing and the backline had to be reshuffled. Most importantly, the depleted Lions pack with

Mulcahy, Rowlands and Meredith especially prominent, earned high honours, and Dickie Jeeps flourished as in Kimberley when the chips were down.

H. J. C. Brown was flown out as Richard Sharp's replacement. When he arrived in Johannesburg, he was taken to meet the unfortunate Sharp in hospital. He said that Sharp's face was an absolute mess due to the tackle from Roux, and that he looked as if he had been in a car crash.

The First Test and to the Coast: A Fair Start

For the first Test at Ellis Park in Johannesburg on 23 June, the Lions played Gordon Waddell of Scotland in the crucial position of fly-half. His tactical and touch-kicking style of play actually suited the forward-oriented game envisaged by Vaughan. The Springboks fielded two new caps in wing Ormond Taylor and centre Melville Wyness. It was no great Test, but at least produced an excellent try on either side, with the contest ending in a 3-all draw. For the Springboks, their fast, hard-running centre John Gainsford was put clear by Mannetjies Roux in the first half; he made a dash for the right-hand corner, only just beating full back Willcox before touching down. In the second half, with only ten minutes remaining, Willcox turned defence into attack, finding Waddell who sent Ken Jones off on a 60-yard run to the line.

On to Natal, at King's Park in Durban, the 'Last Outpost of the British Empire', as the controversial (later) Springbok No. 8 Tommy Bedford would refer to it. In a match where both sides' approach was to play open, attacking rugby, the Lions held the upper hand in the scrummages and ran out 13-3 winners in front of a crowd of 30,000. The visitors scored two tries to the home side's sole penalty by their Springbok fly-half, Keith Oxlee. The margin between the teams, however, was much narrower than the score suggested.

Still at the coast, the Lions faced Eastern Province in Port Elizabeth on 30 June. The previous encounter between these sides in 1955 was catastrophic for the visitors, going down 20-0 to the men from 'The Friendly City'. This time around, however, after leading only 5-3 at half-time, the Lions cut loose in the second half, scoring three tries in the match. A feature of the match was the goal-kicking of Willcox, who converted all three tries and kicked two long penalty goals for the best place-kicking performance of the tour to date. Final score British Lions 21, Eastern Province 6.

Free State in Bloemfontein was a very tough affair, and the Lions only scraped through for a 14-all draw with a last-minute conversion of Haydn Morgan's try off the last scrum of the match, while 30,000 spectators looked on. The Lions led 6-3 at the break through two Willcox penalties, and increased their lead early in the second half with a try by Richard Sharp's replacement, H. J. C. Brown, playing in the centre. But a 20-minute golden patch for Free State saw them surge into a 14-9 lead with two tries by their speedy wing Gert Cilliers and further points from the boot of full back Strydom, until Morgan's try at the death denied them victory.

More stiff opposition was to follow. Up north in Pretoria, in front of 37 000 spectators, they faced the Junior Springboks and were trailing 3-11 in the early part of the second half before their forwards came increasingly into the picture and tries by Morgan and Jones and the boots of Weston and Tom Kiernan saw them through 16-11. The Junior Boks had the consolation that they outscored the Lions by three tries to two. Scrum half De Villiers had another fine game against the visitors, in fact playing himself into the scrum half berth for the second Test.

In a match marked by very robust play, the Lions then defeated the Combined Services – with a few Springboks in the side – 20-6 at Potchefstroom. The latter's forwards failed to stay the pace and the Lions' pack, the same as the combination fielded in the first Test, put up a very encouraging performance with a view to the second Test waiting around the corner.

In contrast to the robust affair at Potchefstroom, their fourteenth match against Western Province at Newlands turned out to be the finest of the tour up to that stage. Fielding nine Springboks/future Springboks, Western Province were sure to give them a run for their money. But trailing 8-13 at one stage, the visitors stunned the local crowd of 30,000 by scoring 13 points in the last eight minutes to win 21-13. For the Lions, their pack of forwards had become the mainstay of their success, while the backs, with Waddell at the helm, made good use of their attacking opportunities. Amongst the loose forwards, Pask had an excellent game. Not surprisingly, the Newlands crowd invaded the field after the final whistle to cheer both teams off.

The Second Test: Remember Cardiff!

Welshmen in the touring squad would remember the Springbok fly-half Keith Oxlee as the man who kicked a winning penalty goal in the clinging mud of Cardiff Arms Park in 1960. Now, in the second Test at King's Park, Durban, on 21 July, he repeated this performance to clinch the game for the Springbks and put them 1-0 up in the series, while the visitors failed to register a single point.

With 43,000 spectators watching, the Springboks dominated the first twenty minutes, with Oxlee coming close with a drop goal. But the Lions launched attacks of their own, with Jones once stopped just 10 yards short of the Boks' try line. When half-time came, there was still no score. Some penalties and drop goals were missed on either side, and five minutes from time the climax came when Rowlands was blown for offside, and from 35 yards out, and 7 yards infield from touch, Oxlee slotted the crucial penalty.

But that was not the end of it. With literally seconds to play, Waddell kicked for the corner flag, and with the ball just going into touch, referee Ken Carlson called a final line-out. Roux's throw-in was skew, and a scrum was awarded to the Lions. Jeeps put the ball in, Mulcahy called for a 'hold and wheel', and when the wheel collapsed on the Springboks' line, the Lions celebrated what they thought was a try by Keith Rowlands. But Mr Carlson, later claiming he was unsighted, blew his whistle for a scrum 5 yards and then immediately for full time. Rowlands was completely convinced that he had fallen on the ball as the scrum collapsed and that it was grounded inside the in-goal area.[3] Springbok scrum half Dawie de Villiers, who was right by the action at the time, many years later also conceded that it was a try.[4] No one could blame the visitors for feeling that they at least deserved a draw.

An interesting fact regarding this Test was that in Dawie de Villiers at scrum half for the Springboks and Gordon Waddell at fly-half for the Lions, you had two potential opposition MPs of the South African Parliament. De Villiers of course went on to become a ruling party MP and Cabinet Minister, while Waddell sat in the Opposition benches for the Progressive Party.

Before the third Test, the Lions still had to take care of the Northern Universities and Transvaal. The students gave them a good run for their money at Springs and the match ended in a 6-all draw, with the Lions scoring a try and a penalty and the Universities a try and drop goal. For the match, Sharp returned for the first time since his mishap against Northern Transvaal. Next up was Transvaal, which boasted a good, solid pack of forwards including a few Springboks, and another in Mickey Gerber among the backs. But the Lions returned to their finest form and leading 8-3 at the break, outplayed their opponents to win 24-3. In the process, they scored three goals, a drop goal and two penalties to the try of Transvaal. For the Lions, Mulcahy and Smith (2) scored tries, with Sharp adding two penalties, three conversions and a drop goal. After this match, the Lions would have felt ready to take on the Springboks down south in Cape Town.

Third Test: Last Chance

A loss would mean the end of their chances of a series victory, which had eluded them since 1896. During the week before the Test it rained hard with frost on the Friday night, and Saturday 4 August was clear but cold. This would be the first Test at Newlands for the legendary Frik du Preez, who went on to play thirty-eight Tests for the Springboks until 1971 – not many these days, but a lot in that era.

When it became apparent that Richard Sharp would play, black market prices for tickets shot up to unheard-of prices. Traditionally 'non-Europeans' were allowed to sit only on the South Stand behind the goalposts, yet even some of these seats were reserved for 'Europeans'. On the afternoon of the Test many more spectators of colour appeared at Newlands, very eager to support the Lions. Chaos erupted after the gates were closed and those outside began to climb over the turnstiles. In excess of 100 spectators or would-be spectators had to be treated for injuries by the St John Ambulance volunteers on a cement area.

Both sides made several attacks before Sharp missed a goalable penalty, before Springbok wing Jannie Engelbrecht crossed the try line, only to be called back for a forward pass. The Lions put first points on the board when Sharp put over a drop goal from 30 yards. Then just before half-time Oxlee levelled the scores with a penalty against Campbell-Lamerton for hands-in. The Lions pack won the battle up front but their backs were kept under pressure. About thirty minutes into the second half, Sharp attempted to run the ball from near his try line and Ken Jones was tackled in possession; the loose ball was snapped up by Keith Oxlee who crashed over for a try, which he converted for an 8-3 lead. For the remainder of the match the Lions played their hearts out but to no avail.[5]

Having lost the series, it was a disappointed Lions team that left Cape Town for Bloemfontein en route to Burgersdorp, where they were to play North Eastern Districts. It was an easy match, which they won 34-8. Probably for the first time since the opening match at Salisbury, the Lions backs were let off the leash and allowed to run as free as the wind, scoring seven tries after leading 16-5 at the break. From here it was on to Port Elizabeth where they faced the Central Universities, and it was evident that they were coming towards the end of a long tour. Leading 6-0 at half-time, they eventually won 14-6. Their last match against Eastern Transvaal at Springs was to end in disappointment, losing 16-19 against the Red Devils, who played an attacking game and outscored them four tries to three. The Easterns' fly-half Norman Riley was to make his Springbok debut the next season against the Wallabies.

The Fourth Test: Uninhibited Rugby

More than 60,000 spectators braved the heat of Bloemfontein for the fourth and final Test at the Free State Stadium on 25 August. But they were well rewarded by handling and running of a

GORDON WADDELL: A REMARKABLE MAN

Between 1957 and 1962, Gordon Waddell (12 April 1937–13 August 2012) won eighteen caps for Scotland, five of which as captain, including the Test match against South Africa in Port Elizabeth in 1960. In 1962 he was the main influence in Scotland's first win in Wales since the 1930s, an achievement not repeated for another twenty years. During his eighteen caps he was never dropped, although he had to leave because of injury, and his record for a Scotland fly-half was only later broken by John Rutherford. Waddell and his father Herbert Waddell are one of the very few examples of a father and son having played for the same teams in the same position. Both were fly-halves for Scotland and the British Lions. Waddell twice toured with the British Isles: to New Zealand in 1959 when university examinations and injury limited his appearances to ten (including seven tries) and South Africa in 1962 when his twelve appearances included the first Test and he also scored 17 points. He played twelve times for the Barbarians between 1957 and 1960.

Waddell was a Director of E[rnest] Oppenheimer & Son Ltd, 1967–87; Executive Director of the Anglo American Corporation of South Africa Ltd, 1971–87; Chairman of Johannesburg Consolidated Investments Ltd, 1981–87; Rustenburg Platinum Mines Ltd, 1981–87; South African Breweries Ltd, 1984–87; Fairway Group PLC, 1989–98; Ryan GP 1991-95; Gartmore Scotland Investment Trust, 1991–2001; Tor Investment Trust, 1992–96; Mersey Docks and Harbour Company, 1992–2006; Shanks Group PLC; Director Cadbury Schweppes, 1988–97; Scottish National Trust 1988–96; London and Strathclyde Trust 1989–96.

Waddell was elected to the South African Parliament in April 1974, winning the constituency of Johannesburg North for the Progressive Party. Waddell was one of seven new Progressive Party MPs who won election to Parliament that year, and acted as spokesperson for Economic Affairs for the Progressive Federal Party during his term. He became known as the tycoon Harry Oppenheimer's chief fixer on cross-border deals, deploying the convenience of his UK passport to go where other South Africans at the time could not. He returned to Scotland in 1987. His wife Mary, daughter of Oppenheimer, once said: 'He'll be much more of an Oppenheimer than I'll ever be.'⁹

superlative skill and support play of the highest order. Keith Oxlee, who kicked excellently in windy conditions, was to better the Test record of Okey Geffin of 15 points in a Test that had stood since 1949 against the All Blacks, scoring 16 points with two penalties and five conversions. Tries from Ron Cowan, Rowlands and Mike Campbell-Lamerton and a conversion and penalty from John Willcox were not enough to save the match for the Lions as the Springboks ran in six tries, five conversions and two penalties to win the final Test 34-14 and take the series.

Leading only 10-6 at the break and with the visitors well in the match, South Africa scored 13 points in only five minutes in the second half as they hit a purple patch which simply blew the Lions away. One of the tries was scored by wing Mannetjies Roux, who ran from his own half of the field and swerved his way past several defenders to score in a long, arching dive. The spectators also enjoyed the sight of a rampant Frik du Preez bursting through one tackle after another for some 50 yards before delivering a final pass for Hugo van Zyl's try.⁶ It was indeed a case of, as that great BBC man Bill Mclaren would put it, 'running like a stag'. A legitimate criticism of the Lions was that they lacked true loose forwards in a wide-ranging game and there was no one to match the pace of the Springboks' Doug Hopwood.

Away from the Tests, the Lions had won sixteen matches, drawing three and losing two. Compared to the 1955 Lions who scored ninety-four tries, the Lions of 1962 scored sixty-two tries. From a total of 351 points, full back John Willcox scored sixty-seven. They did, however, concede fewer points than Robin Thompson's 1955 team. Lions captain Arthur Smith, with eight tries from fourteen matches, was the most successful finisher.

For the Springboks, Keith Oxlee played a crucial role in the Springboks' success during the series, but not only in terms of all the points he scored at critical times. Welsh rugby scribe J. B. G. Thomas summed up the Springbok fly-half:

> Oxlee was a modern outside-half in approach, although not quite as brilliant or elusive as Cliff Morgan [the Welsh fly-half]... He had an excellent pair of hands and a good eye for an opening near the scrum, as well as being an excellent tactical kicker. He did not score many tries on this tour [the 1960-61 UK tour], but obviously he was another player who, if properly encouraged in open play, would have had an even better tour. He was dependable and fitted in with the normal Springbok tactics, which were based on winning at all costs within the laws.[7]

His old centre teammate John Gainsford said of Oxlee:

> Keith Oxlee would be my number one Springbok fly-half of the 1960s – by the proverbial mile. But while most people remember him as a brilliant running fly-half and the mainstay of what was to become known as "Natal rugby", I always rated him as a far better kicking fly-half. At least at international level. His best games in the Springbok jersey, as far as I am concerned, were those in which the games were tight and he had to do a lot of kicking... Keith was a magnificent footballer and a cunning tactician. He also booted many vital Test points for us and I think if he had been a yard or two faster he would have been absolutely devastating.[8]

1962 BRITISH LIONS

Manager – D. B. Vaughan (England)
Coach – H. R. McKibbin (Ireland)

Backs
Dewi Bebb (Wales)
Niall Brophy (Ireland)
H. J. C. Brown (Blackheath and RAF)
J. M. Dee (England)
Ronnie Cowan (Scotland)
David Hewitt (Ireland)
Raymond Hunter (Ireland)
Dickie Jeeps (England)
Ken Jones (Wales)
Tom Kiernan (Ireland)
Tony O'Connor (Wales)
Richard Sharp (England)
Arthur Smith (Capt., Scotland)
Gordon Waddell (Scotland)
Mike Weston (England)
John Willcox England)

Forwards
Mike Campbell-Lamerton (Scotland)
Glyn Davidge (Wales)
John Douglas (Scotland)
H. O. Godwin (England)
Stan Hodgson (England)
Kingsley Jones (Wales)
Willie John McBride (Ireland)
Bryn Meredith (Wales)
Syd Millar (Ireland)
Haydn Morgan (Wales)
Bill Mulcahy (Ireland)
David Nash (Wales)

Alun Pask (Wales)
Budge Rogers (England)
David Rollo (Scotland)
Keith Rowlands (Wales)
T. P. Wright (England)

1962 BRITISH LIONS TOUR PROGRAM & RESULTS
May 26 v Rhodesia W 38-9
May 31 v Griqualand West D 8-8
June 2 v Western Transvaal W 11-6
June 6 v Southern Universities W 14-11
June 9 v Boland W 25-8
June 12 v South West Africa W 14-6
June 16 v Northern Transvaal L 6-14
June 23 v South Africa D 3-3
June 27 v Natal W 13-3
June 30 v Eastern Province W 21-6
July 4 v Orange Free State D 14-14
July 7 v Junior Springboks W 16-11
July 11 v Combined Services W 20-6
July 14 v Western Province W 21-13
July 17 v South West Districts W 11-3
July 21 v South Africa L 0-3
July 25 v Northern Universities D 6-6
July 28 v Transvaal W 24-3
August 4 v South Africa L 3-8
August 8 v North East Districts W 34-8
August 11 v Border W 5-0
August 15 v Central Universities W 14-6
August 18 v Eastern Transvaal L 16-19
August 25 v South Africa L 14-34
August 28 v East Africa W 50-0

9

THE 1968 BRITISH LIONS: CLOSE BUT NO CIGAR

The 1968 British Lions will be remembered as a team that was highly successful in the provincial matches, but failed to achieve its real mission, to become the first British side to win a Test series in South Africa since Johnny Hammond's team in 1896. With the exception of the Transvaal match, they won fifteen of their sixteen provincial matches. In terms of the Tests, the best they could do was a draw. In the twenty matches they played on tour – the fewest of any overseas team on a long tour of South Africa since the visit of W. E. Maclagan's side in 1891 – they scored 339 points with 120 against.

Up to their seventh match, when the British Lions played their first Test, they had South African supporters quite worried with six successive wins. The only British Lions side who had achieved this before was Maclagan's men in 1891. The 1960 All Blacks managed to win five and draw one of their first six matches. While morale was high, seasoned campaigners like Tom Kiernan, Willie John McBride, Syd Millar and the coach Ronnie Dawson did not get carried away. Former Springboks were nevertheless quite impressed with the Lions' victories over Western Province and Natal, two of South Africa's strongest provinces. The Lions could not know that the Springboks were streets ahead of any provincial side they had encountered. This applied particularly to the forwards, where they would come up against super players like Frik du Preez, Mof Myburgh, Hannes Marais, Jan Ellis and Tommy Bedford. Behind this pack, they fielded an experienced and well-established half-back pairing in Dawie de Villiers (the captain) and Piet Visagie, and speedy three-quarters.

The touring party was captained by Tom Kiernan, coached by Ronnie Dawson and managed by David Brooks. As well as South Africa, games were played against South West Africa (now Namibia) and Rhodesia (now Zimbabwe). Unlike the previous two tours to South Africa, this team did not stop off in Nairobi, Kenya, to play East Africa on the way home. The squad boasted such great talents as Gareth Edwards, Barry John, Mike Gibson and Gerald Davies, but the party was ravaged by injury and the four of them never appeared in a Test team together. Gibson became the Lions', and international rugby's, first replacement when he came onto the field to win the first of his eventual twelve Test appearances for the Lions on five tours. Six of the squad would ultimately change codes and play professional rugby league: Mike Coulman, Ken Goodall, Keith Jarrett, Keri Jones, Maurice Richards, and Bryan West.[1]

It was interesting that the Welsh flanker John Taylor was prepared to tour South Africa with the Lions in 1968, but the very next year gave up his place in the Welsh team that had to play South Africa because of his views on apartheid. He was also invited on the 1974 Lions tour to South Africa but made it clear he would follow his conscience and he refused to tour.[2]

Jim Telfer's leadership qualities were once again put to good use on this tour. Apart from skippering the side in four of the provincial matches, Telfer acted as pack leader in each of the last three Tests against the Springboks. His selection for the tour had been very much in doubt after injury had interrupted his Scotland career until the Six Nations match with England, when a typically industrious performance secured his place. Despite suffering a knee injury against Western Province that ruled him out of contention for the first Test, he started the remaining three internationals.

There were two changes from the original selection: England centre Bob Lloyd stayed behind for study reasons, and was replaced by Keith Jarrett of Wales, while England loose forward Bryan West could not recover from an ankle injury in time and had to be replaced by Scotland's Rodger Arneil. Arneil grabbed the opportunity with both hands and played in all four Test matches.[3]

Some fifty years later, Arneil recalled:

As a young lad from Scotland it was a great honour to be picked to go with the Lions in 1968 to South Africa and our focus was on rugby. I was even more thrilled to be selected for all four Tests and was so impressed with the hospitality and friendship we received in SA. Playing on the firm grounds of South Africa suited my game well and I enjoyed every minute of it. Playing against the likes of Jan Ellis, Tom Bedford and Piet Greyling was a great experience and for me they were world class. Whilst aware of the apartheid situation and the many problems my view was that politics had no place in sport. Sport is a way of making friends and reaching people of all classes and colour. Courtesy of SA Rugby we were asked back in 2018 with our wives for a most wonderful visit. What was evident was the enormous sporting talent in the townships we visited from the youngsters we met and talked to. They saw sport as a way forward and the work being undertaken by various organisations was absolutely marvellous.

Following a few days training at Eastbourne, the Lions boarded a SA Airways Boeing on 12 May bound for Johannesburg. On their arrival the next day, manager David Brooks told the news conference that the Lions would be playing 'attacking, but not suicidal rugby'.[4]

Their first match was against Western Transvaal, who had beaten the 1955 Lions 9-6, but this Western Transvaal side was not as strong as the one from those glory days. After a week of drizzle, the day of the match was bright and sunny, and became even more bright when Western Transvaal took a 6-0 lead after a second penalty in the twenty-sixth minute. The Lions only scored after thirty-seven minutes when Jim Telfer pounced on a wayward line-out ball to score in the corner. First try of the tour then to Jim Telfer. Kiernan's conversion failed, but the Lions took control in the second half to score 17 more points, including three tries (a second one by Telfer). The *Mielieboere* added two penalties for a final score of British Lions 20, Western Transvaal 12. A feature of the match was the introduction of the new substitute law when Barry Bresnihan came on for the injured Mike Gibson, who later on tour himself became the first Test substitute when he replaced the injured Barry John in the first Test.

In only their second match of the tour, the tourists had to face the strong Western Province team, the Currie Cup champions, who fielded ten Springboks/future Springboks in their line-up. A crowd of 45,000 had showed up to cheer on their team. It was the Lions, though, who opened the scoring after twenty minutes when left wing Richards went over in the corner after the Lions had pounced on a loose ball and sent it along the line. Kiernan's conversion made it 5-0. Western Province struggled to get going and then, in the thirty-sixth minute of the first half, Barry John exhibited his brilliance. From a scrum 5 yards from his own try line, he broke straight upfield instead of kicking for touch, kicked ahead, collected again and linked with Bresnihan, who sent Savage in for a fantastic score.

A penalty by their captain Tiny Naudé brought the score closer, and in the second half the local side came more and more into the game. In the 33rd minute the exciting Province full back H. O. de Villiers breached the defence and sent centre Johann van der Merwe in close to the posts. The conversion, however, was missed and it was a relieved Lions side that left the field 10-6 winners. But the score could have been more convincing, had Kiernan not fluffed a few penalties and John two drop goal attempts. Injuries to Telfer and Davies didn't help their cause, either. There was general consensus among former Springboks that this Lions side could become hard to beat in the Tests.

A much easier outing awaited them in Mossel Bay where South Western Districts were no match for them, and went down 6-24 to the visitors who led 9-3 at the break. The Lions scored four tries, while Hiller added three conversions and two penalties. From here it was on to the Boet Erasmus Stadium in Port Elizabeth (now demolished) to face Eastern Province, that had a useful pack led by Springbok Gawie Carelse. Cliff Morgan of 1955 fame was there to commentate for the BBC and sure to revive memories of the 0-20 debacle thirteen years before. As expected, the red-and-blacks gave them a difficult time and leading only 15-14 with thirteen minutes to go, the Lions had to produce a strong finish to reach a 23-14 final score. Playing McBride at No. 8 was not a success. Hiller contributed a try, conversion and three penalty goals, Turner two dropped goals and Hinshelwood a try, while the home side managed a try and three penalties.

For their fifth match, the Lions travelled to Durban to play Natal, whose stalwart Springbok fly-half Keith Oxlee had retired the year before. But they still fielded a competitive side with players like Springboks Tommy Bedford and Don Walton and Junior Springbok prop Willem Labuschagne. In front of a crowd of some 35,000, the Lions ran up an unassailable lead of 17-0 by half-time; in the first twenty minutes or so, they were already 14-0 ahead. The scoring was opened in only the fifth minute by Gareth Edwards, who slipped past the loose forwards Tommy Bedford and Ian Grant and then full back Rodney Gould (who was to become a Springbok in the Test series) to score under the posts for Kiernan to convert. Kiernan followed up with a penalty and then from a 5-yard scrum John flung out a long pass to Savage who fed Turner who had cut outside to score. Soon McBride and Millar breached the defence before Bresnihan took Millar's long pass to score far out. In the twenty-sixth minute, Gareth Edwards initiated a fourth try from a line-out when he broke, linked with Turner and the centre sent Richards over in the corner. Kiernan missed several kicks, otherwise the score would have been much higher. It was only in the last twenty minutes that Natal started a revival among the forwards and after half an hour McIntosh scored behind the posts for Swanby to convert. In the last ten minutes it was all Natal but they could not add to their score, and the match ended in a 17-5 victory for the Lions. It was regarded as the visitors' best performance on tour to date, with Edwards and John superb as half-backs.

Match number six for the Lions, and all the way north to Rhodesia. Even though they made far too many elementary errors in the first half, they still ran in five tries, O'Shea scoring two. Jarrett and Kiernan contributed a penalty and two conversions each, while Gibson added a drop goal. Rhodesia scored one try and a penalty. Among the backs, Edwards once again had a good game.

First Test

After Rhodesia, it was back to the Republic and time for the real thing – the Springboks at Loftus Versfeld in Pretoria on 8 June. According to the groundsman, the field was faster and harder than it had ever been. The two teams took the field in front of around 74,000 spectators on a windless afternoon. Initially, the Boks looked the more purposeful side and sadly for the Lions, their star fly-half Barry John had to leave the field with a fractured collarbone after the first quarter. The home side took a 6-0 lead through penalties by Naude and Visagie, the first a monster of almost 60 yards. The Lions were back in the game soon when Willie John McBride crossed for a try following a wayward pass by Dirksen on the wing, and Kiernan made no mistake with the conversion. John was then replaced by Mike Gibson in the thirty-first minute, who thereby became international rugby's first replacement.

He had hardly settled in when Naude scored a gift try from a sloppy Lions line-out, crashing over from 15 yards out, with Visagie's conversion increasing the Boks' lead to 11-5. Kiernan reduced the deficit with a penalty, before Bok captain De Villiers scored his first Test try from just inside the Lions' half. Engelbrecht started a move from a loose ball, who fed Olivier, the ball went to Bedford who drew Kiernan and sent De Villiers in next to the posts. With the conversion, the lead stretched to 16-8. But Kiernan kept them within distance with a penalty just before half-time.

This was cancelled out in the twelfth minute of the second half by a Visagie penalty, against the run of play.

Then came the highlight of the Test – Springbok lock Frik du Preez's long-distance try early in the second half, and the sight of the lock thundering down the touchline, his thick mop of dark hair bobbing up and down as he ran, is still imprinted in fans' minds to this day.

Many people did not realise for quite a while that I scored only one Test try throughout my entire career [38 Tests]. So, when they asked me which Test try was my best, I would reply, tongue-in-cheek, that it 'undoubtedly must have been the one at Loftus against the Lions'! I remember we led 16-11 at half-time through tries by Dawie [de Villiers] and Tiny [Naudé], and penalty goals by Tiny and Piet Visagie. After the break Piet added another penalty goal, and then it was my turn for a try. We had practised the move a few times previously at Northern Transvaal and decided to try it out in the Test, too. We were awarded a line-out some 40m out from the Lions' goal-line. I was in the No 5 position and when Mof Myburgh secured the ball at the front, I peeled around and ran off him. I bolted down the touchline past several defenders on my way to the goal-line, and Tom Kiernan was the last man to beat, but there was no way he was going to stop me that day. The huge Loftus cheer when I dived over the line is something I will never forget. My team-mates were immediately on hand to congratulate me, but the din was so loud that I could not hear what they were saying. For years I still got a kick from just thinking about it.[5]

With the Boks leading 22-11, they seemed home and dry, but Kiernan kept the scoreboard ticking with three more penalties and another monster from inside the halfway line by Naude kept the home side ahead by five. Final score South Africa 25, British Lions 20. British scribe Vivian Jenkins summed the match up well when he commented: 'It was the Springboks' power that did it once again. I had thought that the Lions pack would be strong enough to provide their backs with at least 40 per cent share of the ball, but they were never able to do in the open exchanges, and the writing thereafter was always on the wall.'⁶

Dawie de Villiers recalled:

On the day of the Test, there were 75,000 spectators after temporary pavilions had also been erected. The British Lions were still unbeaten and the atmosphere was loaded. Our forwards had the Lions on the back foot from the start and behind such a pack Piet Visagie and I could play our best game. In addition, the star fly-half of the Lions, Barry John, had to leave the field in the first half already with a broken collarbone. It was my day and I scored my first Test try shortly before half-time when we were only leading 11-8. It was also the day when Frik du Preez scored his famous try when he burst around a line out and ran 40 yards for an outstanding score. We won 25-20, and it was only the boot of Tom Kiernan that kept the Lions within range. All agreed that we could have won even further.⁷

Before the Test, there had been criticism of De Villiers in the north of the country, but after the final whistle enthusiastic supporters carried him shoulder-high from the field.

From Loftus the Lions flew to Upingtꝏn to take on the North-West Cape, one of the smaller unions, and ran out easy winners 25-5. They scored five tries, with Hiller adding the rest with the boot. South West Africa led by Jan Ellis were next, who they put away 23-0. Showing great form, Gareth Edwards scored two tries, while Hiller, Savage and Raybould scored the others. Here in Windhoek they were also joined by replacement loose forward Ken Goodall.

Transvaal at Ellis Park in front of 42,000 spectators was a different matter altogether, and they lost their unbeaten record against provincial sides with a 6-14 defeat to a well-balanced team with a strong pack and midfield and cover defence. The Lions earned 15 penalties against them, of which the home side could aim 10 at the posts and succeeded with three. They also did not take their chances and made too many mistakes and the only try came from Mike Gibson as early as the fourth minute when he feinted a drop and dummied his way through to score.

Second Test: Holding Out

The Boks had a setback when their star flanker Piet Greyling was unavailable because of injury, and his place was taken by the Northern Transvaal loose forward Thys Lourens, the only change to the side from the first Test. Richards and John were out of contention for the Lions because of injury, and replaced by Hinshelwood and Gibson. Amongst the forwards, Pullin, Horton, Larter and Telfer replaced Young, O'Shea, Stagg and Doyle.

The Springboks had last lost a Test in Port Elizabeth as far back as 1910 – against the British Isles – at the old Crusaders Ground. This time, on 22 June, they were at the Boet Erasmus Stadium. Dr Danie Craven predicted that this would be the hardest Test of all for the Springboks to win,[8] and how right he was. The South African forwards won so much possession that it seemed impossible for the Lions to hold them out all day, but that the tourists did. At half-time the score was 3-all, courtesy of a penalty by Visagie and one by Kiernan. In the second half, Kiernan succeeded with another one and Naude with one for South Africa to bring the score to 6-all, and that's how a disappointing Test ended for 50,000 spectators at the ground. The Lions, though, had to be admired for their staunch defence. They were also fuming about the handling of the game by the referee, Mr Hansie Schoeman, whose interpretation of the laws at scrum time came under heavy fire.[9] About the second Test, Springbok captain Dawie de Villiers recalled: 'The second Test ended in a 6-all draw even though we had a lot of possession, but the Lions defended very well and their forwards were a lot more effective than in the first Test.'[10]

The Lions had a good break at the popular Kruger National Park before their match against Eastern Transvaal at Springs. On the previous tour in 1962, the Red Devils had beaten the Lions 19-16, but this time around it was a convincing 37-9 win after the Lions had quickly run up a 13-0 lead in the first twenty-six minutes. The match was unfortunately overshadowed by the referee Mr Bert Woolley's sending off of John O'Shea, the Welsh prop, after he had thrown several punches at Johan Brits, the Eastern Transvaal flank forward. Near the exit gate a spectator punched O'Shea; Willie John McBride promptly rushed from the stand to O'Shea's assistance before the police grabbed hold of O'Shea's assailant. For the record, Taylor, Gibson, Roger Young, Doyle, Richards and Davies scored tries, while Hiller landed five conversions and a penalty. Eastern Transvaal replied with two tries and a penalty.

Northern Transvaal at Loftus Versfeld was always going to be a hard nut to crack, with a great pack of forwards – including Mof Myburgh, Frik du Preez, the hard hooker Gys Pitzer and Thys Lourens – and an experienced Springbok scrum half in Piet Uys. With the Lions trailing 8-16 at the break, the Northern Transvaal supporters had visions of a famous victory, but the Lions gradually took control with Mike Gibson reading the game so well, first tiring out the heavier Northern Transvaal forwards with great tactical kicking before opening up the game. As Frik du Preez remarked, 'We ran out of petrol.' While Northerns could only add a penalty in the second half, the Lions scored a converted try by Coulman and Kiernan added three penalties during the same period. Thoughtfully, the Lions allowed John O'Shea to lead them off the field. With a well-deserved 22-19 victory, the tourists understandably felt confident leading up to the crucial third Test.[11]

The Griquas at De Beers Stadium in Kimberley were always hard to beat, and the Lions had their work cut out against a side skippered by Mannetjies Roux and boasting the Springbok fly-half Piet Visagie. The game had little sparkle, but Gareth Edwards, who scored their only two tries, was outstanding. The Lions won comfortably enough (11-3), but it was always going to be difficult to so soon raise their game to the level against Northern Transvaal.

Next up was Boland, the *Wynboere* (winefarmers) led by Springbok skipper Dawie de Villiers, and again a comfortable victory of 14-0 with the Lions – captained by Syd Millar – scoring three tries. The match was marked by the Lions' finest individual try of the tour by Davies who received the ball from Raybould, moved outside, then inside, jinking and side-stepping his way past the cover defence before straightening and accelerating clear to score to the left of the post. On the dark side, Gareth Edwards tore a hamstring that put him out of the tour permanently.

Third Test

For this crucial 13 July clash at Newlands the Lions made five changes: Roger Young in for the injured Edwards, and Richards, Davies, Coulman and Stagg in for Hinshelwood, Bresnihan, Millar and Larter. For the first time since the Second World War, the Lions fielded an all-England front row. For the Boks, Gert Brynard came in for the injured Jannie Engelbrecht on the wing. On a mild, sunny afternoon, on a firm and dry surface and with 46,000 spectators looking on, the Lions played their best rugby of the four-Test series, but failed to take their opportunities. Unfortunately, Coulman had to be carried off after only five minutes with an ankle injury that put him out of the tour, and for thirteen minutes McBride had to pack in the front row until Delme Thomas came on at tight head. During this period, Visagie put the Boks in front with a penalty before Kiernan levelled the scores just before half-time with an easy penalty.

Only three minutes into the second half, the Boks scored the vital try that eventually clinched the match for them. Just outside the Lions 25, Richards threw in deep, the ball was tapped back untidily to Young who was dispossessed and next moment Lourens snapped up the loose ball on the bounce and crossed over in the right-hand corner. Visagie converted excellently and the Boks were leading 8-3. It took the visitors a while to recover from this setback, but they then severely tested the Boks defence. At a line-out, Pullin was poleaxed by Gys Pitzer, who was lucky that the ref missed the punch, otherwise he would have been sent off. Pullin had to be revived but played on. In the twenty-eighth minute, South Africa stretched their lead – against the run of play – to 11-3 with a 50-yard penalty by Naude. With three minutes of extra time still left, Kiernan landed a penalty from just outside the Boks' 25 to reduce the deficit to five points, and there was still time to salvage a draw to keep the series alive. But try as they might, it was not to be and the match finished at 11-6 for the Springboks to clinch the series. Sadly for the Lions, on a day that their pack raised their game to great heights, the Lions' lack of combined skill and thrust in midfield let them down. Ronnie Dawson said:

> When a side fails to take what the gods offer it doesn't deserve to win. British players tend to do the wrong thing or make mistakes in a crisis. The All Blacks and also the Springboks – presented with the chances we had at Newlands – would, in all probability, have accepted them, or some of them.[12]

More bad luck crossed the Lions' path when in East London, against Border, scrum half Roger Young suffered two fractured ribs, which ended his tour. Beating Border 26-6, they only scored one try (Gibson) while Hiller kicked 23 points, consisting of five penalties, a conversion and two dropped goals. Young was replaced by Kiernan in the second half and Gordon Connell, the Scotland scrum half, had to be summoned immediately to join the squad. Connell arrived in time to start in the next game against Free State in Bloemfontein. On the previous tour in 1962, Free State managed a 14-all draw with the Lions. Winning a lot of possession at forward, Free State opened up the game where Joggie Jansen really tested the Lions defence. But it was nevertheless the Lions who led 6-0 at half-time following a Kiernan penalty and a drop goal by Gibson. In the second half, Richards scored midway out before Free State answered with a penalty for an unconvincing win for the Lions of 9-3.

One more game remained before the final Test in the Eastern Cape town of Cradock, home of North East Cape. Leading 17-9 at the break, the Lions finished with a 40-12 victory, which included seven tries. Hiller's 16 points in the match took him to his tour century of 104 points, achieved in only eight matches. They were now at the end of their journey, with just the last Test waiting in South Africa.

Fourth Test: 'Sparkling Rugby'

The Test side for Ellis Park on 27 July showed two changes from the third Test: Connell came in at scrum half, and Bresnihan for Davies in the centre. For the Springboks, Tiny Neethling came in for Mof Myburgh. The last time a touring team had won a fourth Test in South Africa was forty years earlier, when Maurice Brownlee's All Blacks won at Newlands in 1928. But at this stage of the tour, not many gave the visitors a chance to repeat that feat.

Having won the series, the Springboks were in a relaxed frame of mind and therefore approached the fourth Test looking to attack. By now, the Lions were tour-weary, the several injuries had taken their toll and, as the saying goes, they already had one foot in the plane bound for Britain. The Springboks led 6-3 at half-time and in the second half took control to score a runaway victory of 19-6. Not a big score nowadays, but a fair margin way back in 1968. In fact, this score could have been even higher with better finishing. At least the Lions did not crack like their predecessors in 1962 in the fourth Test in Bloemfontein.

It was a good game to watch because both teams, especially the Springboks, were prepared to run the ball, while the referee, Dr Bertie Strasheim, applied the advantage law to good effect. In the first ten minutes the Lions were swamped by the Springboks but held out until in the fourteenth minute; Mannetjies Roux made a break, deceiving Mike Gibson from a standing start, before beating Kiernan on the inside to dive over for a marvellous try. Visagie could not convert. The Lions then enjoyed a long spell on the attack but Richards could not finish from a long pass by Telfer. After twenty-two minutes the Lions drew level from a penalty by Kiernan, but South Africa took a 6-3 lead when Gould gathered a weak relieving attempt by Bresnihan and put over an excellent drop goal.

The second half saw mainly one-way traffic with the Lions front row obviously in trouble. With Bedford and Ellis linking well with the backs, the Boks scored three tries through Ellis, Nomis and Olivier, Visagie converting two of these. Kiernan scored the last points of the series with a penalty, finishing on 35 points for the series, which bettered Springbok Okey Geffin's 32 points of the 1949 All Blacks series in South Africa. Springbok captain Dawie de Villiers was elated and recalled: 'In the fourth and last Test at Ellis Park we played sparkling rugby and scored four tries to win 19-6 and seal the series 3-0. I captained the Springboks for the eleventh time, which was a new South African record for a captain.'

Although the Lions drew the second Test 6-6 and lost the first and third both by a mere five points, their hosts scored eight tries to one over the four matches. Only Kiernan's boot kept the Lions within touching distance as the Irish full back thumped over a record 35 points in the Tests to account for all but three of his team's total. Of the total of 377 points, no fewer than 182 came from the boots of Tom Kiernan and Bob Hiller, of which 120 came from penalty goals.

Their coach, Ronnie Dawson, said after the tour:

I regard the results of the tour basically as a failure in that we did not succeed in our primary object, which was to win the Test series. However, as the record states, our results generally have been satisfactory and it was no mean achievement for the team to have the best record of a touring side in South Africa for some time. Our provincial successes and Test failures may be a reflection not only of the limitations of our rugby, but the relative position of the game in South Africa. Most of the provincial games we won quite well, but some of the results should have been more impressive had the Lions capitalised on their leads. Likewise, the South African Test team and immediate reserves are strong and generally very effective... Generally the side did come up to expectations. We knew at the outset of the tour, and following a very poor home international championship, that the pattern of rugby and its basic skills were poor and that we lacked really quality players. It would be ridiculous to think that you can completely change a rugby way of life in 13 short weeks, but I can give nothing but the highest praise to Tom Kiernan and the team for the way in which they attempted to improve the individual and team performances. Perhaps expectations should have been hopes, because this in my opinion is all a British isles tour can do at present – work hard and live in hope... In my opinion the approach in the Home countries has been too casual and we have become too good losers too often.[13]

JIM TELFER

James Telfer was born on 17 March 1940 in Melrose, the son of a local shepherd. From a young age he developed a taste for the game of rugby, of which he never grew tired. Born into the amateur era, Telfer worked as a chemistry teacher to earn a living while rugby remained a passion on the side. Telfer earned his first cap for Scotland against France at Murrayfield on 4 March 1964, and played his last match for Scotland on 28 February 1970 at Lansdowne Road against Ireland, having gained twenty-two caps for Scotland. The first game he played for Scotland was also his first in the back row, as he played in the second row for Melrose, so it was a big step up for the debutant. If not for injury, he might have gained several more caps for Scotland. Allan Massie writes of him: 'Telfer is a man of innate authority. (There's a wealth of quiet reserve and self-knowledge, touched by that form of self-mockery which appears as under-statement, in the way he will describe himself as being a "dominant personality").'

Telfer played back row for Scotland and for the Lions in 1966 and 1968. Impressed by the All Blacks' style of the game, he was heavily influenced by New Zealand rugby. Unfortunately, after a cartilage operation he slowed up, but he played twenty-three games for the British & Irish Lions on their 1966 tour to Australia and New Zealand, and eleven games on their 1968 tour of South Africa. Between 1963 and 1967, he also played eight times for the Barbarians FC. George Crerar said of Telfer, 'The great thing about Jim Telfer is that he makes sure that if he isn't going to win the ball the other side won't get it either.'

Telfer was head coach to the British & Irish Lions on their tour of New Zealand in 1983 but the series was not a success with the Lions losing 4-0. The 'land of the long white cloud' had since his playing days always fascinated him with the wealth of rugby experience that it offered, and he used the tour to chalk up invaluable knowledge as a young coach. An opportunity would come again in 1997 as assistant coach to Ian McGeechan, with particular responsibility for the forwards on the British Lions tour to South Africa. It was on this tour, prior to the crucial first Test, that he made his now well-known motivational 'Everest speech' to the forwards. 'Very few ever get a chance in rugby terms to get for the top of Everest. You have the chance today... If you put in the performance, you'll get what you deserve.' The Lions won that match against all expectations.

Telfer coached Scotland to the Grand Slam in 1984 and, as assistant to Sir Ian McGeechan, to his second Grand Slam in 1990. In his third term as head coach 1998–99, Scotland won the final Five Nations Championship. In 2014 he was still coaching the Melrose RFC Under-18 team, the Melrose Wasps.

1968 BRITISH LIONS SQUAD
Backs
Barry Bresnihan (Ireland)
Gordon Connell (Scotland)
Gerald Davies (Wales)
Gareth Edwards (Wales)
Mike Gibson (Ireland)
Bob Hiller (England)
Sandy Hinshelwood Scotland)
Keith Jarrett (Wales)
Barry John (Wales)
Keri Jones (Wales)
Tom Kiernan (Capt., Ireland)
Billy Raybould (Wales)
Maurice Richards (Wales)
Keith Savage (England)
Jock Turner (Scotland)
Roger Young (Ireland)

Forwards
Rodger Arneil (Scotland)
Mike Coulman (England)
Mick Doyle (Ireland)
Ken Goodall (Ireland)
Tony Horton (England)
Peter Larter (England)
Willie John McBride (Ireland)
Syd Millar (Ireland)
John O'Shea (Wales)
John Pullin (England)
Peter Stagg (Scotland)
John Taylor (Wales)
Bob Taylor (England)
Jim Telfer (Scotland)
Delme Thomas (Wales)
Bryan West (England)
Jeff Young (Wales)

1968 TOUR PROGRAM & RESULTS

Lions 20-12 Western Transvaal
Lions 10-6 Western Province
Lions 24-6 South West Districts
Lions 23-14 Eastern Province
Lions 17-5 Natal
Lions 32-6 Rhodesia
Lions 20-25 South Africa (Pretoria)
Lions 25-5 North West Cape
Lions 23-0 South West Africa
Lions 6-14 Transvaal
Lions 6-6 South Africa (Port Elizabeth)
Lions 37-9 Eastern Transvaal
Lions 22-19 Northern Transvaal
Lions 11-3 Griqualand West
Lions 14-0 Boland
Lions 6-11 South Africa (Cape Town)
Lions 26-6 Border
Lions 9-3 Orange Free State
Lions 40-12 North East Cape
Lions 6-19 South Africa (Johannesburg).

IO

THE 1974 BRITISH LIONS: THE INVINCIBLES

The 1974 British Lions became the first touring team to beat the Springboks in a four-match series in South Africa in seventy-eight years. Although the last Test was drawn, the first three were won by the Lions with convincing ease. Few would argue that they have been the best side ever to visit South Africa, and that includes the great All Blacks side of Brian Lochore in 1970. The 1974 Lions were a side without any weaknesses, from full back through to the front row. Led by Willie John McBride and coached by Syd Millar – both of them from Ballymena – they believed that Tests were won up front. Not that their backs lacked brilliance. And they came to South Africa with a series win against the mighty All Blacks in the New Zealanders' own backyard three years earlier.

Of all the Lions tours, the 1974 one stands out as the most controversial. Not only was it controversial on the pitch but also off it, as the question of whether or not the tour should go ahead was a bone of contention between the rugby fraternity and the Anti-Apartheid Movement led by Peter Hain, who vehemently opposed it. Hain was already known for his role in the occasionally violent demonstrations during the 1969–70 Springbok tour of the UK. There was also pressure from the British Labour Government under the premiership of Harold Wilson not to undertake the tour, but it went ahead regardless. As mentioned earlier, Welsh flanker

John Taylor declined to tour owing to his stance on apartheid – even though he had toured South Africa in 1968.[1]

Tour skipper Willie John McBride said decades later: 'There was never any question in my mind that we should go, and I don't think that politics should be using sport, whether it's rugby, any sport, politics should not be using any sport in any way, because sport is about people. And it's about bringing people together, it's not about isolating people.'[2]

Peter Hain (now Lord Hain) did not agree:

> I think they should have said no. I don't think they should have gone. I cannot defend any player who participated in that team and went to apartheid South Africa and where rugby was infected with apartheid. I don't see how you can justify that.[3]

Once the tour had begun it was clear that Willie John McBride's Lions team had started where they had left off in New Zealand in 1971 and that they were determined to win the four-Test series. The brains trust of Syd Millar and Willie John McBride planned to beat the Springboks up front by nullifying the power of the Springbok forwards with a better scrum technique and dominate the forward exchanges, with the half-backs – Gareth Edwards and Phil Bennett – then controlling the game with tactical kicking to keep play in the opponents' half of the field. Despite this approach, the 1974 Lions still managed to score 10 tries in the Test series to the Springboks' solitary try in the final Test (the latter, by centre Peter Cronjé, was the first 4-point try to be scored by a Springbok).

The manner in which the tourists played shook the confidence of the South African rugby fraternity and surely dented their belief that the Springboks were the best team in the world. The Springbok selectors were continually unsure as to the best team to pick during the Test series and paid the price, only managing a controversial draw with the Lions in the final Test. The Lions left South Africa unbeaten having played twenty-two matches, winning all eighteen provincial games, and three of the four Tests.

'We were all amateurs, we had other jobs, we went with a manager and a coach and 30 players,' Ian McGeechan recalled. 'That was it.' He was a secondary school teacher at the time:

> When we went into a place we would find a local doctor and a local physio and we had to go in the waiting rooms and queue if we wanted treatments. So it was very different from all the logistics that go into a tour now. You know, I had to train on my own before the tour, and I trained every day, with my wife holding a stopwatch, to make sure I would be as fit as anybody else in the party. The Lions was the closest you got to being professionals. Because that was the only time when you woke up in the morning and the only thing on your mind was your rugby and the training.[4]

Before their departure in early May, McBride, a huge farming man from Northern Ireland, confronted his teammates in a hotel in London where they had gathered to leave for South Africa. He was readying himself for an immense challenge against a world-class side which the Lions had not beaten in a series for seventy-eight years. 'I know there are pressures on you,' the captain said. 'But if you have any doubts, I would ask you to turn around and look behind you.' At the back of the room there were two large open doors. As WJB remembers in his foreword to this book, he continued:

> Gentlemen, if you have any doubts about going on this tour, I want you to be big enough to stand up now and leave this room. Because you are no use to me, and you're no use to this team. There will be no stain on your character, no accusations if you do so, but you must be honest and committed. I've been in South Africa before and there's going to be a lot of physical intimidation, a lot of cheating. So if you're not up for a fight, there's the door.[5]

Outside the team hotel, hundreds of demonstrators were making a big noise. They had come to express their anger that the Lions were 'condoning' a murderous apartheid regime.

McBride, an intelligent Ulster Protestant who had experienced the rise of paramilitary terrorism in Northern Ireland and the wrecking of the Sunningdale Agreement by Unionists opposed to power-sharing, needed no lectures on social cohesion. He argued that a sports boycott of South Africa would not help the disenfranchised black majority. The tour would, in fact, include in the itinerary for the first time matches against an all-black team (the Leopards) and a coloured team (the Proteas). The thirty-two players, tour manager Alun Thomas and coach Syd Millar left the hotel together and boarded the plane to Johannesburg.

The tour also became known for the so-called '99 call'. During previous tours of South Africa, provincial sides had tended to use their physical size and over-robust play to deliberately intimidate Lions players prior to Test matches. McBride – who had toured the country in 1962 and 1968 – decided on the call that was meant to show that the Lions would act as one and fight unsporting play with more of the same, while the referee would be unlikely to send off all of the Lions players if they all got stuck in. A famous example was the so-called 'Battle of Boet Erasmus', referring to the stadium in Port Elizabeth where one of the most violent matches in rugby history played out. Famous video footage showed full back JPR Williams running over half the length of the pitch to launch himself at big Moaner van Heerden – one of the hardest, most robust locks of his era – after such a call.

According to the former Wales international and Lion John Taylor, the '99 call' was the result of an incident that occurred during the Lions' 1968 South Africa tour that saw the Welsh prop John O'Shea become the first and to-date only Lion to have been sent off during a Lions tour. Taylor recalled that during a Lions tour match against Eastern Transvaal at Springs, a scuffle broke out among the forwards and O'Shea got isolated by half a dozen home forwards. When the dust had settled the home referee (Mr Bert Woolley) singled O'Shea out and gave him his marching orders. Willie John McBride rushed down from the stand to offer him protection against local fans. This was the genesis of the infamous '99 call' when the Lions toured again in 1974.[6]

Looking back decades later, it can be seen that the 1974 Lions contained some of the greatest players in rugby history. Led by the inspirational Irish second row forward and veteran of two previous Lions tours to South Africa in 1962 and 1968, Willie John McBride, other superstars of this remarkable side were the exciting and daring full back JPR Williams; John James (JJ) Williams on the wing, a former sprinter who represented Wales at the Commonwealth Games in 1970 and who scored two tries in each of the second and third Tests; the half-back pair Phil Bennett and Gareth Edwards; and the No. 8 Mervyn Davies from Wales; the centre Ian McGeechan, who later coached the British Lions; prop Ian McLauchlan, known as 'Mighty Mouse'; the converted full back Andy Irvine on the wing from Scotland; the marauding Irish flanker Fergus Slattery; and the formidable English forwards Fran Cotton and Roger Uttley. It says a lot about the strength of the touring party that players of the calibre of the Irishmen Mike Gibson and Tom Grace and the tall English No. 8 Andy Ripley were unable to gain selection for any of the Tests.

A Good, Tough Start

The Lions kicked off their tour with a match against Western Transvaal in Potchefstroom on 15 May, but the poor Western Transvalers were no match for the might of this touring side and lost heavily, 13-59. Next up were South West Africa (now Namibia) in Windhoek where they won 23-16 in a much harder game, before taking on Boland in Wellington for a comfortable 23-6 victory. Their toughest match of the tour so far was against Eastern Province, a very competitive team on the South African provincial scene led by Springbok captain Hannes Marais. Tensions were electric, violence flared up and at the shout of McBride's '99 call', the Lions swarmed over opposition players to show that the days of being bullied by burly South Africans were over. With these events, the spirit of the tour was forged. Of course the violence attracted the most attention, but for the record, the Lions won 28-14.

Another hard game waited at Newlands where they had to take on Western Province in front of nearly 44,500 spectators, only a week before the first Test at the same venue. The Province side boasted eight Springboks and offered strong resistance; WP wing Alan Read scored two tries, but three penalties made the difference for the Lions and they emerged 17-8 victors (tries counted four points then).[7] Five of the WP backs and two of the forwards were chosen for the first Test. Four days before the Test, they trounced the SA Federation (the Proteas) in Goodwood, Cape Town, 37-6.

On 8 June, their first real challenge waited with the first Test against South Africa at the same venue. The last time the Lions had won at Newlands was in 1938. Newlands had always been special to McBride.

> I have wonderful memories of Newlands; in fact I played my first Test there – it was the third Test of the 1962 British Lions tour. So that was the biggest day of my rugby life. I was only 21 years old then. I again played there for the British Lions in 1968 and in 1974 it was also very special as I was the captain and we played the first Test there.[8]

The South African selectors appointed the experienced prop Hannes Marais as captain for the Springboks, the man who had led the Springboks on their unbeaten tour of Australia in 1971 where they played in a three-Test series. Like McBride, Marais was a farm boy, and hailed from the Somerset East area in the Eastern Cape. He played rugby at school and listened to Test commentaries on the radio, and when the British Lions toured South Africa in 1955, he was perched on empty brandy bottles at the old St George's Park Ground in Port Elizabeth. 'Theunis Briers (Springbok wing) made his great tackle on Tony O'Reilly in front of us,' he recalls. 'I was 14 and, when we walked out of St George's Park at the end, I was literally lifted off my feet.'[9]

The First Test: A Perfect Beginning

For a whole week it had rained on and off so the field was very muddy on 8 June at Newlands. In the changing room before the game, Gareth Edwards warned the younger players about the

Newlands roar. 'When you run onto the field, you will hear the most deafening roar in the world. It will hit you straight in the face and go right to your knees. But when the Boks run out, it will be like an atomic explosion. You will feel like fainting. You will wonder if we can ever beat them. We can.'[10] England prop Fran Cotton, who played in all four Tests, recalled:

> So it was to Cape Town for the first Test and we came down to the captain's room. It was half full and nobody was saying a word, not a word. It was probably another five minutes before everyone arrived, and still nobody's saying a word. Willie John arrives, nobody says a word. And then twenty minutes passed – twenty minutes! Well, you can imagine the atmosphere in the room, and he just looked at us all and said: 'Right then, we're ready,' and we got on the coach. It was the most unreal thing I've ever been through. But the tension that had built up was fantastic.[11]

The Lions beat the Springboks 12-3 in the mud, and McBride was obviously very pleased with the result, 'which was very important, because it set the tone for the rest of the series'.[12] Playing with the wind in the first half, the Springboks took the lead with a drop goal by Dawie Snyman, but Bennett responded with one for the Lions, to take the score to 3-all at half-time. The Lions dominated up front in these wet conditions, and two penalties by Bennett gave the Lions more breathing space before Edwards put over a crucial drop goal. Ian McGeechan knew they had the game in the bag when Edwards's drop cleared the crossbar; he knew that the Boks could not run the ball at them 'in a bog like that'. The victory gave everyone in the side the feeling that they were dominant and they were believing in themselves.

En route to the second Test at Loftus Versfeld in Pretoria the Lions had to see off the Southern Universities (26-4), Transvaal (23-15) and Rhodesia (42-6). The England prop Mike Burton remembers their resolve growing by the game, as McBride and Millar quietly spread confidence through the squad:

Willie John said before one game, against Transvaal at Ellis Park, 'I need him to be demoralised,' he says. He was talking about the big Transvaal prop [Johan] Strauss, a real good'un. At the end of it, we won 23-15. As we're taking our boots off afterwards, Willie John leaned over to me and said, 'I see that man was done. His heart will never be mended. With the Springboks, something like that stays with them for ever.' He was right. We had broken a Springbok's heart.[13]

The Springbok selectors had become panicky and made the first of many changes for the second Test; it would eventually lead to thirty-three players being used in the series, of whom twenty-one gained their colours for the first time.

Second Test

For the Lions, the second Test was the chance to go 2-0 up in the series and make sure they could at least draw the series. They surely had the team to do it and the resolve to show what it means to be a British Lion. Gareth Edwards tried to explain it:

It's hard to put in so many words what is special about the Lions... Suffice to say every player aspires to play for his country. Then you realise there is a further step to take. You read about it and, OK in later years, you're able to see these tours on TV. But we grew up reading about them, Cliff Morgan, Jeff Butterfield, Tony O'Reilly and all those guys on these long, long trips to the far side of the world. It's a gathering of the clans, isn't it. And there's the uncanny factor, too, that you battle and try to tear each other apart only weeks before and, all of a sudden, you are standing shoulder to shoulder against a common enemy a long way from home.[14]

On this day they would be standing shoulder to shoulder, as Edwards said, to fight for the man on your left and to fight for the man on your right. When the team bus pulled up to Loftus Versfeld, Pretoria, a confident group of Lions were belting out the rousing lyrics of *Flower of Scotland* and that spirit manifested on the field of play. The Lions were dominant, winning the second Test 28-9 in front of a shocked crowd of 63,000 to go up 2-0 in the series. For the Lions, the flyer J. J. Williams scored two tries, Bennett a truly marvellous one after jinking and side-stepping his way through the Boks, while Brown and Milliken also scored one each. Bennett also added a conversion and a penalty and McGeechan a smart drop goal. South Africa's points came from two penalties and a drop goal by the new fly-half, Gerald Bosch. It was South Africa's biggest-ever defeat and the next Test saw no less than eleven changes for the Springbok team.

Going up to the third Test in Port Elizabeth, the Lions had some close games and the Quaggas in Johannesburg (20-16), Orange Free State (11-9) and Northern Transvaal gave them a good run for their money. Griquas in Kimberley (69-16) and the Leopards, an all-black team, in East London (56-10) were easily dispatched.

Third Test

13 July 1974 saw the sides clash in the vital third Test at the Boet Erasmus Stadium in Port Elizabeth. Following the humiliation of Loftus Versfeld, the Springbok selectors kept only five players from the previous match in the starting line-up. One of the most bizarre changes was bringing in Free State loose forward Gerrie Sonnekus to play out of position at scrum half, a move that had disastrous consequences. In the opening half hour, the Springboks played with desperation and much like the earlier match against Eastern Province at the same venue, the match was marred by outbreaks of violence, such that the match has since been dubbed the 'Battle of Boet Erasmus'. Despite the Springboks having the better of most of the first half, they still trailed 3-7 at half-time. For the Lions, Gordon Brown had snatched the ball from a line-out and crashed over the line in injury time.

After the break, the Lions regrouped and as the big, heavy Springboks began to tire, they took complete control, the forwards beginning to assert themselves and the backs launching attack after attack on the Springbok line. Again, winger J. J. Williams scored two superb tries, the first coming from a brilliant one-two pass combination with J. P. R. Williams, and the second from of a brilliant kick-and-chase. Andy Irvine added a conversion and two penalties and Bennett two drop goals. The final score, 26-9 to the Lions, and the second biggest defeat in South Africa's rugby history.

At the end of the match, victorious Lions captain McBride was carried off on the shoulders of Bobby Windsor and Gordon Brown. It was the first time since 1896 that the British Isles had won a series in South Africa, and the first time since 1910 that a touring side had beaten the Springboks in Port Elizabeth (at the old Crusaders Ground).

Three more provincial matches remained before the final Test in Johannesburg. Border in East London was easily beaten 26-6, Natal in Durban 34-6 and Eastern Transvaal in Springs 33-10. The match against Natal was also marred by some violence and Tommy Bedford at one stage was hit repeatedly by an aggressive JPR after the full back was tackled into touch. Bottles, tins and naartjies (tangerines) were tossed onto the field by furious spectators.

Fourth Test: Firm Favourites

Obviously the unbeaten Lions were firm favourites to win at Ellis Park. They had used only seventeen players in the four Tests and had made just one enforced change from their victorious third Test side. The dynamic Scottish second-row forward Gordon Brown, who was responsible for much of the Lions' line-out ball thus far and scored a try in both the second and third Tests, had unfortunately broken his hand during the third at the Boet Erasmus Stadium. He was replaced by the England lock Chris Ralston, whose selection did not necessarily weaken the Lions line-up. For the last Test, the South African selectors made only three changes to the side who were beaten convincingly in Port Elizabeth, including one new cap – the Free State No. 8 Kleintjie Grobler – in the starting line-up.

The final Test was attended by 75,000 spectators who were packed to the rafters at Ellis Park to see if the Springboks could work a miracle and beat the all-conquering British Lions. Jackie Snyman, the Springbok fly-half who had taken over from Gerald Bosch for the last two Tests (and brother of Dawie Snyman, fly-half for the first Test in Cape Town), opened the scoring with a penalty goal after only five minutes. But Roger Uttley then put the Lions on the scoreboard when he dived on a ball that had gone loose at the back of the Springbok scrum, and Bennett converted for a 6-3 lead. Shortly afterwards, Jackie Snyman landed a second penalty goal to level the scores at 6-all. Then it was that man Gareth Edwards again: he broke sharply on the blind side and flung out a long pass to Andy Irvine on the right wing, who crossed over untouched. Phil Bennett missed the conversion but at half-time the Lions were leading by 10 points to 6.

The second half was nearly twenty minutes old when the Springboks – who up to the final Test had not yet scored a try against the Lions – finally broke the tourists' defence. After a long line-out throw, the loose forwards Kleintjie Grobler and the veteran Jan Ellis secured the ball; it went down the three-quarter line to the strong-running Chris Pope on the right wing. Pope stepped on the gas, powering past the Lions cross defence and on being blocked by JPR Williams just short of the try line, flung the ball infield. Somehow, the Lions defence failed to clear and the centre Peter Cronjé picked up the loose ball and threw himself over the try line for the Springboks' first – and only – try of the series. Snyman missed the conversion and the scores were tied at 10-all, but before long he kicked a third penalty goal to give South Africa a 13-10 lead with ten minutes to go.

The final minutes of the Test were dramatic. First, Andy Irvine landed a crucial penalty to level the scores at 13-all. A fine break by Jackie Snyman then created a golden chance for the experienced Gert Muller on the left wing, but the speedster overran the ball with the try line at his mercy. Shortly afterwards, the enterprising JPR took off on a powerful run into the Springboks 25 and was stopped just short of the try line. Williams managed to release the ball and it was picked up by the ubiquitous Fergus Slattery, who drove for the Springbok line and crossed over to the left of the posts in spite of being tackled head on by Cronjé. The Lions jumped for joy in celebration of what they thought was the winning try, but the referee, Mr Max Baise, disallowed the try and awarded a 5-yard scrum to the Lions instead.

The Lions protested furiously and some outright insults were directed at the referee, but to no avail. It didn't help that Peter Cronjé, the player who tackled Slattery head-on, afterwards said that he thought that Slattery should have been awarded the try. Unfortunately, the Lions could not profit from the ensuing five-yard scrum, after which Mr Baise blew his whistle – four minutes too early, it was said – with the powerful Lions pack only a few yards from the Springboks' try line. Mr Baise's whistle signalled the end of the Test and a Test series steeped in controversy. The 1974 British Lions thus preserved their unbeaten record but were denied a series and tour whitewash. At the same time, they had deflated the legend of the Springboks' invincibility at home.

The 1974 British Lions team was arguably the best touring side to have visited South Africa. They played the game as rugby should be played, but when they had the chance they could have fun, too. When they broke off from rugby to have a week in the Kruger National Park, the largest game reserve in South Africa, they really enjoyed themselves, as Stuart McKinney recalled:

Imagine that on a modern-day tour. What it really was, we were on the drink for a week. Today you'd be watching videos of the other team. We had every afternoon free to do your standard leisure things, fishing or shooting or wee cruises up the Zambezi. I'm not jealous of the players these days. Ours was a different game from a different era. I think we had a lot more enjoyment. I'm actually jealous of the guys who toured in the fifties. They went by boat for a month there and back. They were gone for six months; that would've been my idea of heaven![15]

When they had left Britain earlier, it was under a cloud of political censure, but the performances of the 1974 British Lions in South Africa had an impact. Fergus Slattery recalled the difference:

> At the beginning of the tour, the British government told the diplomatic corps in Pretoria not to get involved with us at all, to stay away from the games, not to host functions. Then we landed at Heathrow on the way back and there was an invitation to go to Downing Street. Where did it all change? What happened when we were out there? Apartheid certainly hadn't changed one little bit at that time. But the attitude of the British government had changed.[16]

THE LION KING: WILLIE JOHN MCBRIDE

William James McBride, CBE, was born on 6 June 1940 at Toomebridge, County Antrim. His father's death when he was only five years old meant he spent most of his spare time helping out on his family farm, and therefore he did not start playing rugby until he was seventeen. He was educated at Ballymena Academy and played for the school's First XV, joining Ballymena R.F.C. afterwards.

He was first selected to play for Ireland in 1962, making his debut on 10 February 1962 against England at Twickenham, and later that year he was selected to tour South Africa with the British & Irish Lions. McBride continued to play for Ireland throughout the 1960s and played when they first defeated the Springboks in 1965 on South Africa's short tour of Ireland and Scotland, and when Ireland defeated Australia in Sydney – the first time a Home Nations team had defeated a major Southern Hemisphere team in their own country. He was again selected for the Lions in 1966, this time touring New Zealand and Australia, and toured South Africa again with the Lions in 1968.

He was selected to play for the Lions in their 1971 tour of New Zealand and despite being criticised by some as being 'over the hill', McBride acted as pack leader and helped the

Lions to a Test series win over New Zealand – their first and last series win over the All Blacks. He received an MBE in 1971 for services to rugby.

McBride's leadership qualities led to him being appointed as captain of the British & Irish Lions on their 1974 tour to South Africa. The Test series was won 3–0, with one match drawn; the first Lions series ever won in South Africa. It was one of the most controversial and physical Test match series ever played, after the Lions management concluded that the Springboks dominated their opponents with physical aggression, and so decided to match fire with fire. McBride initiated an approach of 'one in, all in', meaning that when one Lion retaliated, all other Lions were expected to join in the melee.

At the time, a player could only be substituted if a doctor agreed that a player was physically unable to continue; there were no video cameras and sideline officials to monitor punching and kicking. The infamous '99 call' was a signal for the Lions to clobber their nearest rivals. In spite of the order for disorder during the tour, he has remained a great friend of South Africa and has always been highly respected and appreciated by the South African rugby fraternity. He played his last game for Ireland at Lansdowne Road in 1975 against France, and near the end of the match scored his first Test try for Ireland. His last international game was against Wales in Cardiff on 15 March 1975.

After retiring from the game, McBride coached the Irish team and was manager of the 1983 Lions tour to New Zealand. Although the Test results were mainly poor, some good wins were recorded in other games. In 1997 he was an inaugural inductee into the International Rugby Hall of Fame. He now lives in Ballyclare and has often been asked to present Test jerseys and give motivational speeches to Lions players prior to matches. In 2004 he was named in *Rugby World* magazine as 'Rugby Personality of the Century'. He is a major supporter of the Wooden Spoon Society. He was also awarded a CBE in the 2019 New Year Honours list for services to Rugby Union.

THE 1974 LIONS SQUAD
Manager – Alun Thomas (Wales)
Coach – Syd Millar (Ireland)

Backs
J. P. R. Williams (London Welsh and Wales)
Andy Irvine (Heriot's FP and Scotland)
Tom Grace (St Mary's College RFC and Ireland)
J. J. Williams (Llanelli and Wales)
William Steele (Bedford and R.A.F. and Scotland)
Clive Rees (London Welsh and Wales)
Alan Morley (Bristol and England) as replacement
Richard Milliken (Bangor and Ireland)
Ian McGeechan (Headingley and Scotland)
Roy Bergiers (Llanelli and Wales)
Geoff Evans (Coventry and England)
Phil Bennett (Llanelli and Wales)
Alan Old (Leicester and England)
Mike Gibson (North of Ireland FC and Ireland) as replacement
Gareth Edwards (Cardiff and Wales)
John Moloney (St. Mary's College and Ireland)

Forwards
Bobby Windsor (Pontypool and Wales)
Ken Kennedy (London Irish and Ireland)
Ian McLauchlan (Jordanhill College RFC and Scotland)
Sandy Carmichael (West of Scotland and Scotland)
Fran Cotton (Coventry and England)
Mike Burton (Gloucester and England)
Willie John McBride (Capt., Ballymena and Ireland)
Chris Ralston (Richmond and England)
Gordon Brown (West of Scotland and Scotland)
Roger Uttley (Gosforth and England)
Fergus Slattery (Blackrock College and Ireland)
Stewart McKinney (Dungannon and Ireland)
Tom David (Llanelli and Wales)

Tony Neary (Broughton Park and England)
Andy Ripley (Rosslyn Park and England)
Mervyn Davies (Swansea and Wales)

1974 BRITISH LIONS TOUR PROGRAM & RESULTS
Lions 59-13 Western Transvaal
Lions 23-16 South West Africa
Lions 33-6 Boland
Lions 28-14 Eastern Province
Lions 97-0 South Western Districts
Lions 17-8 Western Province
Lions 37-6 SAR Federation XV
Lions 12-3 South Africa (Cape Town)
Lions 26-4 Southern Universities
Lions 23-15 Transvaal
Lions 42-6 Rhodesia (Salisbury)
Lions 28-9 South Africa (Pretoria)
Lions 20-16 Quaggas
Lions 11-9 Orange Free State
Lions 69-16 Griqualand West
Lions 16-12 Northern Transvaal
Lions 56-10 Leopards
Lions 26-9 South Africa (Port Elizabeth)
Lions 26-6 Border
Lions 34-6 Natal
Lions 33-10 Eastern Transvaal
Lions 13-13 South Africa (Johannesburg)

II

THE 1980 BRITISH LIONS: INJURIES, INJURIES

The British Lions' next journey to Africa took place in 1980, six years after South Africa had been annihilated by Willie John McBride's men, who returned to the UK unbeaten. The tour was not much of a success for the Lions, as they lost the first three Tests before salvaging some pride with a win in the fourth. They also won all fourteen of their provincial matches on tour, a feat that not many touring sides can achieve considering the length of the tours in that era, the effect of injuries on the squad and the strength of several provincial sides.

As was the case in 1974 with Willie John McBride's Lions, the 1980 Lions tour went ahead in the face of opposition from the British government and groups opposed to sporting contact with the apartheid regime in South Africa. Britain was a signatory to the 1977 Gleneagles Agreement in which Commonwealth governments agreed to discourage sporting contacts with South Africa. The government of the Republic of Ireland was also against the tour. But in November 1979, the Four Home Unions committee that organises British Lions tours decided to go ahead, despite this opposition, and the rugby unions of England, Ireland, Scotland and Wales had all approved the tour by January 1980.

The Springbok captain for the series, Morné du Plessis, looking back on that controversial era, said: 'It was the time we lived in. Looking back at it now you can't believe we lived in those times. This country was in a deep, dark place. We, rugby guys, unfortunately just look out for your own territory, your own sport. You get a chance to play and you do.'[1]

After all these years, John Robbie, who had come on tour as a replacement scrum half and played in the fourth Test, seems to have regrets about it. As a young man of twenty-four he didn't think so at the time, but he now believes it was wrong to come to a SA in the grip of a repressive regime. 'It is something I have to live with,' he said some forty years later. 'I have this great contradiction that it was a great rugby experience and highlight of my rugby career. Later in life I would be interviewing people who were in jail while I was touring here. I've learnt to forgive myself and move on.'[2]

The Lions were captained by England lock Bill Beaumont, who had made an impression in New Zealand on the 1977 British Lions tour and had led England to the Triple Crown and the Grand Slam in 1980. He toured South Africa with the North West Counties in 1979, so he was familiar with South African conditions. Of the thirty players originally selected, ten had previous Lions tour experience. Derek Quinnell had toured New Zealand in 1971 and 1977; Andy Irvine and Fran Cotton had toured South Africa in 1974 and New Zealand in 1977; while Bruce Hay, Bill Beaumont, Allan Martin, Graham Price, Jeff Squire, Peter Wheeler and Clive Williams had all toured New Zealand in 1977. Elgan Rees, added to the party before it left the UK, and Phil Orr, a replacement during the tour, had also toured New Zealand in 1977. When Quinnell toured New Zealand in 1971, he had yet to be capped by Wales, and he was selected for the 1980 tour despite not playing in the 1980 Five Nations Championship.[3]

Knees, Shoulders, Necks, Ribs, Heart

The tour party was disrupted by an unusually high number of injuries and replacements throughout the ten-week tour. Eight players flew to South Africa to reinforce the original thirty tourists, namely Gareth Williams, Tony Ward, Ian Stephens, John Robbie,

Phil Orr, Andy Irvine, Paul Dodge and Steve Smith. Smith joined the tour as cover prior to the final Test after Patterson was injured and did not appear in any games. Andy Irvine was selected for the original squad but withdrew due to injury prior to leaving the UK. He was replaced by Elgan Rees, but joined the tour later when Mike Slemen withdrew.

Nine players left the tour early, including Slemen who went home owing to family illness. The eight players who were ruled out by injury were Rodney O'Donnell (neck), David Richards (shoulder), Gareth Davies (shoulder and knee), Terry Holmes (shoulder and knee), Stuart Lane (knee), Phil Blakeway (rib) and Fran Cotton (suspected heart trouble). The Welsh forward Stuart Lane's injury occurred after a mere 55 seconds of the opening game against Eastern Province in Port Elizabeth, which handed him the shortest career of any British Lions tourist in history. Sadly, he never played international rugby again. Rodney O'Donnell's neck injury ended his rugby career completely. And poor Colin Patterson suffered a knee injury in the penultimate game against Griqualand West in Kimberley which also proved career-ending in the end.

One of the replacements on tour, the Irish scrum half John Robbie, who later settled in South Africa and played for Transvaal, said of their manager and coach:

> Syd Millar was a truly great manager. Of course, he knew South African rugby, having toured as a player and later as coach to the legendary 1974 Lions side... He was scrupulously fair as well, and at times could impose discipline with only a word when it was needed. He was no mug, either. We called him Mallett Head. It sounds unkind, but I assure you it was good-natured affection. We all loved him. Noel Murphy was the coach and I think at first a few of the non-Irish players were a bit disappointed in Noel, or Noisey, as he's always known. Noel was a world-class flanker and a great Lion himself. As a coach, he was always a bit disorganised. He was great fun but sometimes he addressed the troops in a very roundabout way that is typical of the natives of the city

of Cork. But as the tour went on I think the players began to figure that under all the rambling was a very committed man who will put the players first. He would have died for us, and at the end we would've done the same for him. Unlike some Lions coaches, he showed no favouritism to the players from his country, and when Tests are being lost that is crucial. His style of coaching was, I believe, too conservative for the collective talents of the team. But with a bit of luck that series could easily have been drawn, and for any side to do that in South Africa is an achievement.[4]

A Good Start

The Lions' first match of the tour was against Eastern Province at the Boet Erasmus Stadium, the home of some wild violent scenes during the previous tour when Willie John McBride's men came up against Eastern Province and also against the Springboks in the do-or-die third Test. But things had changed and the match, though hard, was played without any nasty incidents, the Lions winning comfortably 28-16. Next up was the SARA Invitation XV, which faced them in East London at the Border Rugby Union Ground. Again, the visitors had a comfortable win, 28-6. From here they went up the east coast to Durban to play Natal at Kings Park Stadium. They got a good run for their money, but were still 21-15 winners. Then it was over to the Highveld where they came up against the South African Invitation XV in Potchefstroom, a game they narrowly won 22-19; but as they say, a win is a win.

The match produced perhaps the Lions' finest moment of the tour in the final minutes when the home side was leading 19-16. David Richards at fly-half broke from his own 22-metre line to take play deep into the opponents' half. He was stopped but the Lions won the ruck and continued to attack. They won four more rucks in succession and numerous players handled the ball before Mike Slemen rounded off an incredible try under the posts.

Now the games did not become any easier, as they had to face Orange Free State in Bloemfontein, a match touring sides usually found quite tough. This time it was the same, the Lions winning

21-17. In their last match before the first Test in Cape Town, they played the South African Rugby Football Federation Invitation XV in picturesque Stellenbosch, the home of so many Springboks, and had a hard time in beating the Federation 15-6. One of the talking points of the game was the good play of the Federation fly-half, Errol Tobias. Tobias was to become the first black Springbok in SA rugby history not long afterwards when he was selected for the Springboks' controversial tour to New Zealand in 1981, characterised by similar demonstrations as those the Springboks encountered on their UK tour of 1969–70.[5]

Everybody was looking forward to the Tests to gauge the real strength of the Springboks, who through the isolation imposed on the apartheid government had not faced opposition of top international standing for four years. They did play a one-off match against a World XV in 1977 – captained by former Lion Willie John McBride – with the inauguration of the new Loftus Versfeld Stadium, but that was no real Test, in spite of some big names who were finding themselves out of season. The Boks also had two Tests against a South American side earlier in 1980, but those matches would never be a true yardstick by which Springbok rugby could measure itself. The World XV was easily dispatched 45-24 and the South Americans, led by the legendary Hugo Porta, by margins of 24-9 and 18-9.

The visit of Bill Beaumont's team would now provide an opportunity to see more or less where the South Africans were in the pecking order of world rugby. During the British Lions' last visit to the country in 1974, the Boks were annihilated, beaten up front and beaten in the backs and that reflected badly on the scoreboard. The Springbok captain for the 1980 British Lions series, lanky loose forward Morné du Plessis, had experienced that humiliation, having played in the first Test at Newlands as a young player. 'It was a drubbing. There is no other way for me to describe it. That was the best touring side to come to South Africa.'

Looking back on the 1980 series, Du Plessis said: 'We wanted to prove we could still play rugby. We didn't want to be caught off guard again.' He was referring in part to the fact that they only made two changes in the four Tests in 1980, as opposed to the 1974 series when they used no fewer than thirty-three players through the series. 'There was understanding and cohesion,' he added. 'We were a more settled team. We were a happy team. Playing with Theuns [Stofberg] and Rob [Louw] in 1980 was something else. We also had Naas [Botha] and Divan [Serfontein] in their prime.'

Whereas the 1974 Test series was marked by sporadic battles on the field, Du Plessis's men showed restraint and tried to focus on the game as much as possible. It also has to be said that in this respect, Lions captain Bill Beaumont – while not turning the other cheek – had the composure to avoid free-for-alls on the park. The series could have started off on an ugly note when the Springbok captain received a haymaker from the Lions' No. 8 Derek Quinnell in the opening minute of the first Test. But they got on to concentrate on playing the game and entertained the crowd to an exhibition of enterprising running rugby as seldom seen in international rugby.

'We've seen each other through the years and we chuckle about it,' Du Plessis said about the incident with Quinnell. 'I was more worried as captain not seeing out of one eye.' And out of one eye Du Plessis saw 'some incredible tries' from his teammates as they kicked off the series.[6]

First Test: One to Remember

With Ollie Campbell unavailable, the Lions were obliged to play the replacement fly-half Tony Ward. On the South African side, their most experienced centre Peter Whipp was troubled by injury and the South African selectors opted for Rhodesia's David Smith. For the Springboks, full back Gysie Pienaar, centre David Smith, scrum half Divan Serfontein, hooker Willie Kahts and prop Martiens le Roux had their first outings in the Green and Gold.

The Lions team for the first Test at Newlands on 31 May was: O'Donnell, Carleton (replaced by Gravell), Richards, Renwick, Slemen, Ward, Patterson, Quinnell, O'Driscoll, Squire, Colclough, Beaumont (c), Price, Wheeler, and Williams. By now, the emphasis in British rugby had shifted to the forwards, but unlike the 1974 Lions, there was no Gareth Edwards or Phil Bennett to take advantage of good work done up front. The result was that there was an overdependence on the rolling maul and forcing second phase.

The Newlands Test, played in front of some 38,000 spectators, turned out to be one of the most exciting internationals in the history of the game. As mentioned above, it started off sensationally when Derek Quinnell sent the Springbok captain Morné du Plessis staggering with a punch that closed his eye. Nowadays it probably would have been passed on to the TMO, but times were different then and the game went on. The Lions forwards held the edge, but the backs could not take advantage of that possession. The Springboks, showing exceptional flair on the attack, made the most of every opportunity and were quick to counter the Lions' fumbles. For the Lions, Tony Ward kept them in the game all along with five penalties and a drop goal, while Graham Price scored the Lions' only try.

For the Springboks, Rob Louw scored their first try with his remarkable speed, followed by tries from centre Willie du Plessis and lock Moaner van Heerden. Gerrie Germishuys scored their fourth try, taking an awkard pass above his head at full speed. Naas Botha converted three of these and with the score tied at 22-all, it was anybody's game. Right at the death, the Springboks drove up to the goal line, where scrum half Divan Serfontein got the ball and dived over for the winning try. Newlands erupted. Final score Springboks 26, British Lions 22.[7]

Springbok coach Nelie Smith explained their strategy.

It was balanced rugby. We wanted to play the ball wide away from the powerful Lions pack but to do that, we needed quick wings and loose forwards who were fast enough to support on the outside. We had both. That was our plan. In 1974, I think South Africa had gone into the series confident that natural ability would see them through. We were not going to fall into the same trap.[8]

A few days after the Test, the Lions flew to South West Africa to play a South African Country Districts XV in Windhoek. It was an easy match for them, winning 27-7. From Windhoek they flew to Johannesburg to play Transvaal at the Wanderers Stadium, a match that they won comfortably 32-12. Eastern Transvaal were beaten 21-15 in Springs before they took on the Springboks again at the Free State Stadium in Bloemfontein.

Second Test: Pienaar's Touch

For the second Test at Bloemfontein on 14 June, the Lions kept their pack of forwards unchanged, but in the backs they brought in Irvine for the injured O'Donnell, also Ray Gravell, Clive Woodward, Bruce Hay and Gareth Davies at fly-half for Ward. The Lions team for the second Test was Irvine, Carleton, Gravell, Woodward, Hay, Davies (replaced by Campbell), Patterson, Quinnell, O'Driscoll, Squire, Colclough, Beaumont (c), Price, Wheeler, Williams.

With the excitement of the first Test at Newlands still fresh in the memory, 57,000 spectators packed into the Free State Stadium hoping to see some more of the same. And they were not disappointed. It will undoubtedly always be remembered for the superb play by full back Gysie Pienaar from the Free State, who on his home ground made the most of every poor kick which came his way. At the end of the series, in fact, the Lions singled him out as the Springbok player who had caused them the most problems. The ubiquitous Rob Louw again had a great game, scoring the Springboks' first try, and so did Germishuys, who scored the third try for the Springboks.

The Springboks were leading 16-15 when Pienaar scored the try that broke the Lions' hearts. From a loose ball, Morné du Plessis booted upfield and Pienaar followed up, grabbed the ball as the defence faltered, dummied and accelerated without a hand being laid on him to score a marvellous touchdown. He showed his elation holding the ball triumphantly above his head while the Free State cheers could be heard miles away. The try was only the fourth scored by a Springbok full back in a Test. Stofberg also scored a try for the Boks; two of the tries were converted by Naas Botha, who also contributed two penalties.

For the Lions, the industrious O'Driscoll and Gravell scored tries, of which Davies converted one. Davies also kicked two penalties and Irvine another. That made the final score 26-19. The result meant that the Springboks could not lose the series.

Between the second and the third Test, two tough matches awaited the tourists: the Junior Springboks at the Wanderers Stadium in Johannesburg, followed by Northern Transvaal at Boet Erasmus in Port Elizabeth. The Junior Springboks gave it a good go but still lost 17-6. The Blue Bulls, usually a tough side to overcome at Loftus Versfeld, were also defeated, the final score 16-9.

Third Test

The Test was to be the eighteenth match of the tour, played in front of almost 50,000 spectators at the Loftus Versfeld Stadium, Pretoria, on 28 June. In came Paul Dodge and Ollie Campbell in the backs, while up front, Irishman Colm Tucker came in for Quinnell on the flank. Their team list read: Irvine, Woodward, Gravell, Dodge, Hay, Campbell, Patterson, Squire, O'Driscoll, Tucker, Colclough, Beaumont (c), Price, Wheeler, Williams.

In a howling wind and with rain pouring down – weather which suited the British Lions better than the locals – the Lions pack looked well in control. Springbok flanker Rob Louw recalled:

Conditions were atrocious. It was raining so hard that, as we arrived at the ground, we could see spectators leaving. The rain had been too much for them. They obviously weren't surfers. The wet, muddy conditions were to the liking of the Lions. They were used to them – we weren't. Throughout the match their tight forwards had control ... the Lions certainly had scoring opportunities, but last-second desperate tackles and their own handling errors kept them out...with the possession that the Lions had enjoyed in this match they ought to have won. But they didn't take their chances. We had far fewer chances but they were enough. That's what Test rugby is about.[9]

At half-time the Lions deservedly led 7-3 through a try by Bruce Hay and a penalty by Ollie Campbell. The Springboks could only reply with a drop goal by Naas Botha, who struck the sodden ball well to steer it through the sticks. With less than ten minutes to go, the Lions had an unforgivable lapse in concentration which would cost them the match. A cross kick by Naas Botha almost went into touch in the Lions 25, and Clive Woodward, instead of hoofing it into the stand, casually side-footed the ball into touch. Reacting quickly, Germishuys took a quick line-out to Stofberg with the Lions caught napping. Stofberg then ran a few paces, drawing the defence and passed back to Germishuys who went over in the corner for a soft try, very much against the run of play. Everything now hinged on Botha's conversion, but in the atrocious conditions not many would have given him a chance from the touchline. Lo and behold, he nailed it, the ball keeping low but going straight, and the Boks won 12-10. With that, the Lions' hopes of salvaging the series disappeared.

The conversion in those awful conditions was just typical of the BMT of Naas Botha. In his time, he dominated the game in South Africa and was known as the 'Golden Boy'. Unfortunately, his career overlapped with most of the country's rugby isolation. As a drop-kick master he had no equal in the history of the game. During his first-class career from 1977 to 1995 he put over 210 drop goals, and in his twenjty-eight Tests Botha landed an impressive eighteen.

Springbok captain Morné du Plessis later acknowledged that his side had been fortunate. 'At half-time I was preparing a losing speech. We know we played a match today where Lady Luck played a great part. It would be silly to say I feel sorry for what has happened to them in the Tests, but I do feel sympathy. The Tests could have gone either way, believe me. I know how close they were. I was there.'[10]

Before the match, replacement fly-half Tony Ward had some anxious moments when he realised he had forgotten his boots at the hotel. Ollie Campbell was to wear the No. 10 jersey and Ward was in line to replace him, and take over as goal-kicker, should Campbell need to come off. Fellow replacement and fellow Irishman John Robbie recalled that it was raining and sleeting in Port Elizabeth on the day and the roads to the stadium were jammed and everything was rushed. At the very last minute he and Ward were getting ready to leave the team in the changing room, when Ward told him that he had forgotten his boots! As Ward has tiny feet he could not borrow another pair. Robbie told him to stay quiet amidst all the tension. As the crowd had crammed back under the roof of the grandstand to avoid the rain, the two substitutes had to scramble around the back of the stadium to take their places on the bench, already hearing the roar of the crowd as the teams ran on. As they emerged from the car park to their places they could see in the gloom that a Lions player was lying injured. Oh dear, it was Ollie Campbell, who had a bad cut on his head, and coach Noel Murphy, shouted at Ward to warm up. Angrily Ward asked Robbie what to do next, to which Robbie replied that he should start praying immediately. Fortunately for Ward, Campbell recovered and an anxious Noel Murphy avoided a heart attack by not learning that his reserve fly-half and goal-kicker had forgotten his boots.

Two weeks before the final Test in Pretoria, the Lions had to face the Barbarians in Durban; the match turned out to be the most spectacular of the tour outside the first two Tests. The Barbarians fielded several Test players, including the legendary Hugo Porta from Argentina and the Australian loose forward Mark Loane. The Lions won an exciting, carefree match 25-14. They then travelled down to Cape Town to take on the Western Province, which had several Springboks in their line-up, but they totally outclassed the men from the Cape to win 37-6. Their last match before the fourth Test in Pretoria was against Griqualand West in Kimberley, which proved a tough assignment as they only won 23-19.

Fourth Test: Facing a Whitewash

The Lions now faced the prospect of becoming the first British Isles side ever to suffer a whitewash in South Africa. The only changes to the side for the last Test on 12 July at Pretoria were Carleton coming in for Woodward and John Robbie for Patterson, while the pack of forwards remained intact. So the Lions team for this final Test was Irvine, Carleton, Gravell, Dodge, Hay, Campbell, Robbie, Squire, O'Driscoll, Tucker, Colclough, Beaumont (c), Price, Wheeler, Williams.

With the Boks having won the third Test in a wet Port Elizabeth 12-10 to sew up the series, they then arrived at Loftus Versfeld full of confidence. But they had a surprise when the South African rugby boss, Doc Danie Craven, showed up at their change room only minutes before kick-off and warned them against complacency. 'He told us we were going to lose that Test,' Naas Botha recalled. 'We were all taken aback but he was proved right.'[11]

In front of 68,000 spectators, the Lions outscored the Springboks by three tries to one, the three coming from Williams, Irvine and O'Driscoll, with Ollie Campbell adding a penalty goal and a conversion. The Springboks' try was scored by Willie du Plessis, while Gysie Pienaar added two penalties and Naas Botha, who had an off day with the boot, adding another.

In total, the Lions used thirty-eight players on tour which, considering the number of injuries, was understandable. Over the four Tests they used three different fly-halves – Tony Ward, Gareth Davies and Ollie Campbell; not a situation to build consistency for a series.

Speaking of fly-halves, looking back on the 1980 series, Bok fly-half Naas Botha said: 'I don't think we played on emotion. We were inexperienced (in the Test arena) and, in fact, I don't think we had anything to lose. Also, Morné's captaincy really shone through in that series.'

Irish scrum half John Robbie, who was called up as a replacement while on tour in the newly formed Zimbabwe, believes the quality of the Springboks' attack made a big difference in deciding the outcome of the series. 'You had Rob Louw's speed and impact all around the park, while Gysie (Pienaar) was so dynamic in their attacks from full back.'[12]

FRAN COTTON

Francis Edward Cotton was born on 3 January 1947 in Wigan, Lancashire, as the son of a good rugby league player and went to Loughborough University to study physical education. It was said that Cotton was ahead of his time in terms of physical preparation. It was during these years that Cotton won the Glengarth Sevens at Davenport Rugby Club (Stockport Rugby Club) along with Steve Smith and Clive Rees.

Cotton made his England debut against Scotland in 1971, and eventually won thirty-one caps for the Roses. During that time, he also captained the English team three times. His clubs included Coventry R.F.C. and Sale. With his 6ft 2in frame he was an outstanding prop who could play on either side of the scrum. He had both brains and brawn and a hard edge, and on the 1974 British Lions tour to South Africa earned the Test spot among fierce competition in the front row, and played a key role alongside Bobby Windsor and Ian McLauchlan for the unbeaten tourists. Windsor said of him, 'Frannie was massive on that 1974 Lions tour, like a great English oak.'

Cotton's versatility meant he played loosehead in England's Grand Slam-winning team in 1980 and on the 1977 British Lions tour to New Zealand, when he was part of a pack so dominant that the All Blacks resorted to three-man scrums in a bid to get the ball straight out. It was during the game against the Junior All Blacks on the 1977 tour of New Zealand that the famous 'Mudman' image of Cotton, waiting for the ball at a line-out while caked in mud from head to toe, was captured, and it became one of the most iconic images of rugby union.

An interesting fact is that the man from Wigan never lost a match in South Africa, having played there with England in 1972 when they beat the Boks 18–9 and in 1974 with the 'Invincibles' of Willie John McBride, and returning with the Lions in 1980, when he had to head home after four appearances due to a heart condition. His playing career ended with a leg injury in 1981.

After retiring, he remained in rugby administration and in July 2007 Cotton returned to his former club Sale as a member of the club's board. Cotton was banned for a decade by the RFU for earning money from writing a book, but was welcomed back to Union in time to become manager of the 1997 Lions tour to South Africa. His success as a Lions player, his understanding of the Springbok mentality and his management expertise and attention to detail meant he played a key role as the Lions upset the odds and won the series 2-1 against all expectations. He is still involved in charitable work and is an honorary president of the rugby charity Wooden Spoon, improving the lives of disadvantaged children and young people in Britain and Ireland.

THE 1980 BRITISH LIONS SQUAD
Manager – Syd Millar (Ireland)
Coach – Noel Murphy (Ireland)
Team Doctor – Jack Matthews (Wales)

Backs
Rodney O'Donnell (Ireland)
Bruce Hay (Scotland)
Andy Irvine (Scotland) as replacement
Mike Slemen (England)
John Carleton (England)
Elgan Rees (Wales)
Peter Morgan (Wales)
Jim Renwick (Scotland)
Ray Gravell (Wales)
David Richards (Wales)
Clive Woodward (England)
Paul Dodge (England) as replacement

Gareth Davies (Wales)
Ollie Campbell (Ireland)
Tony Ward (Ireland) as replacement
Terry Holmes (Wales)
Colin Patterson (Ireland)
John Robbie (Ireland) as replacement
Steve Smith (England) as replacement

Forwards
Peter Wheeler (England)
Alan Phillips (Wales)
Fran Cotton (England)
Clive Williams (Wales)
Ian Stephens (Wales) as replacement
Phil Orr (Ireland) as replacement
Graham Price (Wales)
Phil Blakeway (England)
Bill Beaumont (Capt., England)
Maurice Colclough (England)
Alan Tomes (Scotland)
Allan Martin (Wales)
John O'Driscoll (Ireland)
Colm Tucker (Ireland)
Jeff Squire (Wales)
Stuart Lane (Wales)
Derek Quinnell (Wales)
John Beattie (Scotland)
Gareth Williams (Wales) as replacement.

THE 1980 BRITISH LIONS TOUR PROGRAM & RESULTS
May 10 v Eastern Province W 28-16
May 14 v SARA Invitation XV W 28-6
May 17 v Natal W 21-15
May 21 v South African Invitation XV W 22-19
May 24 v Orange Free State W 21-17
May 27 v South African Federation XV W 15-6

May 31 v South Africa L 22-26
June 4 v South African Country Districts XV W 27-7
June 7 v Transvaal W 32-12
June 10 v Eastern Transvaal W 21-15
June 14 v South Africa L 19-26
June 18 v Junior Springboks W 17-6
June 21 v Northern Transvaal W 16-9
June 28 v South Africa L 10-12
July 2 v South African Barbarians W 25-14
July 5 v Western Province W 37-6
July 8 v Griqualand West W 23-19
July 12 v South Africa W 17-13

12

THE 1997 BRITISH LIONS TOUR: LAST HURRAH OF AMATEURISM

The 1997 British Lions tour to South Africa followed the Lions' 1993 tour to New Zealand and preceded their 2001 tour to Australia. It was the last Lions tour in the sport's amateur era. In 1993, the Lions lost the first Test match, but won the second to level the series, with New Zealand winning the deciding third Test. The tour manager was Geoff Cooke, the coaches were Ian McGeechan and Dick Best and the Lions were captained by Scotland's veteran full back Gavin Hastings. The much-anticipated 1997 tour was the first after the end of apartheid in South Africa, and the first Lions tour since rugby union turned professional. These Lions achieved what few others have: they were only the third touring side to win a Test series in South Africa, the others being the 1974 Lions and the 1996 All Blacks.

South Africa had won the 1995 Rugby World Cup, but were in decline at the time of the Lions tour. The inaugural Tri Nations in 1996 had been comfortably won by New Zealand, captained by Sean Fitzpatrick, with South Africa winning only one of their four matches in the tournament. There was also some disarray in the management of the game in South Africa with the resignation of the coach André Markgraaff, who had taken over from the highly successful Kitch Christie, and the controversial replacement of the World Cup-winning captain Francois Pienaar. But still the Lions were seen to be underdogs. An editorial in the South African sports magazine *SA Sports Illustrated* read: 'The British Lions arrived in South Africa rated – by their own media, South African media and supporters – as nothing more than rank underdogs. A nice bunch of blokes who were making a bit of history and, in so doing, winning friends rather than matches.'

The Lions couldn't have asked for a more experienced coach to lead them. It was Ian McGeechan's fifth British Lions tour. A member of Willie John McBride's all-conquering Lions of 1974 in South Africa, he played centre in all four Tests and three years later in all four Tests against New Zealand. He was a Lions coach in 1989 (Australia) and 1993 (New Zealand) and now was in charge of the expedition to South Africa. At the time, he was regarded as the most innovative and deep-thinking coach in the British game.

John Dawes said of Martin Johnson: 'An automatic selection for the tour and the Test matches, but a somewhat surprising selection as captain. The respect that he has from friend and foe suggests he's a good choice and there are enough "officers" to him to help if needed. His line-out play alone can go a long way to clinching the series.'[1]

Former British Lions captain Finlay Calder predicted that it would be the hardest tour the Lions have ever undertaken:

The quality of the opposition is outstanding and because of the history behind the Lions, and the fact that South Africa have been starved of international competition, the Springboks will be thirsting for this squad. South Africa like playing New Zealand and Australia, but nothing compares to the Lions. The early Seventies was a magical period for the Northern Hemisphere and a lot of people in South Africa still remember that. So the Lions carry the unwelcome baggage of being probably the 'biggest' team to go to South Africa... You never know what will happen on tours. But the beauty of this team is that there are few guaranteed Test places, so there will be a lot of competition at training. If everyone's fit, you have a marvellously powerful pack and the Lions have some very, very hard tacklers at centre. Gibbs and Bateman are an important force, but if they are separated the Lions' midfield won't be nearly as effective... If everybody stays fit and we have hugely competitive training sessions, the Lions will do well. If we steer clear of injury, I wouldn't be surprised if we won the series. But if we have injuries, well ... it will be hard. And no one remembers the teams that lose.[2]

The Lions convincingly won the first Test at Newlands with Neil Jenkins kicking five penalties, and Matt Dawson and Alan Tait scoring tries. Despite scoring three tries in the second Test at Durban, the Springboks suffered from some woeful goal-kicking and failed to land any penalties or conversions, while the Lions' Neil Jenkins once again kicked five penalties to level the scores at 15-15 before a Jeremy Guscott drop goal for an 18-15 lead for the Lions. The Lions then held off a ferocious South African fightback, Lawrence Dallaglio putting in a magnificent try-saving tackle, to win the match 18-15 and take the series. The third Test at Ellis Park proved a match too far for the Lions squad and they lost 35-16.

The tour was a triumph for the Lions management of Fran Cotton (Manager), Ian McGeechan (Head Coach), Jim Telfer (Assistant Coach) and especially the captain Martin Johnson. It was the last occasion on which the Lions returned victorious from a tour until the tour of Australia in 2013.

In his autobiography, Springbok skipper Gary Teichmann conceded that they had expected to take the series:

The appalling record of northern hemisphere teams against the three southern giants in recent years kindled speculation that we would cruise to a 3-0 series win, and, to be honest, we expected nothing less. Perhaps an element of complacency did creep in. I recall reading articles about the Lions' preparation, where they trained with the Royal Marines, and the various measures being taken by manager Fran Cotton and coach Ian McGeechan, but my conviction remained we would have too much quality in our team. They would be well prepared, well managed and well coached, but they surely lacked the talent to beat us.[3]

A notable feature of the tour was that the first two Tests of the series were played at the coastal stadiums of Newlands (Cape Town) and King's Park (Durban), before the action moved to the Highveld of Johannesburg for the final Test.

First Test: 'I Had Never Considered It Possible'
Before the match at Newlands on 21 June, a fired-up forwards coach Jim Telfer delivered a speech to the players that, judging by the result, must have motivated them to exceptional heights:

The easy bit has passed. Selection for the Test team is the easy bit. You have an awesome responsibility on the eight individual forwards' shoulders, awesome responsibility. This is your f***ing Everest, boys. Very few ever get a chance in rugby terms to get for the top of Everest. You have the chance today... To win for the Lions in a Test match is the ultimate, but you'll not do it unless you put your bodies on the line. Every one jack of you for eighty minutes. Defeat doesn't worry me. I've had it often and so have you. It's performance that matters. If you put in the performance, you'll get what you deserve. No luck attached to it. If you don't put it in, then we're second-raters. They don't respect you. They don't rate you. The only way to be rated is to stick one on them, to get right up in their faces and turn them back, knock them back. Outdo what they do. Outjump them, outscrum them, outruck them, outdrive them, out-tackle them, until they're f***ing sick of you. Remember the pledges you made. Remember how you depend on each other at every phase, teams within teams, scrums, line-outs, ruck ball, tackles. They are better than you've played against so far. They are better individually or they wouldn't be there. So it's an awesome task you have and it will only be done if everybody commits themself now.

You are privileged. You are the chosen few. Many are considered but few are chosen. They don't think f*** all of us. Nothing. We're here just to make up the f***ing numbers. No one's going to do it for you. You have to find your own solace – your own drive, your ambition, your own inner strength, because the moment's arrived for the greatest game of your f***ing life.[4]

Some 51,000 spectators had packed into the Newlands Stadium to see how the Springboks were going to wipe the floor with the British Lions – or so they thought. The Springboks start the match with grim purposefulness and after twenty-four minutes, Os du Randt scores from a line-out when in tandem with Hannes Strydom he powers through the Lions pack. But the Boks give away penalties and the dead-eye Neil Jenkins gathers one point after the other to keep the scoreboard ticking for the Lions. At the break, the Lions lead 9-8, having defended like Trojans. The longer the game lasts, the more the lighter pack comes into its own; Tom Smith, Keith Wood and Paul Wallace are outstanding in the front row. Martin Johnson, Jeremy Davidson and Lawrence Dallaglio are doing great work in the line-outs.

Soon after the break, Henry Honiball moved the ball to his left, and when Gibbs mistimes his tackle on Teichmann, the Bok captain sends Russell Bennett – who had come on for the injured Edrich Lubbe – over in the corner. Rain starts to fall and the battle intensifies. With eight minutes remaining, the Boks are leading 16-15. The critical moment of the match comes when Matt Dawson, who had been elevated into the No. 9 jersey following the injury to Rob Howley, slips around the blind side past Ruben Kruger, and holds the ball aloft as if to flop a high pass inside. Teichmann and Joost van der Westhuizen buy the dummy, and away goes Dawson, high-stepping into the corner for a marvellous try. The try clearly stunned the Springboks.

The Lions are now leading but it is not over yet. In injury time, Tim Rodber and Dawson contrive a sniping burst, and when the ball is played back, Gregor Townsend sends the pocket battleship

Scott Gibbs thundering into the midfield. The ball comes back again, Rodber throws a high pass to Jenkins and sends Alan Tait arcing into the corner for another stunning try. The Lions win 25-16, and no one can complain about the result.[5]

As mentioned, it was only due to injury to Howley that Dawson started the first Test. And how well did he take his chance. He recalled his try:

> My face from the end-on camera of running into the corner is just eyes wide open at the thought they had just fallen for that. I was doing that to get myself out of a hole, not because I was trying to trick the opposition. I remember saying it felt like a little bit like a schoolboy dummy – as if you were throwing a dummy to the touchline and they still fell for it – but all of the things just aligned at that one time. You can't ever allow for however many South Africans just sort of stopped in their tracks. They wanted to mark Ieuan Evans. It was just one of those split-second moments where you know they have gone for it and there was disbelief from me really.[6]

Looking back, Springbok captain Gary Teichmann found it hard to comprehend their loss:

> There was a period after half-time when we could have ended the contest but we let a couple of chances slip by, a couple of passes didn't go to hand, and, all of a sudden, it started to rain at Newlands and we found ourselves involved in a dogfight. We had displayed the classic signs of a team lacking the confidence to make opportunities count and finish off the opposition. We led 16-15 with eight minutes left, but I purchased a dummy from Matt Dawson following a lack of communication between the flanker, the full back and me, and the Lions's scrum half scrambled clear to score in the corner; in injury time their centre, Alan Tait, scored again. In a blur, we had lost 27-16 [25-16]. The result absolutely shocked me, maybe because I had never considered it possible.[7]

Second Test: 'That Magic Moment'

Some 50,000 spectators looked on at King's Park, Durban, on 28 June as poor goal-kicking let the Springboks down badly and it is probably fair to say that it cost them the game. Henry Honiball tried twice, Percy Montgomery tried twice and Andre Joubert tried twice, but none of them succeeded. The Springboks scored three tries by Joost van der Westhuizen, Percy Montgomery and Andre Joubert, of which none were converted, while the reliable Neil Jenkins again kicked five penalties. With about five minutes left on the clock, the score was tied at 15-all.

Then came a hack out of the breakdown from hooker Keith Wood, chasing downfield to force a line-out deep in the Springboks' half of the field. A burst from fly-half Gregor Townsend who headed into contact resulted in a loose maul in front of the Boks' posts, with Matt Dawson taking up possession at scrum half. With Townsend out of action, the usual kicking option was gone but the drop goal was still on. Teichmann shouted for his boys to mark Jenkins and thought they had him covered, but the ball was passed to Jeremy Guscott at centre. He instinctively launched a drop goal and as Teichmann later described it, 'The ball squirted over the crossbar like a deflating balloon.' It counted three points, nevertheless, and suddenly the Lions were in the lead 18-15. With two minutes left on the clock, he told the Boks to stay calm, but the Lions held on until the final whistle to gain a famous victory that made them only the second British Lions side in the twentieth century to score a series victory over South Africa.[8]

Of course it's not the kind of score one would ever forget. Guscott certainly didn't:

It was so nice to see that drop goal go over – I struck it pretty well for someone who doesn't normally hit them. It went right through the middle but boy was I keen to get everyone back to defend in those last three minutes! It was a great feeling, a great moment and a great achievement for everyone involved in that Tour. I'm just pleased to be part of that magic moment. Things could have been so different – Austin Healey was outside of me, if I'd passed the ball to him, he might have been the one talking! To see Keith Wood try and hack that ball, it could have gone anywhere – you don't know what the bouncing ball will do in rugby. They kicked it into touch, we had a line-out and before you knew it, I was in the fly-half position – I should never have been there. You can almost see in his [Dawson's] eyes 'what are you doing there?' – I've got my hands up, ready to go. I'd have looked up, scanned the outside and thought, 'drop goal'. They played all the rugby, we did all the kicking. But we got what we deserved – every time we pushed, they penalised. If they didn't, we would have probably gone through the phases and scored tries. But Jenko kicks that ball so sweetly, every time it sailed through the posts, the Boks players must have wondered if he'd ever miss.[9]

Guscott continued: 'The tour was magical. It was a fantastic moment, we weren't just expected to lose that game but we weren't given a chance on the whole tour. We were outplayed, we froze a bit – the whistle went and we'd won both the game and the series. We were going to have a good time and enjoy a moment that many people thought wouldn't come. Coming together, we walked around the stadium, applauded the support that was there. The red Lions jerseys were everywhere and we just wanted to show our appreciation for them, following us and supporting them so well.'[10]

Bok skipper Gary Teichmann was devastated.

On the most disappointing day of my entire rugby career, we lost 18-15, victims of a late, late drop goal. The series was lost. Even now, I find it hard to understand how we failed to win the Durban Test. The atrocious goal-kicking obviously didn't help our cause but, on the balance of play, we deserved to win by 20 points. That is not an exaggeration. We had been the better side in every phase of the game ... but we lost.[11]

Third Test

Having been let down by poor goal-kicking in the second Test, the Springbok selectors had little choice but to play a highly reliable kicker at Ellis Park on 5 July, and the choice fell on Free State's Jannie de Beer. De Beer will of course be best remembered for his world record five dropped goals against England in the World Cup quarter-final in Paris in 1999, when the Boks humiliated the Poms by 44 points to 21. Jannie scored 34 points in the match, setting a South African record for most points in a Test, which still stands today. His inclusion for the third Test proved justified as he kicked 13 points in a convincing 35-16 Springbok win, and South Africa at least regained some pride despite having lost the series.[12]

Even though the series had already been decided, the match still drew a lot of interest and 62,000 turned up at Ellis Park to watch the game. On the day, the Springboks were just too good for the visitors, scoring tries by Joost van der Westhuizen, Percy Montgomery, Andre Snyman and Pieter Rossouw. The Lions replied with a try by Dawson, converted by Jenkins, and three penalties by Jenkins.

After the tour, Gary Teichmann stated: 'The 1997 Lions will be remembered as a squad who made the absolute most of the players at their disposal. Their management and coaching were exceptional, and the team clearly developed a spirit that was remarkable.'[13]

Springbok lock Mark Andrews revealed that the Lions tour had been an 'unhappy' time in his rugby career, but he was looking forward to the visit of the British & Irish Lions in 2021. 'It's always a phenomenal series against the British & Irish Lions – it's probably second only to a World Cup,' Andrews said, who as a member of the 1995 RWC Springbok squad knows what it's like to win one:

> For a spectator it's phenomenal. You've got those crazy Lions fans coming out here, and they will give it everything – the stadiums are packed and there is a huge amount of vibe and atmosphere. Looking ahead to next year, I hope the pandemic

can blow over. If there is one series that I think is even bigger than a series between the Springboks and the All Blacks, it's between the Springboks and the British & Irish Lions. At this stage, it's difficult to know who will be available and in form next year. But I would like to think that the guys will know what it will take to win and that we will have a core of players from last year's World Cup win who will be guiding our side next year. I just hope that culture and ethos of what it takes to be a successful Springbok is instilled in the players next year, and if that is the case, I'm sure it will be a great series.

Looking back at 1997, Andrews admits it was a tough time:

There is not many things I regret in my career – I was lucky enough to win the World Cup, Tri-Nations, Currie Cup – but one of my saddest moments was the 1997 Lions tour. SARU had appointed two legends – players who were my heroes when I was younger – to coach the Springboks, in Carel and Gert Smal. It wasn't a happy time for me or for South African rugby supporters. Losing to the Lions was frustrating to me, because in my opinion that wasn't the best side to come here, but we were in such turmoil as a team – we should have won convincingly. It became a very unhappy period in my life, and I regret it.[14]

An important factor in the Lions' success on this tour was the presence of the players with rugby league experience, where they learned their mental hardness, an attribute that was felt would stand the squad in good stead on the South African scene. Scott Gibbs was one, who went by the nickname of 'Car Crash', a Welshman who, following his highly influential role in midfield, was named 'Player of the Series'. On his return to union in 1996 it was sometimes joked that he was the fastest prop in world rugby, though in fact he was an inside centre. He became known as the world's hardest tackler and this was exemplified by his performance in the Lions tour. The Lions produced some memorable defensive performances with Gibbs at the centre of the action pulling off some devastating tackles. Alan Bateman gained four caps for Wales in 1990 before moving to rugby league with Warrington Wolves and returned to rugby union after it went professional in 1996 to gain a further thirty-one Wales caps and one for the British & Irish Lions in 1997. John Bentley was an English former dual-code international rugby union and rugby league footballer who played club rugby union as a wing for Otley, Sale, Newcastle and Rotherham and in rugby league he played at club level for Leeds, Halifax, Balmain Tigers and Huddersfield Giants as a wing. He won five international caps for England, and two for Great Britain. Of course he will be remembered for his iconic 60-metre 'try of the tour' vs the Gauteng Lions.

About his time with the British Lions, Bentley said:

> The Lions experience in South Africa was better than anything I have experienced in rugby league or rugby union. I never expected to be picked, I was in the right place at the right time with the right people who they thought was the right type of player to go to South Africa. I think there were six league boys who went and what I think what the rugby union boys, without been rude, took from it was the approach to professionalism. Professionalism isn't about being paid money. It's about how you conduct yourself on and off the field. And importantly the attitude towards training which had a real positive influence on that group of players in '97. We set some high standards in training in the build-up to the games, were very competitive and the competition for places was fierce. Which stood [us] in great stead for probably one of the greatest challenges in world rugby, against the Springboks.[15]

Another dual-code rugby footballer was Alan Tait, who played outside centre for Scotland (RU), and the British & Irish Lions. He played club rugby union for Kelso and the Newcastle Falcons, and club rugby league for Widnes and Leeds. David 'Dai' Young was a former rugby union and rugby league footballer who won fifty-one

THE KICKING MACHINE: NEIL JENKINS

Neil Jenkins was born in Church Village near Pontypridd to a scrap dealer and his wife and attended Llanilltud Faerdref Primary School and then Bryn Celynnog Comprehensive School in Beddau.

Jenkins joined Pontypridd in 1990, making his First XV debut on 14 April, and made his Wales debut aged 19 on 19 January 1991 against England during the Five Nations Championship in Cardiff. Wales lost 25–6, but Jenkins scored his first three points through a penalty. Unfortunately for him, he missed out on a place in the Welsh World Cup squad.

Jenkins' main strength was his kicking, and although he had described himself as 'not as twinkle-toed' as the like of Phil Bennett and Jonathan Davies, he was deceptively quick in his early career. He tailored his game to the demands of the modern game, developing his tackling, passing and running skills especially under the coaching of Graham Henry. In November 1993 he scored an international record eight successful penalty kicks at goal in Wales's 24–26 defeat to Canada. He was only twenty-three when he passed Paul Thorburn as Wales's record Test point scorer in a 29–19 win against Italy, also equalling the record of 24 points in a game he had set against Canada.

Jenkins went on the 1997 British Lions tour to South Africa, playing full back in all three Tests, and his accurate goalkicking helped the Lions to secure the series 2–1, scoring 41 points. In 1999 he also equalled the international record by converting nine penalties in a World Cup warm-up game against France. In October 2000, Jenkins was given an MBE for services to sport. He became the first ever rugby player to break the 1,000 international points mark in 2001, with a 28-point haul featuring a full house of a try, conversion, drop goal, and penalty against France in Paris. Jenkins went on the 2001 British & Irish Lions tour to Australia, but only gained his fourth Lions cap as a late replacement in the second Test.

His final match for Wales was on 1 November 2002 in Wrexham against Romania, after an eleven-year career in international rugby. During his eighty-seven caps for Wales he scored 1,049 points (11 tries, 130 conversions, 235 penalties and 10 drop goals) and a further forty-one points (1 conversion and 13 penalties) for the British & Irish Lions. He retired as the only player to score over 1,000 points in international rugby, his world record subsequently broken by Jonny Wilkinson.

In 2004, Jenkins returned to the Welsh Rugby Union in the capacity of Kicking Skills Coach, and in 2006 he returned to the National Squad setup as Skills Coach, where he first worked under Gareth Jenkins during the 2007 Rugby World Cup campaign and subsequently Warren Gatland. In 2009, he joined the British & Irish Lions as specialist kicking coach on their tour of South Africa, and was reappointed as a coach for the Lions in 2017 under head coach Warren Gatland.

caps for Wales in rugby union between 1987 and 2002, three caps for the British Lions, and fourteen caps for Wales in rugby league and captained Wales in the 1995 Rugby League World Cup.

Then there was Scott Quinnell who was a No. 8 for Wales, Llanelli RFC, Llanelli Scarlets, and Richmond, and won fifty-two caps for Wales and in 1994 changed rugby football codes when he transferred from Richmond F.C. to Wigan, and won two caps for Wales.

The top Test point scorer was Welsh fly-half/full back Neil Jenkins with forty-one. Tim Stimpson finished as top point scorer for the tour with 111 points. The top Test try scorer was scrum half Matt Dawson with two, while the top try scorers for the tour were John Bentley and Tony Underwood with seven apiece.

1997 BRITISH LIONS SQUAD
Backs
Neil Jenkins (Wales)
Tim Stimpson (England)

Nick Beal (England)
John Bentley (England)
Ieuan Evans (Wales)
Tony Underwood (England)
Allan Bateman (Wales)
Scott Gibbs (Wales)
Will Greenwood (England)
Jeremy Guscott (England)
Alan Tait (Scotland)
Paul Grayson (England)
Gregor Townsend (Scotland)
Matt Dawson (England)
Austin Healey (England)
Rob Howley (Wales)

Forwards
Paul Wallace (Ireland)
Jason Leonard (England)
Graham Rowntree (England)
Tom Smith (Scotland)
Dai Young (Wales)
Mark Regan (England)
Barry Williams (Wales)
Keith Wood (Ireland)
Martin Johnson (Capt., England)
Jeremy Davidson (Ireland)
Simon Shaw (England)
Doddie Weir (Scotland)
Neil Back (England)
Lawrence Dallaglio (England)
Richard Hill (England)
Eric Miller (Ireland)
Scott Quinnell (Wales)
Tim Rodber (England)
Rob Wainwright (Scotland)

Replacements
Tony Stanger (Scotland)
Mike Catt (England)
Kyran Bracken (England)
Tony Diprose (England)
Nigel Redman (England)

1997 BRITISH LIONS TOUR PROGRAM & RESULTS
May 24 v Eastern Province XV W 39-11
May 28 v Border W 18-14
May 31 v Western Province W 38-21
June 4 v Mpumalanga W 64-14
June 7 v Northern Transvaal L 30-35
June 11 v Gauteng Lions W 20-14
June 14 v Natal W 42-12
June 17 v Emerging Springboks W 51-22
June 21 v South Africa W 25-16
June 24 v Free State W 52-30
June 28 v South Africa W 18-15
July 1 v Northern Free State W 67-39
July 5 v South Africa L 16-35

13

THE 2009 BRITISH LIONS: OH, SO CLOSE!

The 2009 British & Irish Lions tour to South Africa took place from May to July 2009, following on from the 2005 British & Irish Lions tour to New Zealand coached by Sir Clive Woodward. It was not a happy tour, with the Lions losing the Test series 3-0, the first time in twenty-two years that a Lions team had lost every Test match on tour.

The Lions announced a thirty-seven-man squad on 21 April 2009. Before the start of the tour, Tomás O'Leary, Tom Shanklin and Jerry Flannery all withdrew because of injuries and Alan Quinlan was suspended. The side was also hit by injuries during the tour, and Leigh Halfpenny, Stephen Ferris, Euan Murray, Lee Byrne, Adam Jones, Gethin Jenkins, Jamie Roberts and their star Irish centre, Brian O'Driscoll, were all forced to withdraw from the squad because of injuries. In addition, Ferris's replacement, the Welshman Ryan Jones, was also forced to withdraw from the squad through injury. Their Scottish lock, Nathan Hines, was suspended for one week because of a dangerous tackle in the match against the Emerging Springboks.

The Lions played a three-match Test series against South Africa, in Durban, Pretoria and Johannesburg – one at the coast and two on the Highveld – as well as matches against six provincial teams and a match against South Africa A, the Emerging Springboks.

They won all six provincial matches and drew 13-all with the Emerging Springboks. The first two Tests were quite close but the scoreline in the final one was much bigger. In the end, South Africa won the Test series, defeating the Lions 26-21 in the first Test and then 28-25 in the second Test. With the series already sewn up, the third Test was won convincingly by the Lions 28-9. It is significant that the Lions outscored the Springboks by seven tries to five over the series and notched up 74 points to the Springboks' 63.

The Lions chief executive John Feehan stated in November 2007 that no home Test match would be played prior to departure as in 2005, also that a smaller squad of players and staff would go to South Africa than had gone to New Zealand. The coaching staff consisted of Ian McGeechan as the head coach, Warren Gatland as the forwards coach, Rob Howley as the backs coach, Shaun Edwards as the defence coach, Graham Rowntree as the scrum coach and Neil Jenkins as kicking coach. The tour manager was Gerald Davies, while the squad was to be captained by the Munster captain and Ireland lock, Paul O'Connell. There was a plan for the Lions squad to train in the Spanish city of Granada at the foot of the Sierra Nevada mountains, a high-altitude training camp, but it was cancelled because of players' uavailability. The Lions flew to South Africa on 24 May, arriving the following day.

The format for the tour was similar to that of the Lions' 2005 tour of New Zealand, with six games being played before the first Test, and a midweek game between the first and second Tests. The Lions did not face the formidable Bulls on tour, arguably the strongest provincial side in the world at the time, and having defeated New Zealand's Waikato Chiefs with a record score of 61-17 in the Super 14 Final a few months earlier.

The Lions started their tour on 30 May with a match against the Royal XV at the Royal Bafokeng Stadium in Rustenburg, which they won 37-25. They launched a late fightback to beat the Royal XV, avoiding what would have been their first defeat in the opening tour match since 1971 (against the Queensland Reds). Two tries in quick succession gave the hosts a shock 18-3 lead with the Lions making a raft of mistakes and struggling to gel in the first hour. But Jamie Roberts and Lee Byrne both turned in fine performances and in the end the Lions' greater fitness saw them run in three late tries.[1]

In their next game against the Golden Lions at Ellis Park in Johannesburg, one of the Test venues, the Lions laid down a firm challenge to the Springboks as they totally mesmerised the Golden Lions to win 74-10. They were a totally different proposition from the side which stumbled through the opening match in Rustenburg, and a Jamie Roberts brace and tries from Brian O'Driscoll, Ugo Monye and Tom Croft saw them go in at half-time 39-10 up. After the break, Tommy Bowe scored a double and Monye, James Hook and Stephen Ferris completed the rout.[2]

In contrast, the game against the Free State Cheetahs at Vodacom Park in Bloemfontein, attended by 23,700 spectators, was a very close one. The Lions survived a severe test to just cling on for a 26-24 win, their third of the tour, after having romped into an early 23-14 lead with tries from Stephen Ferris and Keith Earls, converted by James Hook. Hook also landed four penalties but with Ferris sin-binned, the Cheetahs scored two tries. A Cheetahs intercept try from a Shane Williams pass with eight minutes left saw the Lions hanging on desperately.[3]

Next up were the Sharks at Absa Park in Durban, the venue of the first Test. The Lions continued their unbeaten start with a five-try win over the Sharks, the tourists dominating the first half, but they only had a try from Lee Mears to show for their efforts to a penalty for the hosts. The Lions did improve through the match, with Mike Phillips scoring a well-worked try, with Luke Fitzgerald, Lee Byrne and Jamie Heaslip completing the scoring for a big 39-3 victory. While the performance was an improvement from the game against the Cheetahs, it was clear that coach Ian McGeechan still had plenty of work to do before the first Test.[4]

From Durban it was southward to good old Cape Town where the Western Province awaited them. It was a close affair again, as against Free State, running out winners by 26 points to 23. At a wet and windy Newlands, in front of 34,000 spectators, a penalty from replacement James Hook with three minutes to spare kept their unbeaten record intact as they scraped a fifth win of their tour. The Lions were pushed all the way by a hugely committed Western Province side, in spite of the hosts missing their Springboks. The Lions took an 18-12 lead at the break with tries from Tommy Bowe, already his fourth of the tour, and Ugo Monye, after trailing 9-6. Fifteen minutes into the second half, Martyn Williams scored a third try before Western Province came back and levelled the scores with seventeen minutes left. The Lions then endured some shaky moments with a first defeat of the tour looming, but in the end their dominant scrummage pulled them out of a hole when James Hook – who came on as replacement for Rob Kearney – landed a penalty from a scrum 5 metres into the Western Province half in the seventy-seventh minute, despite a swirling wind.[5]

The Lions had one more match to get under their belt before the first Test in Durban, against the Southern Kings at the new Nelson Mandela Bay Stadium in Port Elizabeth, built for the Soccer World Cup scheduled for the next year. The venue was a departure from the old Boet Erasmus Stadium, where the infamous 'battle' had taken place in 1974 with Willie John McBride's men. The occasion was also the launch of the new franchise in the Eastern Cape Province with the goal of a future place in Super Rugby. The partisan crowd of 36,000 was the biggest of the tour for any match up to then.

Obviously the Lions side contained the players who were likely to miss out on the first Test in Durban, but they did their job under difficult circumstances, surviving a battering from the home side. Within the first twelve minutes of the first half, both prop Euan Murray and fly-half James Hook had to leave the field injured in a half of heavy hits that ended 3-all. For the Lions, Ronan O'Gara scored two penalties and Ugo Monye a try converted by O'Gara, while a penalty try with eleven minutes left settled the final outcome, in spite of the late try by the Kings to take their tally to 8. Final score Lions 20, Southern Kings 8.[6]

First Test

As in 1997, the Lions kicked off their first Test of the series at the coast, but this time it was at Durban and not in Cape Town, on 20 June. Perhaps SA Rugby, with the Springboks' loss to the Lions at Newlands in the first Test on the previous tour still fresh in the mind, thought it best not to risk a repeat start to the series.

The Lions side for the match was: Lee Byrne, Tommy Bowe, Brian O'Driscoll, Jamie Roberts, Ugo Monye; Stephen Jones, Mike Phillips; Gethin Jenkins, Lee Mears, Phil Vickery, Alun-Wyn Jones, Paul O'Connell, Tom Croft, David Wallace, Jamie Heaslip. Replacements: Matthew Rees (for Mears, 50), Adam Jones (for Vickery, 45), Donncha O'Callaghan (for Wyn Jones, 68) Martyn Williams (for Wallace, 66), Rob Kearney (for Byrne, 38). Not used: Harry Ellis, Ronan O'Gara. Jamie Roberts became the youngest Lions starter when he lined up in the first Test, and was to be named Player of the Series by the British and Irish media after the tour.

At fly-half the Springboks fielded Ruan Pienaar. Those who had seen the exciting Gysie Pienaar run rings around the 1980 British Lions in 1980 would not have been surprised at the talent his son, Ruan, had displayed from an early age. Like his father, Ruan is a natural footballer, and made his debut for the Springboks at the age of twenty-one in 2006. He was to make 141 appearances for Ulster from the 2010 season onwards. At the time of writing, he was playing for Free State following two seasons with Montpellier.[7]

Around 48,000 looked on as New Zealand referee Mr Bryce Lawrence started the match. The Springboks had a fiery start and a wave of attacks ended with their captain John Smit powering through Croft's tackle for the opening try. Not even five minutes were on the clock. Pienaar added the conversion. From an attacking scrum in a promising position, Phillips feigned right before number eight Jamie Heaslip went left, and Jones and O'Driscoll combined to send Monye over in the left corner. His momentum seemed to carry him over, but after several minutes of deliberation the TV match official ruled he had not grounded the ball. Where they had been strong in the scrum on tour to date, the Lions then conceded the first of a series of penalties at the set-piece. Pienaar's kick made it 10-0 in as many minutes.

When they did get quality possession, the tourists looked dangerous, but it was Frans Steyn who scored the next points when he booted over a penalty from 45m to make it 13-0. Then when the Springboks fumbled a line-out, Jamie Roberts barged straight through the Springboks' midfield, fed O'Driscoll who cut back against the grain before releasing Croft to stretch over. Jones converted. The Springboks were now beginning to make errors, and the Lions had a second try ruled out for crossing when Tommy Bowe went over. But the Lions continued to give away penalties, and Pienaar made no mistake with two of these to take the score to 19-7 at half-time.

Vickery reappeared after the interval but was hauled off five minutes later, to be replaced by Adam Jones. Only six minutes after the restart, the Boks scored their second try in the forty-sixth minute when Victor Matfield won a line-out and flanker Brussow scored from the resulting maul. With Pienaar's conversion successful, the Lions were in trouble at 26-7 down and with more than half an hour left on the clock. Unfortunately for the Lions, they might have reduced the deficit when Phillips stretched over after a series of attacks, but he lost the ball as he was touching down. And on top of it, a penalty to the Lions in front of the posts was then reversed after replacement hooker Matthew Rees was seen aiming a punch at Bryan Habana. The Boks kept conceding penalties, to which the Lions kept kicking to touch or running them. The defence had to give and eventually O'Driscoll put Croft over for his second try, but there were only twelve minutes left after Jones's conversion had reduced the deficit to 12 points. Soon after, the Lions should have scored again when Monye was put clear, but the ball was forced out of his hands when touching down. Then, with only five minutes left, Phillips shot through a gap to score and for Jones to convert to make it 26-21.

The Lions had their chances in the closing minutes, but their spirited comeback fell agonisingly short. Final score South Africa 26, British Lions 21.[8] They would have felt very disappointed, having looked far more dangerous with ball in hand than their opponents, and probably should have scored another three tries. And in the last ten minutes of the game, they had two tries disallowed by the TMO.

Springbok Calves

Prior to the second Test, the Lions still had to face the Emerging Springboks at Newlands in Cape Town. A penalty by O'Gara after eight minutes put the Lions 3-0 in front, and in the fourteenth minute, Keith Earls rounded off a move under the sticks in which Martyn Williams and Riki Flutey handled, and with the conversion the Lions were 10-0 up. That was also the half-time score. Five minutes into the second half, the Emerging Springboks closed the gap with a penalty, followed by another in the forty-eighth minute. A simple penalty four minutes from time from straight in front was kicked by Hook, taking the score to 13-6, but at the death the Emerging Boks snatched a late try in the corner after a few phases. Fly-half Willem de Waal landed the difficult conversion from out on the touchline, with the siren screaming across Newlands as the ball sailed through the uprights. It had to be said that the Emerging Springboks were the more cohesive side in the second half and probably deserved the draw.[9]

Second Test: 53 Metres

The Test at Loftus Versfeld, Pretoria, on 27 June, was arguably the highlight of the series, which at the end of the match had the Lions leading and then again the Springboks, before the sides were even at 25-25 with only two minutes left. Sadly for the visitors, two minutes into injury time, Morné Steyn scored a long 53-metre penalty kick to win the match for South Africa 28-25. The Lions side for the second Test had some changes when Rob Kearney came in for Lee Byrne, Fitzgerald for Monye, Matthew Rees for Lee Mears, and Simon Shaw for Alun-Wyn Jones. The side read: Rob Kearney, Tommy Bowe, Brian O'Driscoll, Jamie Roberts, Luke Fitzgerald, Stephen Jones, Mike Phillips; Gethin Jenkins, Matthew Rees, Adam Jones, Simon Shaw, Paul O'Connell, Tom Croft, David Wallace, Jamie Heaslip. Replacements: Ross Ford, Andrew Sheridan (for Jenkins, blood, 22-31, 45), Alun-Wyn Jones (for A Jones, 45), Martyn Williams (for Wallace, 68), Harry Ellis, Ronan O'Gara (for Roberts 67), Shane Williams (for O'Driscoll, 64).

In front of 52,500 fans, the match got off to an explosive start when flanker Schalk Burger, who led the Springboks onto the field in celebration of his fiftieth cap, was yellow-carded within the first minute. A penalty against the Lions was reversed when touch judge Bryce Lawrence adjudged that Burger had raked his finger across the eyes of Luke Fitzgerald, and some failed to understand why French referee Christophe Berdos did not hand him a red card. Jones nevertheless knocked over the penalty to give the Lions the early lead. This was followed by a try in the seventh minute after a brilliant offload from Stephen Jones out the back of his hand to Kearney, who went over in the right corner. Jones converted superbly from the touchline and after eight minutes, the Lions were leading 10-0.

So while Burger had been off the field, the Boks conceded 10 points, but they scored immediately upon his return. From a line-out ball at the tail, scrum half Du Preez sent away wing J. P. Pietersen, who ran a great angle past Fitzgerald to score to the right of the posts. Strangely, Pienaar missed the relatively straightforward conversion, the first of three costly misses by him before he was replaced on the hour. Sheridan then came on for a bloodied Jenkins. The Lions came close to scoring when Pierre Spies brought down O'Driscoll after Fitzgerald had a run down the left wing, but they recycled patiently and after thirteen phases Jones, with lots of space, put over a simple drop goal from 15 metres out to extend their lead to 16-5. At the interval, Francois Steyn landed a huge 55-metre penalty with the last kick of the half.

The first twenty minutes of the second half were marked by a number of injuries as Jenkins left the field for good following a head clash and then fellow prop Adam Jones also had to go off with a sprained shoulder. This meant uncontested scrums for the final thirty-five minutes. The Lions had a let-off when Pienaar missed two long-range penalties within four minutes, before Jones landed his third penalty to give the Lions an 11-point cushion as they went into the final quarter. A severe collision between O'Driscoll and Danie Rossouw saw both players being forced off the field.

Then, from a good move from the Springboks, Du Preez sent Habana knifing through the Lions midfield before he stretched over for a try that Morne Steyn – now on at fly-half for Pienaar – converted to close the gap to four points. Jamie Roberts was then also injured, so that a new centre partnership of Stephen Jones and Tommy Bowe had to see through the last thirteen minutes with O'Gara coming on at fly-half. Jones kicked his fifth penalty to make it 22-18 to the Lions with ten minutes left, but then came Jaque Fourie's try that swung the momentum in South Africa's favour. O'Gara missed a tackle on the tall, powerful centre and Mike Phillips's last-ditch tackle also failed. After several minutes of deliberation, the TV match official Stuart Dickinson awarded the try to Fourie. Morne Steyn converted from the touchline and that suddenly left the Lions five minutes to produce something to keep the series alive. They did draw level when, after a high tackle by replacement lock Andries Bekker on Stephen Jones, the latter did not allow the shot to upset him and landed the penalty.

It was South Africa who were handed a last chance to win the game when O'Gara fielded a kick and launched a high up-and-under, chased his own kick but only succeeded in stumbling into Fourie du Preez as he claimed it in the air. Referee Berdos regarded it as a penalty and Morne Steyn, from 53 metres out and just inside his own half, struck it perfectly to send it sailing through the uprights.[10] The 2009 Lions had succumbed in the cruellest manner; Steyn's kick at the same time ensured that the Springboks earned some measure of revenge for their 1997 defeat by the Lions.

Third Test: Controversy

The week of the third Test was marked by controversy surrounding the suspended Springbok players Schalk Burger and Bakkies Botha after the very physical second Test. Burger was subsequently banned for eight weeks for 'making contact with the face in the eye area'. He was cleared of gouging as his action was found to be 'reckless' but not intentional. Bakkies Botha was banned for two weeks for a dangerous charge on prop Adam Jones, which left Jones with a dislocated shoulder. SA Rugby expressed their confusion over the reasons for Botha's ban with the coach calling it a 'textbook cleanout'. Lions player Phil Vickery and forwards coach Warren Gatland also lent their support to Botha's case, while the injured Jones himself later came out in defence of Botha.

With 58,000 people watching at Ellis Park, Johannesburg, on 4 July, the Springboks came out for the third Test wearing white armbands with the words 'Justice 4' in protest over perceived inconsistencies in the citing process. The protest was later investigated by the International Rugby Board for allegedly 'bringing the game into disrepute', and the team and management fined accordingly.[11]

The Lions won the third Test, beating the Springboks 28-9, in what *The Times* labelled as 'one of the best and most heroic performances in the history of the Lions'. This was the first Test victory for the Lions in eight years, their last being in Brisbane in 2001.

The Springbok squad had ten changes from the previous week, and the Lions also saw substantial changes. Their side for the final match were: Rob Kearney, Ugo Monye, Tommy Bowe, Riki Flutey, Shane Williams, Stephen Jones, Mike Phillips; Andrew Sheridan, Matthew Rees, Phil Vickery, Simon Shaw, Paul O'Connell, Joe Worsley, Martyn Williams, Jamie Heaslip. Replacements: Ross Ford (for Rees, 37), John Hayes (for Vickery, 55), Alun-Wyn Jones (for Shaw, 67), Tom Croft (for Worsley, blood 30-34, 66), David Wallace (for M Williams), Harry Ellis (for Flutey, 55). Not used: James Hook.

The Lions were faced with the prospect of a first series whitewash by the Springboks in 118 years, but they put the agony of their last-gasp second Test defeat behind them with a superb performance showing the pride and passion befitting a British & Irish Lions side. In the first half, Welsh flyer Shane Williams scored two tries, his first of the tour, and the Lions took a commanding 15-6 half-time lead. In the second half, Ugo Monye's 70-metre intercept try after fifty-four minutes extended the Lions lead before Morne Steyn landed his third penalty for South Africa. The Lions weren't done yet, and two late penalties from Stephen Jones sealed the Lions' first Test win since the victory in Brisbane in 2001. It also meant the Springboks' first defeat at Ellis Park for eight years.

In many quarters, the Test was billed as a dead rubber, but it did not seem as if the players had been aware of that, as they threw themselves into the game with the same intensity as the first two Tests. The Lions made a tremendous start, keeping the tempo high with their offloading game, in which Welsh flanker Martyn Williams was very prominent in his first start for the British Lions in a Test. At the back, Irish full back Rob Kearney picked up where he left off in the second Test, fielding the Springboks' high up-and-unders with ease and looking dangerous on the counter-attack.

Stephen Jones missed an early penalty, but he got the Lions on the scoreboard after nine minutes with a penalty after the Bok hooker Chiliboy Ralepelle popped out of the first scrum. The points were soon cancelled out by Frans Steyn when he landed a penalty. With both sides going at it hell for leather, referee Mr Stuart Dickinson had to speak to both captains to calm things down. The Lions had to scramble desperately when Jaque Fourie came bursting through, but they were first to get on the board again when in the twenty-fifth minute, Irish loose forward Jamie Heaslip barged into Bok centre Olivier, got back to his feet and passed to Shane Williams who ran in under the posts from the 22. As the ball slipped off his kicking tee, Jones was unable to land the simple kick at goal from under the posts. Heaslip again showed his worth, this time in defence, when he saved a try at the other end in gathering Springbok wing Odwa Ndungane's inside pass only 10 metres from the Lions try line when the Boks attacked.

It was the Lions, however, who looked more dangerous in attack, and it came as no surprise when Shane Williams ran in for his second try after a splendid move. The Lions turned over South Africa's ball, swiftly moved the ball to the left where Riki Flutey chipped ahead and gathered the bouncing ball, before passing to Williams who had an easy run-in for his try. Jones's conversion made it 15-3 to the Lions, but they had a bit of a setback when Rees was forced off with an injury. He was replaced by the Scottish hooker Ross Ford, to become the only Scot to play a part in the Test series. The Lions fiery lock Simon Shaw also had to leave the field after being sin-binned for putting his knee into the back of Springbok scrum half Fourie du Preez.

Morne Steyn then reduced his side's deficit to nine points with his second penalty before half-time, the last kick of the half, to reduce the Boks' half-time deficit to nine points. In spite of being down to fourteen men, the Lions launched another series of sustained attacks after the break and they got a decisive try in the fifty-fourth minute as Monye rushed up on defence to intercept Bok centre Wynand Olivier's pass and raced 70 metres to score. The try was loudly cheered by the mass of red-shirted Lions supporters in the lower tier of the stadium. And as the match went into the final 20 minutes, the sounds of *Swing Low, Sweet Chariot* reverberated around Ellis Park. At this stage, scrum half Mike Phillips had to move to centre after Riki Flutey had to go off because of injury, with Harry Ellis coming on at scrum half.

Soon Rob Kearney had a penalty shot at goal from inside his own half but missed, and then Frans Steyn, who was on as a replacement, attempted a drop goal from inside his own half that just fell wide. But with thirteen minutes left on the clock, Steyn was successful with his third penalty, closing the gap to 13 points. It was cancelled out, however, when, following a shove by Frans Steyn on Phillips, referee Stuart Dickinson awarded a penalty to the Lions. Jones made no mistake and with just seven minutes left, he landed another to settle the outcome. Yet it was not the end, as the Springboks manoeuvred their right wing Ndungane over in the right corner; but again the TMO was called upon and after several minutes of deliberation, the try was ruled out for a foot in touch. At the final whistle, the Lions left the field a happy bunch, in spite of a lost series. They had given it their all and gained a well-deserved victory over the world champions.[13]

After the match, coach Ian McGeechan said: 'I was worried that we wouldn't play or might go into our shells a bit but we didn't and we scored some very good tries. There is disappointment still in that we could have been coming into this one 1-0 or 2-0 up. We tried to play in all three games and had the better of four of the six halves in the series.'

Welshman Stephen Jones (with thirty-nine) finished as top Test points scorer in the series, as well as top points scorer for the tour with sixty-five. The top Test try scorers were England's Tom Croft and Wales's Shane Williams with two tries each. England's Ugo Monye, with five, was the top try scorer for the tour.

2009 LIONS SQUAD
Backs
Lee Byrne (Wales)
Rob Kearney (Ireland)
Shane Williams (Wales)
Leigh Halfpenny (Wales)
Ugo Monye (England)
Luke Fitzgerald (Ireland)
Tommy Bowe (Ireland)
Tom Shanklin (Wales)
Jamie Roberts (Wales)
Brian O'Driscoll (Ireland)
Keith Earls (Ireland)
Riki Flutey (England)
Ronan O'Gara (Ireland)
Stephen Jones (Wales)
James Hook (Wales – injury replacement before start of tour)
Mike Phillips (Wales)
Harry Ellis (England)
Tomas O'Leary (Ireland – injured before start of tour),
Mike Blair (Scotland – injury replacement before start of tour)

Forwards
Gethin Jenkins (Wales)
Adam Jones (Wales)
Andrew Sheridan (England)
Phil Vickery (England)
Euan Murray (Scotland)
John Hayes (Ireland – injury replacement)
Tim Payne (England – injury replacement)

Jerry Flannery (Ireland – injured before start of tour)
Lee Mears (England)
Matthew Rees (Wales)
Ross Ford (Scotland – injury replacement before start of tour)
Paul O'Connell (Capt., Ireland)
Alun Wyn Jones (Wales)
Donncha O'Callaghan (Ireland)
Nathan Hines (Scotland)
Simon Shaw (England)
David Wallace (Ireland)
Stephen Ferris (Ireland)
Alan Quinlan (Ireland – banned before start of tour)
Joe Worsley (England)
Martyn Williams (Wales)
Jamie Heaslip (Ireland)
Andy Powell (Wales)
Tom Croft (England – replacement before start of tour)
Ryan Jones (Wales – flew to South Africa as a replacement, but
immediately flew home because of an existing head injury)

2009 BRITISH LIONS TOUR PROGRAM & RESULTS
30 May: Royal XV 25-37 Lions – Royal Bafokeng, Rustenburg
3 June: Golden Lions 10-74 Lions – Ellis Park, Johannesburg
6 June: Cheetahs 24-26 Lions – Vodacom Park, Bloemfontein
10 June: Sharks 3-39 Lions – ABSA Park, Durban
13 June: Western Province 23-26 Lions – Newlands, Cape Town
16 June: Southern Kings 8-20 Lions – Nelson Mandela Bay
Stadium, Port Elizabeth
20 June: South Africa 26-21 Lions (first Test) – ABSA Park, Durban
23 June: Emerging Springboks 13-13 Lions – Newlands, Cape
Town
27 June: South Africa 28-25 Lions (second Test) – Loftus Versfeld,
Pretoria
4 July: South Africa 9-28 Lions (third Test) – Ellis Park,
Johannesburg

BRIAN O'DRISCOLL

Brian Gerard O'Driscoll was born on 21 January 1979 in Dublin to Frank and Geraldine O'Driscoll, both physicians. O'Driscoll's family was steeped in rugby, his father, Frank, having played two games for Ireland and a cousin of his father, Barry, having won four caps. However, it was another cousin of Frank's, Barry's brother John, who really put the O'Driscoll name on the map with twenty-six caps for Ireland and who was a member of the Lions side that toured South Africa in 1980 and New Zealand in 1983. As a child, Brian played Gaelic football before switching to rugby. He attended Blackrock College, where he played in the Senior Cup team in 1996 and 1997.

He was capped three times for Ireland Schools in 1996 and in 1998, and played for the Ireland U-19 side that won the Under-19 Rugby World Championship. After leaving school, he attended UCD on a scholarship and after two years graduated from UCD with a diploma in sports management. O'Driscoll made his Ireland under-21 debut in February 1999, and eventually gained four caps. He made his debut for Leinster in 1999, where he became an explosive force in the Leinster backline. In international rugby, O'Driscoll is the fourth most-capped player in rugby union history, having played 141 Test matches: 133 for Ireland (eighty-three as captain), and eight for the British & Irish Lions. He was selected for the senior squad in 1999 and was on the bench for a match against Italy, and won his first Test cap aged twenty on 12 June 1999 in a 46–10 loss to Australia in Brisbane as part of the tour of Australia. O'Driscoll actually played for Ireland before he played for the senior Leinster team.

He scored forty-six tries for Ireland and one try for the Lions in 2001, making him the highest try scorer of all time in Irish rugby. He is also the highest-scoring centre of all time. O'Driscoll holds the Six Nations record for most tries scored with twenty-six, has scored the most Heineken Cup tries (thirty) by an Irishman, and was chosen as Player of the Tournament in the 2006, 2007 and 2009 Six Nations Championships. He was inducted into the World Rugby Hall of Fame on 17 November 2016.

In 2002, O'Driscoll was handed the captaincy for the first time in Ireland's 18–9 win over Australia, and in 2003, following the international retirement of long-time Ireland captain Keith Wood, was awarded the captaincy on a permanent basis. In that year, he led Ireland to second place in the Six Nations Championship, followed by Triple Crowns in 2004, 2006 and 2007. In 2009, he led Ireland to their first Grand Slam in sixty-one years. O'Driscoll started for and captained Ireland for every match during the 2010 Six Nations Championship and picked up his hundredth Test cap for Ireland against Wales. He played for Ireland in the last four World Cups (seventeen caps, seven tries). On 8 March 2014, in his last home international for Ireland, O'Driscoll achieved a world record for the highest number of international caps, with 140, overtaking George Gregan's record with Australia. In his last international match, the finale of the 2014 Six Nations Championship on 15 March 2014, Ireland beat France in Paris for only the second time in forty-two years.

O'Driscoll appeared in all three British & Irish Lions Tests on the team's 2001 tour of Australia and was named captain of the team for their 2005 tour of New Zealand. O'Driscoll's playing contribution to the 2005 Lions ended in the opening minutes of the first Test against the All Blacks in Christchurch on 25 June 2005, when he was carried off with a shoulder injury following a controversial dual spear tackle. He remained as non-playing captain on a losing tour. In 2009, O'Driscoll was selected as part of the 2009 British & Irish Lions tour to South Africa. He played outside centre in their first Test of the tour against South Africa, but was forced to withdraw from the tour on 30 June before the third and final Test due to a head injury and subsequent concussion he suffered in the second. In 2013, he was named in the squad for his fourth British & Irish Lions tour, only the third player in 125 years of the tournament to achieve this. He was selected at outside centre for the first two Tests but was controversially dropped from the squad for the final Test. He also appeared three times for the invitational Barbarians rugby team.

In 2001, 2002 and 2009, O'Driscoll was nominated for the IRB World Player of the Year. In 2001, he lost out to his Irish teammate Keith Wood; in 2002, to Fabien Galthié; and, in 2009, when widely regarded as favourite for the award, to Richie McCaw by a solitary point.

NOTES

1 *The 1891 British Isles Tour to Southern Africa: The Pioneers*

1. For a good overview of the growth of rugby in the Cape see P. Dobson *Rugby in South Africa...1861–1988*, p. 9–30.

2. R. Bath, *The British & Irish Lions*, p. 2.

3 *The Athletic News*, 4 May 1891.

4. *The Athletic News*, 27 April 1891.

5. *The Athletic News* 22 June 1891.

6. *The Athletic News* 22 June 1891.

7. P.R. Clauss in I. Difford *History of South African Rugby*, p.251–264.

8. *Cape Times*, 10 July 1891.

9. T. Shnaps *A Statistical History of Springbok Rugby*, p151–154 provides a record of all points scored during the tour.

10. *The Sporting Life*, 12 August 1891. Letter dated 20 July 1891.

11. *The Athletic News*, 17 August 1891.

12. *The Sporting Life*, 12 August 1891.

13. A. Trollope, *South Africa*, p. 371–372.

14. *The Athletic News*, 17 August 1891.

15. *The Athletic News*, 17 August 1891.

16. *The Edinburgh Evening News* 31 July 1891

17. *The Sportsman*, 27 August 1891.

18. I. Difford *History...*, p. 254.

19. W. Churchill, *London to Ladysmith via Pretoria*, p. 43.

20. C. van Onselen, *New Babylon New Nineveh*, p. 3.

21. *The Sporting Life*, 31 August 1891.

22. *The Cape Argus*, 5 & 7 July 1891.

23. *The Athletic News*, 5 October 1891.

24. *Edinburgh Evening News*, 7 September 1891.

25. P. Dobson *Rugby in South Africa*, p. 41.

26. I. Difford, *History...*, p. 259.

2 *The 1896 Tour: Hammond's Team Win Nearly Every Match*

1. *The Athletic News*, 10 August 1896.

2. P. Dobson, *Rugby in South Africa*, p. 49.

3. *The Athletic News*, 10 August 1896.

4. P. Dobson, *Rugby in South Africa*, p. 49.

5. *Johannesburg Times*, 12 August 1896.

6. *Johannesburg Times*, 10 August 1896.

7. *Johannesburg Times*, 13 August 1896.

8. *Johannesburg Times*, 17 August 1896.

9. I. Difford, *History...*, p. 269.

10. *Johannesburg Times*, 17 August 1896.

11. F. W. Reitz, *A Century of Wrong*, p. 46–47.

12. C. de Kiewiet, *The Imperial Factor in South Africa*, p. 327.

13. *Johannesburg Times*, 17 August 1896.

14. *Johannesburg Times*, 19 August 1896 & 20 August 1896

15. E. Longford, *Jameson's Raid*, p. 91

16. L. Cohen, *Reminiscences of Johannesburg and London*, p. 73.

17. *Johannesburg Times*, 24 August 1896.

18. *Johannesburg Times*, 1 September 1896 & P. Dobson, *Rugby in South Africa*, p. 51

19. *The Cape Argus*, 7 September 1896.

20. P. Dobson, *Rugby in South Africa*, p. 52.

21. I. Difford, *History...*, p. 277.

22. *Sheffield Daily Telegraph* 30 September 1896.

23. *Yorkshire Evening Post* 30 September 1896.

24. I. Difford, *History...*, p.295–296.

25. W. Reyburn, *The Lions*, p. 48.

26. *The Cape Argus*, 7 September 1896.

27. W. Reyburn, *The Lions*, p. 45.

3 The 1903 Tour: Morrison's Men Struggle

1. I. Difford, *History of South African Rugby*, p. 280.
2. *The Sportsman*, 5 August 1903.
3. I. Difford, *History...*, p. 281.
4. *The Sportsman*, 2 September 1903.
5. *The Sportsman*, 2 September 1903.
6. *The Sportsman*, 9 September 1903.
7. *The Sportsman*, 16 September 1903.
8. *The Sportsman*, 23 September 1903.
9. I. Difford, *History...*, p. 289.
10. I. Difford, *History...*, p. 289–293.
11. *The Sportsman*, 23 September 1903
12. *The Sportsman*, 30 September 1903.
13. Leo Amery (ed.), *The Times History of the War in South Africa*, vol. 4, p. 41.
14. *Times History...*, vol. 4, p. 42.
15. *Times History...*, vol. 4, p. 50.
16. *Times History...*, vol. 4, p. 50.
17. *The Sportsman*, 30 September 1903.
18. I. Difford, *History...*, p. 284.
19. A. C. Parker, *The Springboks*, p. 29.
20. *The Cape Argus*, 12.9.03, p. 3.
21. I. Difford, *History...*, p. 289–293.
22. *The Cape Argus*, 12.9.03, p. 3.
23. D. McLennan & C. Schoeman, *Rugby at Newlands*, p. 28.
24. *The Cape Argus*, 14 September 1903.
25. *The Sportsman*, 5 October 1903.

4 The 1910 British Isles Tour: A Unified South Africa for the First Time

1. Smyth was a good choice as captain. He had grown up in Belfast, gone to university in Scotland and was now practising in Newport and playing for that team. W. L. Sinclair, the editor of *The Athletic News*, felt that Smyth's judgement had 'improved from Welsh associations.' See Cox & Pay, *Records of the Games...*, p. 26.
2. Local unions had paid considerable amounts to be able to host games: Transvaal £1,200, Western Province £1000, Eastern Province £500, Griqualand West £450. The SARFB received £4,400 in total.

3. *The Athletic News*, 1 August 1910. In this edition Cox provides a good overview of this dispute from the first misunderstanding before the tour even began.

4. *The Athletic News*, 4 July 1910.

5. T. Shnaps *A Statistical History of Springbok Rugby*, p. 169.

6. *The Sportsman*, 19 July 1910.

7. *The Athletic News*, 25 July 1910.

8. *The Athletic News*, 25 July 1910.

9. *The Athletic News*, 25 July 1910.

10. *The Sportsman*, 2 August 1910.

11. *The Sportsman*, 2 August 1910.

12. I. Difford, *History...*, p. 296.

13. *The Sportsman*, 9 August 1910.

14. *Rand Daily Mail*, 21 July 1910.

15. *Rand Daily Mail*, 28 July 1910.

16. I. Difford, *History...*, p. 295.

17. *Rand Daily Mail*, 8 August 1910.

18. *Rand Daily Mail*, 11 August 1910.

19. There were 28 players in the full squad, of which Reg Plummer, Ken Wood, Noel Humphreys, Eric Milroy, Tom Smyth, James Kerr, Edward Crean and William Ashby were incapacitated in some way at this stage. Two players, Arthur McClinton, and William Robertson were only selected for a small number of games across the whole tour. That left Crail just eighteen players to choose between in the run-up to the second Test.

20. *Rand Daily Mail*, 15 August 1910.

21. *Westminster Gazette*, 15 August 1910.

22. *Rand Daily Mail*, 18 August 1910.

23. *Rand Daily Mail*, 25 August 1910.

24. I. Difford, *History...*, p. 302.

25. *Rand Daily Mail*, 29 August 1910.

26. I. Difford, *History...*, p. 304.

27. *The Cape Argus*, 3 September 1910.

28. I. Difford, *History...*, p. 305.

29. *The Athletic News*, 26 September 1910.

30. *The Athletic News*, 5 September 1910.

31. Four players who participated in this tour lost their lives during the First World War. On the British Isles side, Noel Humphreys, MC, Eric Milory and Philip Waller. On the South African side Tobias 'Toby' Moll. Waller was one of the four players who remained in South Africa and he lost his life while serving in the South African Artillery in France. Most of the players served during the conflict. Stanley Williams, Arthur McClinton, Cherry Pillman and Tom Richards were all awarded the Military Cross, William Tyrell (later Air Vice-Marshal Sir William) was awarded the DSO and Bar. Dr Charles Timms was awarded the Military Cross four times during the conflict, one of only four soldiers in the British army to be honoured so many times.

5 The 1924 British Lions Tour: Cove-Smith's Blues

1. *The Sportsman,* 3 July 1924.
2. *The Sportsman,* 29 July 1924.
3. *Rand Daily Mail,* 16 July 1924.
4. A. C. Parker, *The Bennie Osler Story,* p. 67.
5. *The Athletic News,* 25 August 1924.
6. *Rand Daily Mail,* 2 August 1924.
7. *The Athletic News,* 4 August 1924.
8. *Rand Daily Mail,* 11 August 1924.
9. *Gloucester Journal,* 16 August 1924 & *Rand Daily Mail, 18 August 1924.*
10. *Leeds Mercury,* 13 August 24.
11. E. Griffiths *The Captains,* p. 53.
12. A. C. Parker *The Springboks,* p. 71.
13. A. C. Parker, *The Springboks,* p. 69.
14. *The Sportsman,* 11 September 1924.
15. T. Shnaps, *A Statistical History of Springbok Rugby,* p. 181.
16. A. C. Parker, *The Bennie Osler Story,* p. 70.
17. *Rand Daily Mail,* 18 August 1924; *The Athletic News,* 18 August 1924 & *The Sportsman,* 11 September 1924.
18. See C. J. van Rensburg *Springbokrugby Spanfotos...,* p. 33–34 & H. Saestad *The First Lions,* p. 65 & 102–103. Saestad describes this team as having a nickname: 'Lint Springbokke' [Ribbon Springboks].
19. *Rand Daily Mail,* 25 August 1924; *The Sportsman,* 16 September 1924; *Athletic News,* 25 August 1924.
20. I. Difford, *History...,* p. 320.

21. I. Difford, *History...*, p. 320.
22. R. Cove-Smith *Rugby Football*, p. 8–9.
23. I. Difford, *History...*, p. 310.
24. I. Difford, *History...*, p. 321.
25. C. Thomas *The History of the British Lions*, p. 68.
26. I. Difford, *History...*, p. 312.
27. *Rand Daily Mail*, 27 September 1924.
28. *Rand Daily Mail*, 27 September 1924 & 14 October 1924.
29. *The Athletic News*, 8 September 1924.
30. P. H. Francis, *British Tour in South Africa; 1925–26 Wisden's Rugby Almanack*, p. 636.
31. The SRU were concerned that the All Blacks contravened the strict amateur rugby codes.
32. C. Thomas, *The History of the British Lions*, p. 70–71.

6 *The 1938 British Lions Tour: The End of an Era and the Blue Jersey*

1. S. Lewis *Last of the Blue Lions*, p. 34.
2. *Rand Daily Mail*, 9 June 1938.
3. *Rand Daily Mail*, 17 June 1938.
4. S. Lewis *Last of the Blue Lions*, p. 62.
5. *Rand Daily Mail*, 1 August 1938.
6. *Rand Daily Mail*, 1 July 1938.
7. *Rand Daily Mail*, 9 July 1938.
8. *Rand Daily Mail*, 29 July 1938.
9. *Rand Daily Mail*, 13 July 1938.
10. D. Craven, *Ons Toets Prestasies*, p. 48.
11. D. Craven, *Ons Toets Prestasies*, p. 49.
12. C. Thomas, *The History of the British Lions*, p. 85.
13. S. Lewis, *Last of the Blue Lions*, p. 151 & *Sunday Mirror*, 7 August 1938.
14. D. Craven, *Ons Toets Prestasies*, p. 44.
15. *Rand Daily Mail*, 15 August 1938.
16. D. Craven, *Ons Toets Prestasies*, p. 97.
17. D. Craven, *Ons Toets Prestasies*, p. 117.
18. S. Lewis, *The Last of the Blue Lions*, p. 228.
19. *Rand Daily Mail*, 8 September 1938.
20. *Rand Daily Mail*, 12 September 1938.

21. *Rand Daily Mail*, 16 September 1938.
22. S. Lewis, *The Last of the Blue Lions*, p. 227–228.
23. *Rand Daily Mail*, 23 September 1938.
24. S. Lewis, *The Last of the Blue Lions*, p. 229.

7 *The 1955 British Lions: Honours Even*
1. Cliff Morgan, *The Autobiography*, p. 136
2. Ibid, p. 137
3. Ivan Fallon, *The Player*, p. 72
4. Cliff Morgan, *The Autobiography*, p. 138
5. Vivian Jenkins, *Lions Rampant*, pp. 56–7
6. Ibid, p. 61
7. Ibid, p. 71
8. Ivan Fallon, *The Player*, p. 73
9. Reg Sweet, *Pride of the Lions*, pp. 119–120
10. *The Coventry Evening Telegraph*, 6 August 1955. "British Team win First R. U. Test."; Reg Sweet, Pride of the Lions pp. 119–125.
11. Cliff Morgan, *The Autobiography*, pp. 140–1
12. Chris Greyvenstein, *Springbokseges*, p. 32
13. Reg Sweet, *Pride of the Lions*, p. 129. Many hats were lost amongst spectators as they threw them in the air in excitement, the *Cape Argus* later reported
14. Vivian Jenkins, *Lions Rampant*, p. 196
15. Reg Sweet, *Pride of the Lions*, p. 117
16. Reg Sweet, *Pride of the Lions*, p. 131
17. Chris Schoeman, *The No. 10s*, pp. 243–6
18. Quoted in Jenkins, *Lions Rampant*, p. 269
19. R. K. Stent, p. 115
20. Cliff Morgan, *The Autobiography*, p. 150

8 *The 1962 British Lions: The Heavy Boys*
1. Reg Sweet, *Pride of the Lions*, p. 145
2. Reg Sweet, *Pride of the Lions*, pp. 149–50
3. Ibid, p. 203
4. Dawie de Villiers, *My Lewensreis*, p. 19
5. Chris Schoeman & David McLennan, *Rugby at Newlands*, pp. 86–90
6. Chris Greyvenstein, *Springbokseges*, pp. 46–52

7. JGB Thomas, *Springbok Glory*, pp. 110–11
8. John Gainsford, *Nice Guys Come Second*, p. 113
9. Interview with Dawie de Villiers

9 The 1968 British Lions: Close but No Cigar

1. See A. C. Parker, *The Lions Tamers*, chapter 4
2. Chris Schoeman, *Rugby Behind Barbed Wire*, pp. 140; 202
3. A. C. Parker, *The Lions Tamers*, chapter 4
4. Ibid, p. 73
5. Frik: *Die Outobiografie van 'n Legende*, p. 116
6. As quoted in A. C. Parker, *The Lion Tamers*, p. 113
7. Dawie de Villiers, *My Lewensreis*, p. 43
8. A. C. Parker, *The Lion Tamers*, p. 129
9. Ibid, pp. 135–136
10. Dawie de Villiers, *My Lewensreis*, p. 43
11. Ibid p. 43
12. A. C. Parker, *The Lion Tamers*, p. 18
13. Ibid, p. 19

10 The 1974 British Lions: The Invincibles

1. Chris Schoeman, *Rugby Behind Barbed Wire*, p. 140; 202
2. Ibid, p. 98
3. Ibid, p. 98
4. 'The Lion Kings'. *The Guardian*, 3 May 2009
5. 'The Lion Kings'. *The Guardian*, 3 May 2009
6. John Taylor, 'We were charging round getting battered.' *ESPN Scrum*. 13 November 2013
7. A. C. Parker, *WP Rugby Eeufees 1883–1983*, p. 128
8. Chris Schoeman & David McLennan, *Rugby at Newlands*, p. 115
9. Edward Griffiths, *The Captains*, p. 242
10. Chris Schoeman & David McLennan, *Rugby at Newlands*, p. 116
11. 'The Lion Kings'. *The Guardian*, 3 May 2009
12. Chris Schoeman & David McLennan, *Rugby at Newlands*, p. 115
13. 'The Lion Kings'. *The Guardian*, 3 May 2009
14. 'The Lion Kings'. *The Guardian*, 3 May 2009
15. Ibid
16. Ibid

11 *The 1980 British Lions: Injuries, Injuries*

1. 'Morne du Plessis reflects on Boks' 1980 Lions series.' *Times Live*, 10 July 2020
2. Ibid
3. See John Hopkins, *British Lions 1980*
4. John Robbie, *The Game of my Life*, p. 87
5. See Chris Schoeman, *The No. 10s*, pp. 158–163
6. 'Morne du Plessis reflects on Boks' 1980 Lions series.' *Times Live*, 10 July 2020
7. Chris Schoeman & David McLennan, *Rugby at Newlands*, pp. 122–6
8. Edward Griffiths, *Naas*, p. 69
9. Rob Louw, *More than just Rugby*, p. 62
10. Edward Griffiths, *Naas*, p. 73
11. 'Morne du Plessis reflects on Boks' 1980 Lions series.' *Times Live*, 10 July 2020
12. Ibid

12 *The 1997 British Lions Tour: Last Hurrah of Amateurism*

1. Rugby World, *The Definitive Guide to the 1997 Lions Tour*, p. 6
2. Ibid, pp. 90–91
3. Gary Teichmann, For the Record, p. 124
4. https://speakola.com/sports/jim-telfer-forwards-everest-lions-tour-1997
5. Chris Schoeman & David McLennan, *Rugby at Newlands*, pp. 154–5; Edward Griffiths, *Joost: for love and money*, pp. 158–9
6. https://www.lionsrugby.com
7. Gary Teichmann, *For the Record*, p. 129
8. Ibid, pp. 131–2; pp. Edward Griffiths, Joost: *For Love and Money*, 160–1
9. https://www.lionsrugby.com/2020/04/19. drop goal hero Guscott reflects on memorable 1997
10. Ibid
11. Gary Teichmann, *For the Record*, p. 131
12. See Chris Schoeman, *The No. 10s*, pp. 186–91
13. Gary Teichmann, *For the Record*, p. 132
14. https://springboks.rugby
15. https://www.vavel.com/ 'John Bentley: The pride and pitfalls of being a British and Irish Lion', 5 July 2017

13 The 2009 British Lions: Oh, So Close!

1. http://news.bbc.co.uk/sport, 30 May 2009
2. Ibid, 3 June 2009
3. Ibid, 6 June 2009
4. Ibid, 10 June 2009; John Smit, *Captain in the Cauldron*, p. 178
5. Ibid, 13 June 2009
6. Ibid, 16 June 2009
7. Chris Schoeman, *The No. 10s*, pp. 229–32
8. Ibid, 20 June 2009; Victor Matfield, *My Journey*, pp. 180–1; John Smit, *Captain in the Cauldron*, pp. 181–3
9. Ibid, 23 June 2009
10. Ibid, 27 June 2009; Victor Matfield, *My Journey*, pp. 181–2; John Smit, *Captain in the Cauldron*, pp. 185–91
11. Victor Matfield, *My Journey*, pp. 183; John Smit, *Captain in the Cauldron*, p. 199
12. 'Lions restore pride with record-equalling win'. *The Times*, 4 July 2009
13. http://news.bbc.co.uk/sport, 30 May 2009

BIBLIOGRAPHY

Books

Amery, Leo (ed.): *The Times History of the War in South Africa,* Sampson Low, Marston and Company, 1900-1909.

Bath, R: *The British & Irish Lions.* Vision Sports, 2008.

Bennett, Phil: *Everywhere for Wales.* Stanley Paul, 1981.

Churchill, Winston: *London to Ladysmith via Pretoria.* Longmans Green & Co, 1900.

Clayton, Keith: *The Legends of Springbok Rugby 1889-1989: Doc Craven's Tribute.* KC Publications, 1989.

Cohen, L: *Reminiscences of Johannesburg and London.* Africana Book Society, 1976.

Colquhoun, Andy & Dobson, Paul: *The Chosen, the 50 Greatest Springboks.* Don Nelson, 2003.

Cox, L A & Pay, F G: *Records of the games and souvenir of the British teams' visit to South Africa 1910.* S.A. Newspaper Company Ltd., 1910.

Craven, Danie: *Die Leeus keil ons op.* Afrikaanse Pers Boekhandel, 1956

Craven, Danie: *Ek Speel vir Suid-Afrika.* Nasionale Pers, 1949

Craven, Danie: *Ons Toets Prestasies.* Afrikaanse Pers Boekhandel, 1955.

Craven, Dr D.H.: *Die Groot Rugbygesin van die Maties.* University of Stellenbosch, 1980.

De Kiewiet, C.: *The Imperial Factor in South Africa.* Frank Cass & Co., 1965.

De Villiers, Dawie (with Chris Schoeman): *My Lewensreis: Springbok, Politikus, Diplomaat.* Penguin Random House, 2019

Difford, Ivor: *History of South African Rugby.* Speciality Press, 1933.

Dobson, Paul: *30 Super Springboks.* Human & Rousseau, 1995.

Dobson, Paul: *Doc, the life of Danie Craven.* Human & Rousseau, 1994.

Dobson, Paul: *Rugby in South Africa 1861-1988.* SA Rugby Board,1989.

Bibliography

Du Preez, Frik (with Chris Schoeman): *Frik: The Autobiography of a Legend.* Don Nelson, 2004).

Du Randt, Os (with Chris Schoeman): *The Autobiography.* Tafelberg, 2006

Edwards, Gareth: *100 Great Players.* MacDonald Queen Anne Press, 1987.

Edwards, Gareth: *Gareth*: Stanley Paul, 1978.

Fallon, Ian. *The Player: The Life of Tony O'Reilly.* Hodder & Stoughton, 1994

Gainsford, John (with Neville Leck): *Nice Guys Come Second.* Don Nelson, 1974.

Greyvenstein, Chris: *Springbok Saga.* Don Nelson, 1989.

Greyvenstein, Chris: *Springbokseges.* Buren Publishers, 1968.

Griffiths, Edward: *Joost: For Love and Money.* CAB, 1998.

Griffiths, Edward: *Naas.* Leo Uitgewers, 1989.

Griffiths, Edward: *The Captains.* Jonathan Ball, 2001.

Hain, Peter: *Don't Play with Apartheid.* Allen & Unwin, 1971.

Hain, Peter: *Inside Out.* Biteback Publishing, 2011.

Hopkins, John. *British Lions 1980.* World's Work Ltd, 1980

Jenkins, Vivian. *Lions Rampant.* Cassell, 1956

John, Barry: *The Barry John Story.* William Collins Sons, 1974.

Lewis, Steve: *The Last of the Blue Lions.* Sports Books, 2009.

Longford, E: *Jameson's Raid.* Jonathan Ball, 1982.

Louw, Rob (with John Cameron-Dow): *For the Love of Rugby.* Hans Strydom Publishers, 1987.

Matfield, Victor (with De Jongh Borchardt): *My Journey.* Penguin Random House, 2012.

McBride, Willie John (with Peter Bills): *Willie John: The Story of My Life.* Portrait, 2004.

McLaren, Bill: *Rugby's Great Heroes and Entertainers.* Hodder & Stoughton, 2003.

McLennan, David & Schoeman, Chris. *Rugby at Newlands 1891-2015.* Burnet Media, 2015.

McLennan, David, Sibul, Hymie & Schoeman, Chris. *Rugby at Ellis Park, a history told through test matches.* Select Books, 2017.

Morgan, Cliff (with Geoffrey Nicholson): *The Autobiography: Beyond the Fields of Play.* Hodder & Stoughton, 1997.

Parker, A C: *The Bennie Osler Story.* Howard Timmins, 1970.

Parker, A C: *The Lion Tamers.* Howard Timmins, 1968

Parker, A C: *The Springboks.* Cassell, 1970.

Reitz, F W: *A Century of Wrong.* Review of Reviews Office, [1900].

Reyburn, Wallace: *The Lions.* Stanley Paul, 1967.

Robbie, John: *The Game of my Life.* Pelham Books, 1989.

Rugby World: *The Definitive Guide to the 1997 Lions Tour.* IPC Magazines, 1997.

Saestad, Hans: *The First Lions.* H. Saestad, 2020

Schoeman, Chris: *Legends of the Ball: Rugby's Greatest Players.* Chosen by Willie John McBride, Frik du Preez & David Campese. CJS Books, 2007).

Schoeman, Chris: *Rugby Behind Barbed Wire.* Amberley Publishers, 2020

Schoeman, Chris: *Seasons of Glory – The Life and Times of Bob Loubser*. CJS Books, 1999, revised edition 2006).

Schoeman, Chris: *South Africa's Rugby Legends: The Amateur Era*. Random House, 2015

Schoeman, Chris: *The No. 10s: South Africa's Finest Flyhalves 1891-2010*. Random House, 2010

Shnaps, Teddy: *A Statistical History of Springbok Rugby*. Don Nelson, 1989.

John Smit (with Mike Greenaway): *Captain in the Cauldron*. Highbury Safika Media, 2009.

Sweet, Reg: *Pride of the Lions*. Howard Timmins, 1962

Teichmann, Gary (with Edward Griffiths): *For the Record*. Willow, 2000

Thomas, Clem: *The History of the British Lions*. Mainstream, 1996.

Thomas, J G B: *Springbok Glory*. Stanley Paul, 1961.

Trollope, A: *South Africa*, A.A. Balkema, 1973.

Van Onselen, Charles: *New Babylon, New Nineveh*, Jonathan Ball, 1992.

Van Rensburg, C J: *Springbokrugby Spanfotos*. Privately Published, 2020.

Williams, JPR: *JPR: An Autobiography*. William Collins Sons, 1979.

Wisden, John: *John Wisden's Rugby Football Almanack for 1925-26*. John Wisden & Co., 1926.

Newspapers and Magazines
Belfast Telegraph
Cape Daily Telegraph
Cape Times
Daily Mirror
Eastern Province Herald
Gloucester Journal
Irish Independent
Johannesburg Times
Leeds Mercury
Mafeking Mail and Protectorate Guardian
Rand Daily Mail
Sheffield Daily Telegraph
Sunday Life
Sunday Mirror
The Athletic News
The Cape Argus
The Coventry Evening Telegraph
The Edinburgh Evening News
The Guardian
The Northern Whig & Belfast Post
The Sporting Life
The Times (London)
Western Mail & South Wales News

Bibliography

Westminster Gazette
Yorkshire Evening Post

SA Rugby Magazine
Rugby World
Rugby XV
SA Rugby News

Interviews
(Lions series in brackets)
Ex-Springboks
Clive Ulyate (1955)
Stephen Fry (1955)
Avril Malan (1962)
Dawie de Villiers (1962, 1968)
Frik du Preez (1962, 1968)
Hannes Marais (1968, 1974)
Eben Olivier (1968)
Piet Greyling (1968)
Thys Lourens (1968)
Tommy Bedford (1968)
Roy McCallum (1974)
Dugald Macdonald (1974)
Ray Mordt (1980)
Theuns Stofberg (1980)
Jannie de Beer (1997)
Rassie Erasmus (1997)
Russell Bennett (1997)
Ex-provincial players
Bertie Gibson – Boland (1955)
Ex-British Lions
Neil Jenkins (1997, 2001)
Peter Larter (1968)
Roger Young (1968)
Bob Taylor (1968)
John O'Shea (1968)
Rodger Arneil (1968)

Internet Sources
https://www.lionsrugby.com
https://springboks.rugby
https://www.vavel.com
https://news.bbc.co.uk/sport
https://www.espnscrum.com

ACKNOWLEDGEMENTS

Chris Schoeman and David McLennan would like to thank rugby icons Willie John McBride and Hannes Marais for agreeing to write the forewords.

They would also like to thank the staff of the National Archives and the National Library for their assistance.

David would like to thank Chavonne Cupido for facilitating access to newspapers during the lockdown in South Africa. He would also like to thank Dave McLennan for technological direction and help, Richard Steel who offered advice and encouragement and Tom Passmore who read his section of the book and provided careful suggestions and recommendations. Karen McLennan acted as a kind and thoughtful sounding board and provided much encouragement, assistance and advice.

Chris would like to thank all those players interviewed over the years for sharing their experiences; some of them have left us, but their names will live on in the hearts of rugby lovers. And finally, thanks to Ronel for her patience, support and thoughts during the writing of the book.

INDEX

Index

Matfield, Victor 254, 275, 277
Matthews, Jack 231
Maxwell, Captain 72–3
Mayne, Robert Blair 145, 148
Maxwell, Frank 39, 49
Maxwell, Reginald 114, 119–20, 128
Mayfield, Edwin 31
McBride, Willie John 6, 11–12, 170–3,
    182, 184–5, 188–9, 193–4, 202–8,
    211, 214–5, 218, 221–2, 230, 235,
    252
McGeechan, Ian 199, 204, 206, 208,
    210, 216, 234–6, 250–1, 260
McKendrick, Jim 28
McKinney, Stewart 12, 213, 216
McLauchlan, Ian 206, 216, 230
McLeod, Hugh 154, 169
McClinton, Arthur 92, 94, 100, 106,
    269–70
McKibbin, Henry 138, 144, 148, 182
McVicker, Jim 119, 122, 126, 128
Meares, Arthur 47, 51, 57
Mears, Lee 251, 253, 255, 262
Meredith, Bryn 153–4, 160–1, 163,
    172–4
Meredith, Courtney 161
Michie, Ernie 156, 160, 169
Millar, Billy 84, 101–5, 123
Millar, Sid 10, 12, 171, 173, 184, 188,
    193–4, 202–3, 205, 208, 220
Miller, Eric 247
Milliken, Richard 210, 216
Milroy, Eric 90, 106, 269
Mitchell, William 21–2, 26–7, 31
Moloney, John 216
Montgomery, Percy 240, 242
Monye, Ugo 251–5, 258, 260–1
Mordt, Ray 280
Morgan, Cliff 149–52, 154–7, 160–6,
    168, 171, 181, 209, 272, 278
Morgan, Eddie 133
Morgan, George 144, 148
Morgan, Haydn 175, 182, 188
Morgan, Morgan 148

Morgan, Peter 231
Morkel, Boy 103, 130
Morkel, Dougie 86–8, 95–7, 101,
    104–5
Morley, Alan 216
Morris, Haydn 152, 168
Morrison, Mark 58–9, 62–5, 68–9,
    74–80, 89, 92
Mortimer, William 57
Mostert, Phil 117, 121, 123, 126, 130,
    133
Mulcahy, Bill 170, 174, 176–7, 182
Muller, Gert 212
Mullineaux, Matthew 47, 49, 56
Mullins, R. C. 49, 51, 57
Murphy, Noel 220, 228, 231
Murray, Euan 249, 252, 261
Myburgh, Mof 173, 185, 190, 193,
    196
Nash, David 170, 182
Neale, Maurice 87, 91, 98–100, 106
Neary, Tony 216
Neil, Robert 75–6, 79
Nel, Philip 130
Nel, Pieter (P. O.) 78
Nicholson, Basil 135, 142, 148
O'Callaghan, Donncha 253, 262
O'Connell, Paul 250, 253, 255, 258,
    262
O'Connor, Tony 182
O'Donnell, Rodney 220, 223, 225, 231
O'Driscoll, Brian 249, 251, 253–6,
    261, 263–5
O'Driscoll, Frank 167
O'Driscoll, John 223, 225–6, 229, 232
O'Gara, Ronan 252–3, 255. 257, 261
Ogilvie, Canon George 14
O'Leary, Tomas 249, 261
Old, Alan 216
Olivier, Eben 189, 197, 280
Olivier, Wynand 259–60
O'Reilly, Tony 150, 152–6, 158–9,
    161, 163, 166–9, 207, 209, 277
Orr, Phil 219–20, 232

285